René Girard

René Girard

Violence and Mimesis

Chris Fleming

Polity

First published in 2004 by Polity Press Ltd

Reprinted in 2008

Polity Press
65 Bridge Street
Cambridge CB2 1UR, UK

Polity Press
350 Main Street
Malden, MA 02148, USA

ISBN 978-0-7456-2947-6
ISBN 978-0-7456-2948-3 (pb)

A catalogue record for this book is available from the British Library.

Typeset in 10.5 on 12 pt Palatino
by SNP Best-set Typesetter Ltd., Hong Kong
Printed and bound in the United States by Odyssey Press Inc., Gonic, New Hampshire

For further information on Polity, visit our website: www.polity.co.uk

Key Contemporary Thinkers

Published

Jeremy Ahearne, *Michel de Certeau: Interpretation and its Other*

Peter Burke, *The French Historical Revolution: The* Annales *School 1929–1989*

Michael Caesar, *Umberto Eco: Philosophy, Semiotics and the Work of Fiction*

M. J. Cain, *Fodor: Language, Mind and Philosophy*

Rosemary Cowan, *Cornel West: The Politics of Redemption*

Colin Davis, *Levinas: An Introduction*

Matthew Elton, *Daniel Dennett: Reconciling Science and our Self-Conception*

Simon Evnine, *Donald Davidson*

Chris Fleming, *René Girard: Violence and Mimesis*

Edward Fullbrook and Kate Fullbrook, *Simone de Beauvoir: A Critical Introduction*

Andrew Gamble, *Hayek: The Iron Cage of Liberty*

Nigel Gibson, *Fanon: The Postcolonial Imagination*

Graeme Gilloch, *Walter Benjamin: Critical Constellations*

Karen Green, *Dummett: Philosophy of Language*

Espen Hammer, *Stanley Cavell: Skepticism, Subjectivity, and the Ordinary*

Phillip Hansen, *Hannah Arendt: Politics, History and Citizenship*

Sean Homer, *Fredric Jameson: Marxism, Hermeneutics, Postmodernism*

Christopher Hookway, *Quine: Language, Experience and Reality*

Christina Howells, *Derrida: Deconstruction from Phenomenology to Ethics*

Fred Inglis, *Clifford Geertz: Culture, Custom and Ethics*

Simon Jarvis, *Adorno: A Critical Introduction*

Sarah Kay, *Žižek: A Critical Introduction*

Douglas Kellner, *Jean Baudrillard: From Marxism to Post-Modernism and Beyond*

Valerie Kennedy, *Edward Said: A Critical Introduction*

Chandran Kukathas and Philip Pettit, *Rawls: A Theory of Justice and its Critics*

James McGilvray, *Chomsky: Language, Mind, and Politics*

Lois McNay, *Foucault: A Critical Introduction*

Philip Manning, *Erving Goffman and Modern Sociology*

Michael Moriarty, *Roland Barthes*

Harold W. Noonan, *Frege: A Critical Introduction*

William Outhwaite, *Habermas: A Critical Introduction*
Kari Palonen, *Quentin Skinner: History, Politics, Rhetoric*
John Preston, *Feyerabend: Philosophy, Science and Society*
Chris Rojek, *Stuart Hall*
Susan Sellers, *Hélène Cixous: Authorship, Autobiography and Love*
Wes Sharrock and Rupert Read, *Kuhn: Philosopher of Scientific Revolution*
David Silverman, *Harvey Sacks: Social Science and Conversation Analysis*
Dennis Smith, *Zygmunt Bauman: Prophet of Postmodernity*
Nicholas H. Smith, *Charles Taylor: Meaning, Morals and Modernity*
Geoffrey Stokes, *Popper: Philosophy, Politics and Scientific Method*
Georgia Warnke, *Gadamer: Hermeneutics, Tradition and Reason*
James Williams, *Lyotard: Towards a Postmodern Philosophy*
Jonathan Wolff, *Robert Nozick: Property, Justice and the Minimal State*

Forthcoming

Maria Baghramian, *Hilary Putnam*
Sara Beardsworth, *Kristeva*
James Carey, *Innis and McLuhan*
George Crowder, *Isaiah Berlin*
Thomas D'Andrea, *Alasdair MacIntyre*
Maximilian de Gaynesford, *John McDowell*
Reidar Andreas Due, *Deleuze*
Eric Dunning, *Norbert Elias*
Neil Gascoigne, *Richard Rorty*
Paul Kelly, *Ronald Dworkin*
Carl Levy, *Antonio Gramsci*
Moya Lloyd, *Judith Butler*
Nigel Mapp, *Paul de Man*
Dermot Moran, *Edmund Husserl*
Stephen Morton, *Gayatri Spivak*
James O'Shea, *Wilfrid Sellars*
Felix Stalder, *Manuel Castells*
Nicholas Walker, *Heidegger*

Contents

Acknowledgements

The writing of this book would not have been possible without the gracious assistance of a whole assortment of friends, colleagues, and sympathetic strangers. First of all, I'd like to thank Steven Maras for introducing me to the work of Girard in the first instance (which is not the same as making him responsible for what happened after that). John O'Carroll has been a constant and singularly invaluable conversation partner in all matters anthropological, epistemological, religious, and ethical. His intellectual openness, scrupulousness, and friendship have been key factors in writing this book. Jane Goodall has consistently been the best scholarly mentor one could wish for. Her indefatigable encouragement of multiple perspectives in intellectual work will hopefully mean that she'll be pleased to see here things with which she would, I have no doubt, strongly disagree. My head of school, Carol Liston, still takes seriously the idea that research is a central part of what academics should do; she provided support by lightening my teaching load during the final preparation of the manuscript. Indeed, the whole team of Humanities at the Blacktown campus have remained in constant dialogue with me about the process and offered advice, encouragement, and sympathy when required – thanks especially to Ruth Barcan, Kath McPhillips, Bob Hodge, and Anthony Uhlmann. And to my research assistant, Karen Enwistle: thanks again for your marvellous efforts in helping me to prepare the references.

To René Girard I am deeply indebted; for being gracious enough to lend his time to talk to me about his work at length – and for providing us all with that work in the first instance. To Jim Williams, for fielding some tough questions and coming up with some of his own; and to Eric Gans, for the same – as well as for making available to all users of the Internet a great forum where questions of the sort he and Girard raise can be seriously discussed. Andrew McKenna, William Johnsen, and Julie Shinnick have each assisted this project at various points by helping me get my hands on resources that would have been otherwise impossible to obtain. Elizabeth Molinari at Polity must also be thanked, most of all for her encouragement of the project and her seemingly limitless patience.

Eris and John Fleming were, again, invaluable supports in more ways than they could probably imagine. Thanks also – for so much – to my singularly wonderful 'new relatives': Hélène, Gil, Zöe, and Nick. And David Haggerty's humour, thought, encouragement and friendship continue to be a genuine blessing. My largest debt of gratitude, however, is to Mindy Sotiri, a partner in all things – confidante, sparring partner, friend, and soul mate. This is for her, of course.

While friends have often not been overly critical of my work, my critics have been unfailingly friendly. Some have drawn attention to a variety of errors; some of these I have corrected, and some I have not. In this respect at least the work remains – perhaps needless to say – something for which I remain ultimately responsible.

Abbreviations

I shall refer to Girard's major texts using the following abbreviations. Where a page reference is followed by a slash and a second reference, the first refers to the page number of the English translation, and the second to the French edition. In most cases, translations are taken from the English edition, sometimes slightly modified for consistency or clarity; titles of Girard's works appear in English in cases where references are given to both French and English editions. Where only one page reference is cited, it refers to the English edition, unless otherwise noted.

DB *'To Double Business Bound': Essays on Literature, Mimesis, and Anthropology.*

DD *Deceit, Desire, and the Novel: Self and Other in Literary Structure* (French: *Mensonge romantique et vérité romanesque*).

GR *The Girard Reader.*

IS *I See Satan Fall Like Lightning* (French: *Je vois Satan tomber comme l'éclair*).

J *Job, the Victim of his People* (French: *La Route antique des hommes pervers*).

RU *Resurrection from the Underground: Feodor Dostoevsky* (French: *Dostoïevski: du double à l'unité*; re-released in 1976 as a chapter in *Critique dans un souterrain*).

S *The Scapegoat* (French: *Le Bouc émissaire*).

TE *A Theater of Envy: William Shakespeare* (French: *Shakespeare: les feux de l'envie*).

TH   *Things Hidden Since the Foundation of the World* (French: *Des
        choses cachées depuis la fondation du monde: recherches avec Jean-
        Michel Oughourlian et Guy Lefort*).
VS   *Violence and the Sacred* (French: *La Violence et le sacré*).

Full information on editions used is listed in the reference section
at the end of the book.

Introduction

It seems to us that Girard's research provides an 'Archimedian point', outside the terrain of classical thought, from which we might profitably de-construct this thought, not in the service of a nihilism which is only the negative image of its failure, but as a *positive* reflection which is capable both of integrating the assets of traditional philosophy and of providing a true anthropological foundation to the 'social sciences.'

Eric Gans, 'Pour une esthétique triangulaire'[1]

Gans may have underestimated the case.

Sandor Goodhart, *Sacrificing Commentary*

While it may be tempting to regard the above reactions to Girard's work as, in the very least, a little overblown, it is less easy – although perhaps equally tempting – to dismiss the body of work that prompted them. Although one would hazard to guess that relatively few contemporary theorists would go so far as to endorse Gans's and Goodhart's assessments, it seems clear to a wide range of scholars that René Girard is one of the most original and influential cultural theorists on the contemporary scene. He is the recipient of honorary doctorates from half a dozen European universities, he has been awarded both the Prix de l'Académie Française (for his book *Violence and the Sacred*), and, more recently, has had the French Academy's Grand Prix de Philosophie bestowed upon him in recognition of his position as one of the outstanding philosophical anthropologists of his generation.

Additionally, there is a substantial and ever-growing body of secondary literature that utilizes Girardian themes and hypotheses to analyse a diverse collection of cultural, social, and psychological phenomena; this literature has utilized Girard's work to open up – or reopen – a host of disciplinary perspectives and questions. Indeed, the impact of his thought has extended across a remarkably wide range of disciplines: from literary theory, anthropology, philosophy, classical studies, and psychology, to systems theory, economics, political science, religious studies, and even musicology. Perhaps more surprising is that there has even been an openness among theorists in biology, chemistry, and physics to Girard's thinking about which they see some parallels with their own.

Additionally, to date, Girard's books have been translated into fifteen languages which, by itself, tends to suggest that his readership – and hence influence – extends far beyond French- and English-speaking audiences. In 1994, an annual scholarly journal – *Contagion: Journal of Violence, Mimesis, and Culture* – was established specifically to discuss Girard's work and the areas with which it intersects; and a wide range of special issues of journals have also been devoted to the discussion of his work, including *Diacritics* (1978), *Esprit* (1979), *Sciences Religieuses/Studies in Religion* (1981), *Schrift* (1985), *Semeia* (1985), *Stanford French and Italian Studies* (1986), and *Helios* (1990); additionally, Girard has been the subject of several Festschrifts, among them *To Honor René Girard* (1985), *Violence and Truth* (1988), and *Violence Renounced* (2000).

And yet, despite this large circle of influence, and by his own admission, Girard's work – both in its method and in its conclusions – is largely out of step with current trends in the humanities and social sciences. The breadth of his endeavour, his synthesizing ambitions – his reticence to abandon the idea that cultural theory should, and indeed can, contribute positive knowledge concerning *la condition humaine* – mark him off somewhat from many of his peers both on the continent and in the Anglo-American academies.

As it stands, however, the charge of atypicality should hardly constitute the basis for any blanket disrecommendation of Girard's work; indeed, it is the above features of his *oeuvre* that provide some of the signal reasons as to why it requires close examination. The character of his work is such that it is possessed of certain nuances that make it difficult to characterize briefly: it is a body of work that is highly systematic, and yet it is not quite a 'system'; its developments have entailed certain disciplinary applications, yet there is no 'Girardian school', 'accreditation procedures', or 'federation'; it is

work that is broadly sympathetic to those currents in the humanities and social sciences that are often described as 'poststructuralist' or 'postmodern' and yet it is highly critical of such tendencies
when they preclude systematic, hypothetical approaches to understanding culture and society; finally, the intellectual orientation
of his work owes little to the main currents of thought in the
twentieth century – Marxism, structuralism, phenomenology,
Hegelianism, and Freudianism – and yet it is worked out in an
intense and sustained engagement with these.

This book attempts to provide a substantial critical introduction
to Girard's work. As I understand it, one of the clear dictates of
the genre, of the introductory monograph, is that the map offered
should not compete with the territory it hopes to elucidate in either
scale or complexity. Nonetheless, this remains a temptation, exacerbated somewhat in the case of the subject of this book, because of
the very nature of his theoretical enterprise. Although his work has
profitably been taken up by philosophers, Girard is, strictly speaking, not a philosopher – and as such it needs to be emphasized that
his cultural and literary hypotheses cannot be properly understood simply through an elucidation and clarification of central
concepts. One of the elements of Girard's work that cannot be
replicated in a book such as this is the extensive amount of anthropological, ethnological, and literary particulars that he brings to
bear on his reflections. The abstract movement of his thought,
that is, cannot be appreciated in the absence of the extremely dense
evidence he enlists to bear out his claims; Girard does not present,
in other words, a theoretical framework that somehow stands
by itself. Given this limitation of the present study, I feel obliged to
make a customary but important caveat – that this book is an
extended *invitation* to Girard's work and by no means a *substitute*
for it.

It is also worth alerting the reader at the outset, in light of my
previous remarks, that the book represents a generally sympathetic
treatment of its subject; it is not without its own reservations or
moments of critical examination, but it takes its task to reside far
more in the realm of *elucidation* than *evaluation*. I hope that my
stance here is little over and above a mirror held up to personal idio-
syncrasies, a stylistic preference that reflects nothing save my own
irritation with books that systematically undermine the figures they
purport to introduce. Capitalizing on the fact that those reading
these books are very unlikely to have encountered much of the
theorist's work itself, one can become quickly convinced that

actually reading them isn't quite worth the trouble. While these books might serve in some ways as introductions to a body of work, they can never be *invitations* to it. Given Girard's somewhat marginal status in the current humanities academy, this danger is multiplied by increasing the probability of conveying the impression that one needn't actually engage with the author as he has somehow already been 'debunked'. In light of this, it would seem that there is, no doubt, a partly apologetic function to an introduction, even if this function is based on little more than the idea that the author thinks that engagement with the subject's work is worth the effort. So while this may be an apologetic of sorts, I sincerely hope that it does not display the paranoia seemingly constitutive of apologetic genres. Others, needless to say, will have to be the judge of this.

René Girard: personal and intellectual biography

René Girard was born on Christmas day, 1923, in Avignon, France.[2] He obtained his baccalaureate in philosophy at the Lycée of Avignon in 1941 and attended the Ecole des Chartres in Paris from 1943 to 1947, graduating as an archiviste-paléographe [a medievalist] with a thesis entitled *La Vie privée à Avignon dans la seconde moitié du XVe siècle* [*Private Life in Avignon in the Second Half of the Fifteenth Century*]. Pursuing an opportunity to study in the United States in 1947, he matriculated from Indiana University in history, receiving his PhD in 1950, with a dissertation entitled *American Opinion of France, 1940–1943*. Girard's early historical work seems a far cry from the kinds of problematics and the breadth of theorizing that would come to characterize his later work. The highly specific questions and micro-historical approaches to socio-cultural patterns appear radically removed from the concerns of a theorist whose interdisciplinarity approach to intellectual questions is renowned, and whose pursuit of what might be termed a 'grand unified theory' of interpersonal relations, religion, and cultural formation has been unrelenting.

The shift in Girard's thinking towards far broader social and cultural questions was prompted by his being assigned to teach courses in French literature at Indiana, an assignment which demanded a thorough familiarity with a range of texts with which he was previously unacquainted. Although Girard's doctoral work had been in history, his fascination with the literature that he was asked to teach made such an impact that by the time of the publication of his first book he would be identified as a literary critic. After completing his PhD at Indiana, he took up a number of successive academic posts, first as an instructor at Duke University, then as an assistant professor at Bryn Mawr from 1953 to 1957. From Bryn Mawr, Girard was appointed associate professor at Johns Hopkins University, chairing its Department of Romance Languages from 1965 to 1968, and becoming a full professor in 1968. In 1966, while still at Johns Hopkins, Girard – along with Eugenio Donato and Richard Macksey – organized a conference which was to have a significant impact on the emergence of critical theory in the United States. The conference, entitled *The Languages of Criticism and the Sciences of Man*, included papers by, among others, Roland Barthes, Jacques Derrida, Lucien Goldman, Jean Hyppolite, Jacques Lacan, Georges Poulet, Tsvetan Todorov, and Jean-Pierre Vernant.

While he was at Johns Hopkins, Girard wrote his first two books: *Mensonge romantique et vérité romanesque* (1961) and *Dostoïevski: du double à l'unité* (1963).[3] The first of these was a study of the works of five novelists: Cervantes, Stendhal, Flaubert, Proust, and Dostoevsky, in which Girard argued – or, rather, professed to allow his subjects to contend – that human desire was anchored neither in (desiring) subjects nor in (desired) objects, but in the *imitation* of the former from which one learns the value of the latter. This is what Girard calls 'mimetic' (*Gk* 'imitation') or 'triangular' desire, and it is one of the key elements of his thought at virtually every level of operation. It is his contention that subjects learn what to desire from observing mediators or models, whose desire for objects is imitated; we learn what to desire, in short, by copying the desires of others. Girard argues that, given certain conditions, this mediation (of desire) happens quite consciously, as is the case with cultural practices such as forms of discipleship, pupilage, and apprenticeship; in other instances, mimetic desire operates more or less undetected – such that the subject believes that his or her desires are 'originary' or authentically individual. (It is this last, false construal of desire, for Girard, that lies at the heart of romantic constructions of subjectivity.) Girard's second central contention concerning desire is that, given the pervasiveness of mimesis, mediators can thus function not only as models for desires, but also as *rivals* in the consummation of those desires. The envy and jealousy attendant upon this (mimetic) structure of desire means that its conflictual potential remains a continual threat to interpersonal relations. The majority of Girard's work can be properly viewed as an exploration of the broad – cultural, religious, and philosophical – ramifications of non-conflictual and, especially, conflictual mimesis.

Girard is one of the very few cultural and literary theorists – indeed, perhaps the first – to emphasize adequately the *appropriative* aspects of imitation. Since Plato, mimesis has been figured almost solely in terms of *representation*; philosophical discussions of mimesis are preoccupied with, for instance, the way in which art, language, or concepts 'imitate', or simulate, reality (or, more recently, fail to do either of these). Girard holds, on the other hand, that mimesis involves not simply representations but intentions and acts of *acquisition*: it is possible not only for us to attempt to mimic reality through philosophical or artistic representations of it, but to mimic the desires of others and thereby bring us into possible conflict with them. Mimesis, that is, often tends to engender conflict between people as the desires of individuals begin to converge on common objects.

Girard's *Mensonge romantique et vérité romanesque* [*Deceit, Desire, and the Novel: Self and Other in Literary Structure*] is somewhat unusual as a book of literary criticism, as it appears to make scant use of most of those categories of analysis common to its era, and has a comparatively small debt to those traditions that were, at the time, thought to constitute legitimate approaches to literature: new criticism, phenomenology and hermeneutics, reception theory, structuralism and semiotics, and Marxism. Rather, Girard's approach – or, at the very least, his avowed approach – was to derive the critical resources for his reading of literature from literature itself. In many of the works that he examines Girard claims to be able to detect an incipient logic that is capable of shedding light not only on the work itself, but on those critical or theoretical approaches usually employed to analyse literature more generally. A plea that he has reiterated throughout his career is that we shouldn't read Proust or Dostoevsky in light of psychoanalytic theory, but rather psychoanalysis in the light of Proust or Dostoevsky. (One is reminded here of Vladimir Nabokov's *Pale Fire*, where a poet, through poetry, provides insightful criticism on the criticism which takes the poetry itself as its object.) He holds that particular late works of those novelists discussed in *Deceit, Desire, and the Novel* make available to us a highly lucid depiction of the machinations of desire and interpersonal relations – works which, through a laborious process of auto-critique, reveal the romantic myopia to which the novelist's earlier works are subject.

Needless to say, the fact that Girard's critical approach stands outside any easily recognizable disciplinary matrix in literary studies, as well as his often highly antipathetic view of much contemporary criticism, has limited somewhat the uptake of his thinking in literary and cultural studies – but there are notable and striking exceptions to this.[4] Girard's theorization of mimetic desire, as well as his critical engagement with psychoanalysis, is the subject of the first chapter.[5]

In 1971, Girard was appointed distinguished professor at the State University of New York at Buffalo, a position he held until 1976. During this time he wrote *La Violence et le sacré* (1972) [*Violence and the Sacred*]. Greeted by something of a fanfare in *Le Monde* – which claimed 'L'année 1972 devrait être marquée d'une croix blanche dans les annales des sciences de l'homme' [The year 1972 should be marked with an asterisk in the annals of the humanities] – it was translated into English in 1977; it is this work with which Anglophone theorists would appear to be most familiar.[6] The result of a decade's research, *Violence and the Sacred* represents the first substantial stage of Girard's exploration of the ramifications of his theory of mimetic desire in relation to anthropology, Greek tragedy, and mythology. More ambitious than his previous two books, this work offers a series of hypotheses concerning the generation and stabilization of cultural order in 'primitive' societies – and, indeed, in communities more generally. Developing the premise that mimetic desire often leads inexorably to rivalry and conflict, Girard posited that the origins of cultural order and stability resided in repeated acts of collective violence against a lone victim (or group of victims) – a scapegoat. It was this postulation of a hypothetical morphogenetic mechanism which accounted for the generation of cultural and social order – the 'surrogate victimage mechanism' – that Girard pursued and developed theoretically in a series of subsequent publications: the first section of *Des choses cachées depuis la fondation du monde* (1978) [*Things Hidden Since the Foundation of the World*]; *'To Double Business Bound': Essays on Literature, Mimesis, and Anthropology* (1978); and *Le Bouc émissaire* (1982) [*The Scapegoat*]. Girard's reading of myth and tragedy and his formulation and application of the hypothesis of surrogate victimage provide the foci for chapters 2 and 3.

In 1976, Girard accepted his second appointment at Johns Hopkins, as John M. Beall Professor of the Humanities, a position he held for the next four years. At this time, following on from the success of *Violence and the Sacred*, Girard released a book which took the format of a series of conversations between himself and two psychiatrists: Jean-Michel Oughourlian and Guy Lefort. The book – *Things Hidden Since the Foundation of the World* – seemed to make Girard, in his native France at least, both a *cause célèbre* and a *bête noire*. Based on a series of discussions which took place at Cheektowaga and Johns Hopkins universities between 1975 and 1977 (supplemented by some of Girard's earlier writing), the book delivered an exhaustive overview and extension of his work to date, including a thesis that had not appeared previously, developed via a sustained reflection on the Judeo-Christian scriptures.

Where *Violence and the Sacred* had seemed to reveal a theorist who was inherently hostile to religion, *Things Hidden* significantly complicated this picture but did not quite *overturn* it – certainly not in any straightforward sense. In the middle section of this book, Girard put forward the striking idea that, far from being texts which advocate the kind of violence associated with the surrogate victimage mechanism – the violence which functions to initiate and maintain social stability and cultural order – the Judeo-Christian scriptures represented a progressive unveiling, repudiation, and critique of this violence. Girard has since developed and extended this controversial thesis in books such as *Le Bouc émissaire* (1982) [*The Scapegoat*], *La Route antique des hommes pervers* (1985) [*Job, the Victim of his People*], and *Je vois Satan tomber comme l'éclair* (1999) [*I See Satan Fall Like Lightning*]. This aspect of Girard's work will be the focus of chapter 4.

In 1981, Girard accepted his next and final academic post, as Andrew B. Hammond Professor of French Language, Literature, and Civilization at Stanford University. Since then, his scholarly output has been steady, including the above mentioned works, as well as a book on Shakespeare – *A Theater of Envy: William Shakespeare* (1991) – a book of conversations with Michel Treguer – *Quand ces choses commenceront* (1994) – and, most recently, *Celui par qui le scandale arrive* (2001). Despite being now over eighty years old, Girard shows few signs of slowing down.

Although his work continues to exert considerable influence in France and, to some extent, in Germany, it is far less familiar to scholars in the English-speaking academy. Some of the possible reasons for this state of affairs are explored in the final chapter, which also takes as its task an examination of some of the applications of Girard's work.[7]

1
Mimetic Desire

Deceit, Desire, and the Novel (1961) represents Girard's first attempts to articulate a concrete theorization of desire through a detailed reading of literature. Aligning himself with neither psychoanalysis, Hegelianism, nor Spinozism, Girard instead claimed to have found an incipient logic of interpersonal relations in a kind of *literary* work that he termed 'novelistic' [*romanesque*]. For him, this literature possessed potentially far greater theoretical and critical resources – greater hermeneutic and heuristic capacities – than most of those theories usually employed to examine *it*. Girard even went so far as to argue for a kind of inversion between literary criticism and its objects: instead of using theories such as psychoanalysis to understand Proust or Dostoevsky, he advised us, no doubt provocatively, to do the opposite: to use the critical insights of Proust or Dostoevsky to understand Freud.

It is the purpose of this chapter to introduce Girard's theorization of 'mimetic' desire and the notions of 'internal' and 'external' mediation; to examine his theory of the novelistic and the romantic literary works; to outline his accounts of psychopathology – of 'pseudo-masochism' and 'pseudo-narcissism'; to place into a broader historical frame some of his reflections on mimesis; and, finally, to elucidate the main features of the nature of Girard's engagement with psychoanalysis. We turn, now, to the notion of 'mimetic desire'.

Desire and mimesis

What is undoubtedly most distinctive about Girard's theorization of desire is that it is based on the notion of imitation, which he refers to by invariably invoking the Greek term – 'mimesis'. Pointing to the obvious centrality of imitative behaviour in human social and cognitive development, Girard makes the (fairly uncontentious) point that, without the ability to copy the behaviour and speech of others – what he calls a 'mimesis of apprenticeship' [*mimétism primaire*] – human socialization, our capacity to inhabit a culture, would be impossible (*TH* 7/15).[1] Socialization and enculturation are contingent on learning 'how to do things' through detailed processes of tacit and explicit imitation; it is, indeed, exceedingly difficult to think of areas of human development that would be able to function without this dimension.

To this, Girard adds – somewhat more contentiously – that human *desire* is also constitutionally imitative. In other words, mimesis, as Girard sees it, involves not simply representation and other forms of cultural memory – it incorporates acts of and intentions towards *acquisition*; here Girard speaks of a 'mimesis of appropriation' [*une mimésis d'appropriation*] (*TH* 7–10/15–18). Girard describes desire as mimetic because of what he sees as the overriding importance of imitation in the constitution of our desires; fundamentally, he suggests, we learn what to desire from copying the desires of others: 'To say that our desires are imitative or mimetic is to root them neither in their objects nor in ourselves but in a third party, the *model* or *mediator*, whose desire we imitate in the hope of resembling him or her' (*RU* 144).[2]

But here it is important to note, however briefly, reservations that Girard has about the term 'desire' [*désir*] itself and the kinds of misleading associations it is likely to invoke. Firstly, he distances his own thinking from psychoanalysis, with its emphasis on the sexual origin and character of desire (*TH* 345/367). Secondly, he warns against those (usually) philosophical approaches to human desire that figure it as thoroughly discontinuous with the kinds of natural propensities exhibited in the animal kingdom. Girard argues that, although mimetic desire as such is distinctly human, this distinctiveness should be seen as emerging from non-human capacities for imitation. Ethological studies have repeatedly tended to suggest that non-human animals have mimetic propensities that are grafted onto more basic needs and appetites (*TH* 283–4/307–8).[3]

Here it is important to note that, although animal needs for hydration, shelter, rest, and nutrition persist at the human level, they do not, in themselves, constitute 'desire' *per se*. Any of these needs may serve as pretexts for the formation of desire, but, by themselves, are not sufficient for it.[4] Needs require satisfaction, but the ways in which they are satisfied take their cues from how *others* meet those same needs; that is, the indeterminate set of objects that might be said to correspond to a (putative) need are invariably transformed and given concrete form by what others desire (or at least what others *behave as if* or *say* they desire). But whereas those drives and needs that are grounded in the biological life of a being are capable of being satisfied – however temporarily – *desire* can emerge in the absence of any genuine appetite at all: 'Once his basic needs are satisfied (indeed, sometimes even before), man is subject to intense desires, though he may not know precisely for what' (*VS* 146/217). This constitutive indeterminacy of desire, Girard argues, takes its cues from others, who mediate desire for us: 'We desire what others desire because we imitate their desires.'[5] Grafted onto the needs and appetites of animal life – but under-determined by them – desire is in large part an *act of the imagination*, involving fascinations with objects and figures that possess not only use values, but *symbolic* values as well – rivalries for symbolically mediated objects made possible by symbolic institutions (*TH* 93/102; cf. 283–4/307–8). What Girard offers us here is an eminently parsimonious hypothesis about human subjectivity; however, as Sandor Goodhart warns us, the 'simplicity and elegance of this theory should not blind us to the enormity of its explanatory power.'[6] Precisely of what this explanatory power consists we shall consider presently, but first, a few further clarifications are in order.

Girard's basic hypothesis concerning desire is most aptly schematized by the triangle; it is not, in other words, a theoretical schema which figures desire as a straight line of force which extends between (desiring) subject and (desired) object, but a complex of lines running from the subject to the mediator of desire and back again.[7] The object is desired neither because of its intrinsic value (like, say, the Freudian 'maternal object') nor as a result of being consciously 'invested in' or 'chosen' by the will of an autonomous subject – it is desired because the subject (consciously or non-consciously) imitates the desire of another (an Other), real or imaginary, who functions as a model for that desire. For Girard, then, desire is *le désir selon l'Autre* [desire following, or according to, the Other], rather than *le désir selon soi* [desire according to one's own unique, intrinsic preferences]: it is neither autonomous nor innate (*DD* 5/13).[8]

The epistemology of literature, or, literature as epistemology?

Girard contends that his ideas concerning desire are the result of a detailed engagement with literature. In *Deceit, Desire, and the Novel*, he discusses what he sees as an incipient logic, concretely if not formally expressed, in certain nineteenth- and early twentieth-century European novels. In selected works of Flaubert, Stendhal, Proust, Cervantes, and Dostoevsky, Girard detects a highly lucid problematic of interpersonal relations that emphasizes the primacy of imitation and rivalry. In Flaubert's *Madame Bovary*, for instance, the author informs us that Emma's desires were learnt by reading while she was at convent school; her models are the romantic heroines typical of the trashy fiction that she devoured (*DD* 5/14). Another example is the character Marcel, in Proust's *Remembrance of Things Past*, who we are told is decidedly underwhelmed by the performance of the famous actress Berma until he hears her praised socially, first by M. de Norpois and then by a reviewer in *Le Figaro*. After this, Marcel is convinced that Berma's performance had been everything that he had expected it would be (*DD* 37/43).

In suggesting that certain literary works are able to provide us with an array of cogent critical tools, Girard is firmly committed to the idea that literary criticism and cultural theory need not always borrow all of their conceptual resources from established disciplines – from semiotics, philosophy, psychoanalysis, or sociology. Rather, he argues that it is possible to find in literary works themselves implicit or half-explicit analytical tools and scenes that criticism itself can utilize and further systematize. And yet, here one should be careful about what is being asserted: Girard's claim concerning the epistemological or cognitive veracity of literature should *not* been seen as signifying the victory of a certain critical intellectual mode over the literature about which it contemplates – he is not of the view that the novel represents a degraded mode of abstraction which merely serves the purpose of illustrating 'theses' (that would perhaps be better expressed in a critical idiom). Girard's point is not that literature is somehow bad (or even latent) theory. Literary theory, rather, is – or at least should be – *an extension of its object*; and its formal rigour should be undertaken out of respect for the

rigour, again, of the literature it contemplates: 'Literary interpretation should be systematic because it is the continuation of literature'
(*DD* 3). Again, Girard argues that, instead of applying modern theories to interpret modern novels, we should criticize the former in
light of the latter, once their 'theoretical voice has become explicit';
therefore, his – and our – relation to novelistic works, he claims,

> cannot be defined as 'critical' in the usual sense. We have more to
> learn from them than they have to learn from us; we must be stu-
> dents in the most literal sense of the word. Our conceptual tools do
> not come up to their level; instead of 'applying' to them our ever
> changing methodologies, we should try to divest ourselves of our
> misconceptions in order to reach the superior perspective they
> embody. (*DB* x–xi)

In light of remarks such as the one above, it should perhaps come
as little surprise that contemporary novelists of the likes of Roberto
Calasso and Milan Kundera have shown far more than just a
passing interest – and more than a begrudging respect – for Girard's
thinking.[9] But Girard is doing far more than demonstrating a finely
honed capacity for flattery; as we will see, he is actually substantially doing what he proclaims to be doing. In any case, his com-
pliments are not haphazardly distributed; the literary detection of
the primacy of imitation in interpersonal relations is not common
to the novel *as a genre*. Girard distinguishes between those works
which function to demystify, or 'demythify', this interpersonal
(mimetic) relation by exposing how the mediation of desire operates – *romanesque* [novelistic] works – and those novels which he
believes bolster notions of desire *selon soi* – *romantique* [romantic]
works (*DD* 16–17/24–5). Further, the *romans romanesques* is not the
domain of a select group of novelists; authors such as Dostoevsky,
who feature heavily in Girard's discussions of the *romanesque* work,
produced novels which do not fit into this category. Nor is the novelistic genre a purely eighteenth- or nineteenth-century phenomenon: it includes, among others, works by Shakespeare, Albert
Camus, Victor Hugo, Franz Kafka, James Joyce, Paul Valéry, and
Virginia Woolf.

For Girard, one of the signal characteristics of the romantic novel
is the way in which it valorizes – through its characters, and their
attitudes and actions – all instances of 'originality' and 'spontaneity', properties which are depicted in such works as indicators of
personal superiority. In terms of its 'geometry', the romantic con-

strual of desire is (again) that of a straight line running between a
desiring subject and (an intrinsically valuable) desired object. For
Girard, the *romans romanesques*, contrary to the romantic work,
shows that the ground of desire doesn't reside in any one subject:
it is, rather, always *between* them. And, in so doing, it throws into
question the intrinsic desirability of the object, recasting its value as
a product of the interpersonal – or, as he prefers, 'interdividual'
[*interdividuelle*] – relation.

As such, Girard's literary theory is somewhat idiosyncratic, given
that his approach to criticism relies neither on theory (extratextual
material) nor on purely formalist modes of analysis (which restricts
itself to intratextual material) – it is, rather, *inter*textual.[10] Girard is,
in other words, concerned with the author's own work at different
stages, and so compares individual works with others and places
each in a writer's *oeuvres complètes*. He has constantly – and no
doubt controversially – dealt with what he believes is a certain kind
of 'conversion' undergone by the author as revealed through the
development of the writer's *oeuvre*, as well as the transformations
of central characters at the end of most novelistic works.[11] For
Girard, the conclusion to the *romanesque* work consists largely in the
repudiation of what he calls 'metaphysical' desire, the 'pseudo-
deification' of pride, substituting a new mode of interpersonal relations not predicated on the slavish but largely unwitting imitation
of others (*DD* 307/305–6). In his work on Dostoevsky Girard argues
that this 'novelistic truth' [*vérité romanesque*] is well encapsulated by
the narrative transformation of the main character in *The Brothers
Karamazov*, whose emergence from the Dostoevskyan 'underground' well captures the novelistic 'resurrection', a late and desperate emergence from the 'romantic lie' [*mensonge romantique*] (*RU*
106–42/104–35).

Dostoevsky's novels, in other words, represent stages in a
cognitive-existential experience. As such, the author systematically
undermines his earlier works: acts which are portrayed as heroic
and expressive of a superior individualism in his first novels are cri-
tiqued in later ones, beginning, Girard argues, with *Notes from the
Underground* and *The Eternal Husband*. The later works depict the
same situations as the earlier ones, but the motives of the characters and the significance of their actions have been significantly
reframed by the author; attitudes and behaviours presented in the
earlier works as worthy of imitation are later shown to stem from
conflict and *ressentiment*, and are, for this reason, rejected. For
Girard, this narrative transformation, a transformation whereby

desire itself is recast, isn't simply expressive of authorial 'cynicism' or disillusionment: it is better knowledge. In Dostoevsky's later works 'passion' as such is not absent – what is absent is the depiction of passion as something spontaneous and individual. Equally, then, such passion is something that Dostoevsky makes the object of his *satire*, not the object of his solemn endorsement (*RU* 62/68).[12]

Yet, despite repudiating 'metaphysical' desire and the unwitting imitation of others, the recurring Dostoevskyan question of whether a person – through either conceit or great acts of heroism – can attain total independence from his or her peers, from their mediators of desire, is answered by him in the negative. For (Girard's) Dostoevsky, the heroism so typical of romanticism is merely the symptom of a more slavish servitude expressed as self-possessed 'pride'. Pride, in this sense, is evinced by those pervasive forms of 'negative imitation': the pursuit of individual distinction by doing what others *don't* do. The most obvious paradox of negative imitation is that it is still thoroughly entangled with the Other – the acquisition of putative 'difference' demands a meticulous observation of others (and perhaps even their approval) so that the romantic subject can distinguish himself or herself *from* them. Thus, fierce individualism leaves the mimetic relation unscathed and even bolsters its obfuscation. This 'romantic individualism', for Girard, is one of the archetypal expressions of cultural as well as literary modernity – a condition which intensifies the mimetic relationship by denying its existence and in so doing exacerbates its pernicious effects. As Girard says, 'the effort to leave the beaten paths forces everyone inevitably into the same ditch' (*DD* 100/105).[13]

Girard sees parallel comprehensions and critiques of romanticism (and even philosophical existentialism) in the work of a host of other novelists and a diverse range of cultural *milieux*. For instance, for Girard, the focus of Camus's *La Chute* [*The Fall*] is not so much some putative 'fictional universe' as his own previous work. The author, through Clamence, critiques Meursault – the central protagonist in *The Stranger* – for his rampant but unacknowledged *ressentiment*; Camus reveals the rigorous homologies between the existentialist anti-hero and the pose of coquette (*DB* 9–35).[14] The existentialist 'individual' is no less romantic (and certainly no less a hero) for his rejection of worldly goods and approval. Archetypally incarnated in Camus's Meursault and Jean-Paul Sartre's Roquentin (of *The Stranger* and *Nausea* respectively), this new romanticism remains even more in denial than its literary precursors, not simply for denying emulation but for *denying the*

heroic quest itself. Predictably, it was, in fact, a more pernicious form
of subjection (*DD* 270–2/271–3) – what Anthony Wilden has called
a 'Jansenism of the anti-hero' – something that Camus himself was
eventually able to see.[15]

Having stated some of the basic hermeneutic strands of Girard's
approach to literature and his assertion of its cognitive import, we
now turn to consider his theorization of mimetic desire and the
dynamics of rivalry in more detail, initially as these notions appear
and are developed in *Deceit, Desire, and the Novel*.

Mimesis and the dynamics of rivalry: internal and external mediation

Girard begins *Mensonge romantique* by citing a section from Miguel
de Cervantes' satire *Don Quixote de la Mancha* in which the hero,
Don Quixote, instructs his page on following the path of knight-
hood. The Don tells Sancho Panza that he himself strives to emulate
those 'knight errants' of chivalric romances; and at the apex of this
hierarchy of knight errants stands Amadis of Gaul, who is, for
Quixote, the very epitome of chivalry:

> I think . . . that, when a painter wants to become famous for his art
> he tries to imitate the originals of the best masters he knows. . . .
> Amadis was the pole, the star, the sun for brave and amorous knights,
> and we others who fight under the banner of love and chivalry
> should imitate him. Thus, my friend Sancho, I reckon that whoever
> imitates him best will come closest to perfect chivalry. (Cited in *DD*
> 1/11)

For Girard, the Don 'has surrendered to Amadis the individual's
fundamental prerogative: he no longer chooses the objects of his
own desire – Amadis must choose for him. The disciple pursues
objects which are determined for him, or at least seem to be determined for him, by the model of all chivalry. We shall call this model
the *mediator* of desire' (*DD*, 1–2/11–12). Girard points out how
Quixote's adventure is essentially mimetic – how his imitation of
Amadis transforms his judgements, his actions, and even his vision.
The Don's imitation of the great knight knows few limits. He
decides that he, like his model, must also have a beloved to whom
he can give himself totally, and through whom he can endure the
agonies of romantic involvement. Quixote chooses an undistin-

guished local farm girl, Aldonza Lorenza – although his desire, mediated through Amadis, transforms her into his hero's lover Dulcinea del Tobosco. Much of the comic impact of the novel, in fact, comes from Cervantes' depiction of Quixote's almost limitless imitative behaviour and the ways in which the Don's love and admiration of Amadis transforms his perceptual field. For instance, although he doesn't even know Aldonza – only admiring her from afar – Quixote dedicates his deeds of chivalry to her and even retires to the Sierra Morena mountains to do penance for her, just as Amadis had been ordered to do so by another of his loves, Oriana.

Cervantes' thematization of mimesis through the Don brings to light the potential for mimesis to shape not only behaviour but also the *perception* of behaviour; it provides not simply a model for how goals are pursued, but exemplars of which goals are actually *worth* pursuing. When Quixote and Sancho set out on their search for glory, inspired by chivalric romances, the banal objects and events of the Spanish countryside are metamorphosed by the two's obsessive attachment to dreams of the adventures of Amadis. For these two, the ordinary surroundings become full of damsels in distress, of evil and treacherous knights; a barber's basin takes on the form of the legendary helmet of Mambrino, windmills become imposing giants before them, and sheep are transformed into maleficent enemy warriors. As Girard says, mimetic desire works to transfigure its objects, and Cervantes has drawn our attention to this by revealing the presence and importance of the mediator of desire (*DD* 17/25).

For Girard, there are two primary possibilities for how desire is mediated: internally and externally. External mediation occurs when there is a sufficient space between the subject-who-desires and their mediator or model such that they do not become rivals for the same desired object; it is when, as Girard puts it, 'the distance is sufficient to eliminate any contact between the two spheres of *possibilities* of which the mediator and the subject occupy the respective centers' (*DD* 9/18). That is, external mediation serves as a bulwark against the degeneration of imitation into *emulation*.[16] Don Quixote himself provides for us a good example of external mediation: the Don does not have to vanquish Amadis of Gaul, his mediator, for chivalric glory to be his. Quixote's desire to become a perfect knight is modelled on Amadis's own chivalry, but the imitation here cannot involve rivalry because Amadis is a fictional character – a figure in a romance; and, even if Amadis were to have walked the earth, the separation in historical time between Quixote and Amadis makes physical rivalry impossible. But it is not simply spatial or temporal distance which determines the presence of external mediation – 'distance' here encompasses prestige or social rank. Therefore, it is not solely – or even primarily – a geographical or temporal matter, but what Girard calls a 'symbolic' or 'spiritual' one (*DD* 9/18). Amadis elicits a kind of respect from Quixote that is commensurate with religious reverence (*DD* 2/12). This also means that Quixote, above all, is *aware* of his mimetic behaviour – the Don makes his imitation an object of reflection for himself; his is a mimetic *apprentissage*.

This symbolic or spiritual distance also exists between Quixote and Sancho, who, although occupying the same spatio-temporal location – the landscape of La Mancha – are separated by a wide disparity in social rank. Quixote functions as an external mediator for Sancho in the same sense that Amadis does for Quixote. Indeed, Quixote's own chivalrous ambitions prove to be highly contagious to his companion, who continually takes for his own the desires shown to him by the Don. Before being subject to Quixote's desires, Panza was a simple farmer whose desires were those of a (stereotypical, literary) peasant. But in the presence of Quixote, Sancho appropriates the Don's desires, those that accord with the ideal images of a squire:

> Some of Sancho's desires are not imitated, for example, those aroused by the sight of a piece of cheese or a goatskin of wine. But Sancho has other ambitions besides filling his stomach. Ever since he has been with Don Quixote he has been dreaming of an 'island' of which he would be governor, and he wants the title of duchess for his daughter. These desires do not come spontaneously to a simple man like Sancho. It is Don Quixote who has put them into his head. (*DD* 3/12)

Girard argues not simply for the importance of the *presence* of mimesis in Cervantes' novel, but for the way in which this mimesis occurs – he argues that we should be sensitive to fact that Quixote's mediator is himself fictional; Amadis, in other words, *is a representation*. Through this, Cervantes renders *literature itself a central protagonist of the novel*, a 'character' even, which exerts a powerful influence on the propulsion of the narrative. (It is in light of this that Girard has repeatedly claimed, therefore, that he by no means *inaugurated* the tradition of reflection on mimetic desire, even at the so-called meta-level.)

So, we can see that external mediation exhibits the main features of mimetic desire: (1) the desirability of an object is predicated as desirable by the mediator, rather than on any intrinsic qualities it possesses; and (2) the objects which are designated undergo a transformation in the perception of the desiring individual so that they are imbued with an 'aura', the properties of which are, again, extrinsic to them. The distinguishing feature of external mediation is related to the field of action that the model and the desiring subject inhabit: although the model exerts a heavy influence on the thought and behaviour of the other, the distance between them in terms of either status or space and time is such that no rivalry develops as a result of the mediation.

In addition to externally mediated desire – and in contrast to it – stands the notion of internally mediated desire: this entails a form of mimesis mediated by a model who is not separated from the desiring subject by space, time, or social/spiritual distance, and thus is more liable to become a rival in the latter's attempts to attain an object. At the heart of internal mediation is a double-imperative: the implicit demand of the mediator is the command 'imitate me'; yet, if this were done 'to the letter', then the rival would need to assume the model's place (thereby placing the mediation itself under threat); therefore, the first message is coupled with another message, a warning: 'do not imitate me.' Internal mediation, then, is *conflictual* mimesis, as it entails the convergence of two or more desires on the same object.[17] However, the primary cause of conflict here is not scarcity – which may be thought to precede the interdividual relation – but the relation itself:

> Rivalry does not arise because of the fortuitous convergence of two desires on a single object; rather, *the subject desires the object because the rival desires it*. In desiring an object the rival alerts the subject to the desirability of the object. The rival, then, serves as a model for the subject, not only in regard to such secondary matters as style and opinions but also, and more essentially, in regard to desires. (*VS* 145/216–17)

Indeed, the antagonism that is produced would thus not be ameliorated by a surplus of goods; the source of conflict in desire is the presence of the contradictory double-imperative, noted above: 'Man and his desires thus perpetually transmit contradictory signals to one another. Neither model nor disciple really understands why one constantly thwarts the other because neither perceives that his desire has become the reflection of the other's' (*VS* 147/219). Girard

calls the mediator who functions both as a model for desire and an
obstacle to its fulfilment the 'model-obstacle' or the 'rival model'.
Internal mediation, in this sense, operates along the same lines as
what Gregory Bateson called the 'double bind', the presence of an
irresolvable contradiction which held (usually) between a message and the behaviour which framed or accompanied it (*VS*
146–7/218–19).[18] In the case of internal mediation, conflictual
mimesis, the model incites imitation *and forbids it* simultaneously:
'As I borrow the desire of a model from whom nothing separates
me, neither time and space, nor prestige and social hierarchy, we
both inevitably desire the same object and, unless this object can be
shared and we are willing to share it, we will compete for it' (*RU*
144–5).[19]

One of the most finely articulated portrayals of internal mediation Girard discusses is taken from Dostoevsky's short story *The
Eternal Husband*. After the death of his wife, Pavel Pavlovitch
Troussotzki embarks upon a perverse journey to seek out, and possibly befriend, her former lovers. In St Petersburg, he finds and
ingratiates himself to such a man – Veltchananov. Within a short
time, Troussotzki finds himself asking his recently acquired 'friend'
to meet his new fiancée and help him select for her an engagement
ring; despite some initial, understandable, reluctance, Veltchananov
accedes to the request. It is not long before we realize that history
will repeat itself; the fiancée, now seemingly unsatisfied with
Troussotzki, allows herself to be seduced by Veltchananov.
Dostoevsky reveals Troussotzki as a man unable to desire anything
outside of the mediation of Veltchananov – neither his partner, nor
the engagement ring that he asks Veltchananov to help him select.
Girard's interest in the story has to do with its capacity to render
pellucid the role of the mediator of desire, of how the mediator
makes the desired object desirable at the same time that he or she
obstructs the desiring subject from attaining it. *The Eternal Husband*
marginalizes the importance of the object and reveals the centrality
of mediation. Indeed, Dostoevsky reveals that the former lovers of
Troussotzki's wife are more important to him than the wife herself,
for it is they who endow her with desirability; Veltchananov's
ability to seduce her attests to his power, his superior being, and,
for this reason, makes him a privileged mediator of desire (*RU*
47–62/55–68; *DD* 45–51/55–7). It is the rival, Girard argues, that is
the ultimate authority in matters of desire; this is the relationship
that the novelistic work detects, of a 'self' that 'imitates constantly,
on its knees before the mediator' (*DD* 298/297).

Like *The Eternal Husband*, the vast majority of relationships por-trayed in Stendhal's *The Red and the Black* [*Le Rouge et le noir*] are internally mediated. From the outset of the narrative, the rivalry between two aspiring bourgeois, Monsieur de Rênal and Monsieur Valenod, takes shape in their concerted individual efforts to hire Julien Sorel as a tutor for their children. Stendhal's depiction makes clear that neither particularly wants a tutor to begin with; all that is required for them to fight over Julien's favour is for each to become imbued with the idea that the *other* wants him (*DD* 6/15). Rênal's decision to hire Sorel as tutor is grounded in little more than the suspicion that his rival, Valenod, hopes to do the same. Valenod then attempts to hire Julien because Julien is in the employ of Rênal. Girard describes this as 'double' or 'reciprocal' mediation: the medi-ator is drawn into the operations of mimesis, imitating the desire of the Other that the Other first located in him or her; it does not require that the desires attributed to the Other are real, or rather real *yet* – double mediation is easily able to *generate* the reality that it believes it perceives: 'Each person prepares himself for the prob-able aggression of his neighbors and interprets his neighbor's preparations as confirmation of the latter's aggressiveness' (*VS* 81/124–5).

In Jean-Pierre Dupuy and Paul Dumouchel's seminal contribu-tion to political economy – *L'Enfer des choses: René Girard et la logique de l'économie* – Dupuy offers the following lucid summation of this kind of scenario:

> It is neither the subject nor society that determines what is desirable, but the *Other*. Or rather, since the subject and his *alter ego* have become perfectly interchangeable doubles, it is their involuntary cooperation that makes the object spring forth from nothing. Each discovers in the desire of the Other the absolute proof of the reality and value of the object. As these rival desires increasingly exacerbate one another as their human bearers become closer, they become capable of creating a world more real and desirable than any object of physical and social reality.[20]

That is, we attribute to the Other certain (real or imagined) desires which actually precede and/or generate the realities to which they ostensibly refer. In the scenario in *The Red and the Black*, referred to above, although each is acutely aware of his rival's desires, neither actually attributes the origin of his desires to the desires – actual or imagined – of his model-rival; these desires are seen, rather, as being founded on the intrinsic desirability of the object.

More than this, each of the rivals uses desire as strategy for individuation – the belief that their own desires are the 'true' and 'original' ones, that it is their rival's desires that are derivative, and that the successful attainment of the object would somehow incarnate this truth and reveal to the rival their patent inferiority. The chief irony, however, as Girard sees it, is that, as internal mediation intensifies, the identities of the subjects involved become increasingly singular; escalating rivalry equates to escalating mimesis, and the result of this striving for differentiation actually works to efface differences: rivals effectively become *doubles* of each other. So, contrary to what one might suspect, extreme interpersonal hostility and rivalry, in other words, do not destroy *reciprocity* (*IS* 22/42). Indeed, these may well exacerbate it. To the extent that internal mediation renders protagonists antagonists, subject to the movements of mimetic rivalry, the putative object of desire loses its centrality in the minds of rivals, becoming little more than a convenient pretext for mimetic struggle.[21] Rivals become for each other the *raison d'être* for their struggle, and the object over which this rivalry is ostensibly produced retains its significance solely by virtue of its place in maintaining the misrecognition that their rivalry is anything but the elimination of the other.

In the second half of *The Red and the Black*, we are again faced with some stark examples of internally mediated mimesis. In the latter part of the novel, Julien Sorel moves to Paris and becomes the secretary of the marquis de Mole. He initially finds the marquis's daughter arrogant and unattractive, but soon changes this assessment while at the ball at the Hôtel de Retz, when he notices the attention lavished on her by a group of other young men. Likewise, Mathilde's interest in Julien does not originate autonomously but is prompted by her (externally mediated) infatuation with an ancestor, Boniface de la Mole. The subsequent love affair between the two illustrates how the triangular model that Girard has constructed (or detected) finds further application when the vertices of a 'love triangle' are reconfigured to represent only two participants.

Although their initial attraction to each other is contingent on the presence of actual third parties, once the affair between Julien and Mathilde begins, another kind of triangulation takes effect. This new triangulation has as its vertices the subject or lover at one corner, the (sexualized) body of the beloved as ostensible object of desire at another, and, finally, the beloved (as mediator). The subject's desire is directed at the body of the beloved, who can accede to this desire if he or she wants to; upon revealing his or her desire for the consummation of the body of the beloved, the beloved copies that desire through a process of self-objectification and self-valuation. Through mediation, therefore, the subject 'realizes' the value of his or her own (sexualized) body such that to allow the lover access to it is tantamount to being beaten by a rival. Girard states that in this form of triangulation the subject will 'desire his own body; in other words he will accord to it such value that to yield possession would appear scandalous to him' (*DD* 159/165).

This dynamic is borne out by the affair between Julien and Mathilde; each time Mathilde gives herself to Julien she is, mysteriously to herself, troubled by her accession, even scandalized by it. Girard argues that the temporary way out of this particular kind of double-bind is for one of the partners to renounce desire or at least give the other the *impression* that desire has been renounced. He calls this act of renunciation the subject's *askesis*, and suggests that its impact resides in the fact that such renunciation of desire is *entirely consonant with it* (*DD* 153/159). In cases of internally mediated desire, it is precisely the presence of the rival that keeps subject and object apart. But it is also the case that the rival's desire is *itself* derived from the subject (both subject and rival mediate each other's desires); thus, the renunciation of desire by either party simultaneously clears the path for the consummation of that desire at the same time that it divests the desired object of its value. Julien's feigned indifference towards Mathilde denies her a mediator to copy, and therefore her self-possession is abated; by seemingly withdrawing his affections, Julien ceases to be Mathilde's (sexual) rival. Indeed, Julien's indifference is precisely that which allows him sexual access to Mathilde's affections. By the same token, Mathilde's desire for Julien escalates enormously after Julien shows indifference towards her; no longer self-absorbed, she begins to desire him intensely simply by virtue of his indifference. It is Julien's feigned self-sufficiency, his seeming lack of need for anyone, especially Mathilde, that makes him so attractive to her; his self-desire becomes the model which provides Mathilde with instructions for where she should direct hers. Julien's state of perceived self-sufficiency – his feigning of God-like independence and indifference – corresponds, Girard suggests, to the condition of the *vaniteux*, so characteristic of Stendhal's novels.

Pseudo-masochism, pseudo-sadism, and 'metaphysical desire'

The hero's *askesis* – the strategic withdrawal or concealment of desire – effects a projection of self-sufficiency or autonomy that attracts the desire of others. Girard calls this attraction to the putative autarky of the other 'metaphysical desire' – a fascination with figures that signify a certain fullness of being, a substantiality that the desiring individual feels that they lack. The figures onto which metaphysical desire is projected mediate 'being' for us; it is via them that we seek to become real and it is through wanting their very being that we come to imitate them. The desired object, therefore, is only the means by which the subject can be reached. Girard argues that desire is ultimately aimed at the mediator's very *existence* in an attempt – or repeated attempts – to absorb it, to assume it (*DD* 53/59; *VS* 146/217). Desire then, in this sense, is that form of mimesis which imbues an appetite with metaphysical or ontological valences (*TH* 296/321–2). Metaphysical desire thus describes a desire not for the objects of desire but for the model's uniqueness, spontaneity – his or her 'qualities': 'Imitative desire is always a desire to be Another' (*DD* 83/89); 'Mimetic desire makes us believe we are always on the verge of becoming self-sufficient through our own transformation into someone else.'[22]

In other words, Girard maintains that the possession of objects is merely a path, the perceived privileged route, to the attainment of the ontological self-sufficiency detected in the rival. In this sense, strategic indifference to another's advances merely taps into that putative self-sufficiency of the model characteristic of metaphysical desire. The desiring subject reasons that, if 'the model, who is apparently already endowed with superior being, desires some object, then that object must surely be capable of conferring an even greater plenitude of being. It is not [simply] through words, therefore, but by the example of his own desire that the model conveys to the subject the supreme desirability of the object' (*VS* 146/217).

In *Remembrance of Things Past*, the narrator Marcel states that he feels that the being of others is somehow more real than his own; and, in *Swann's Way*, he declares that he feels hollow and lacking, that all around him seem more important and substantial than he (*DD* 54–5/59–61). It is in this kind of scenario in which, Girard says, 'men will become gods for each other' (*DD* 119/125). Marcel's search for an appropriate mediator, one who will be able to fill up his felt lack, becomes almost his singular obsession; and, as each mediator ultimately proves disappointing, Marcel's personality decomposes, with a succession of selves tied to the succession of mediators that seem to promise salvation (*DD* 90–1/95–6). Again, as desire becomes increasingly 'ontological' or 'metaphysical', the object falls away and desire is directed at the rival *through* the object.

For Girard, metaphysical desire captures the essence of 'masochism', or rather – given Girard's dissatisfaction with the history of conceptual interpolations of this phenomenon – 'pseudo-masochism', which leads ultimately beyond disappointment to something altogether more grim: 'The will to make oneself God is a will to self-destruction which is gradually realized' (*DD* 287/286).[23] As desire suffers disappointment after disappointment, the metaphysical quest itself is not abandoned: rather, the masochist merely seeks out more powerful mediators from which to attain real, substantial being. Put simply, the masochist understands that the object which can be obtained and held easily is next to useless. Therefore, his or her future resides in the search for an object impossible to attain; in essence, the (pseudo-)masochist only pursues lost causes (*DD* 176/181):

> A man sets out to discover a treasure he believes is hidden under a stone; he turns over stone after stone but finds nothing. He grows tired of such a futile undertaking but the treasure is too precious for him to give up. So he begins to look for a *stone which is too heavy to lift* – he places all his hopes in that stone and will waste all his remaining strength on it. (*DD* 176/181)

In the masochistic relation, desirability is a property constituted by the informal taboo interposed between the desiring subject and the object by the presence of a rival. The prohibition, in other words, renders the object desirable at the same time that it attests to the superiority of the model-obstacle; something about the unworthiness of the desiring subject 'obliges the god to forbid access to the holy of holies, to slam shut the gates of paradise. Far from reducing the divinity's prestige, this new attitude of vengeful spite serves to increase it' (*VS* 175/258). The masochist, then, is a casualty of metaphysical desire; he hopes that realizing the desires that he sees in the Other will bring about the hoped-for self-sufficiency and allow him to participate in his divine being.[24] But since the self-sufficiency, divinity, or plenitude that the masochist attributes to the model is illusory, his project to attain the same is doomed from the outset. The masochist vaguely perceives the fruitlessness of his quest but fails to give it up because to do so would mean that the promise of salvation would have to be given up along with it.

Again, for Girard, Dostoevsky gives some of the most well-articulated novelistic depictions of masochism in literature. The characters in his novels do not enter into rivalry simply because of some ill-defined sense of 'hatred'; they are also attracted to their rivals and even conspire – implicitly and sometimes even explicitly – to help them to achieve victory. There is a double transformation at work in masochism: as the models increasingly become obstacles, desire eventually works to *transform obstacles into models*; that is, eventually masochistic desire is capable of being aroused only by the promise of failure:

> Whenever the disciple borrows from his model what he believes to be the 'true' object, he tries to possess that truth by desiring precisely what this model desires. Whenever he sees himself closest to the supreme goal, he comes into violent conflict with a rival. By a mental shortcut that is both eminently logical and self-defeating, he convinces himself that the violence itself is the most distinctive attribute of this supreme goal! Ever afterward, violence and desire will be linked in his mind, and the presence of violence will invariably awaken desire. . . . Violent opposition, then, is the signifier of ultimate desire, of divine self-sufficiency, of that 'beautiful totality' whose beauty depends on it being inaccessible and impenetrable. (*VS* 148/221)

The ultimate logic is that, rather than the model's desire conferring value on the object, the model's desire itself becomes the most valued thing: the mediator is valuable, in other words, because of the *obstruction he or she is able to provide* (*DD* 176–7/181–2). Masochism lets the desiring subject forget the object and redirects desire towards violence itself: the obstacle *qua* obstacle, that is, becomes the real object of desire (*VS* 148/220–1). In this instance, therefore, rather than obstruction and competition being the results of desire (owing to the presence of a limited number of contested objects of desire), *desire* comes to be determined by *obstruction*. Here one could cite the 'underground man' of Dostoevsky's *Notes from the Underground* – a character who desperately covets an invitation to a school reunion *principally because he has not been invited*.

In this sense, the model-obstacle becomes a lightning rod for *ressentiment* because she has revealed the radical incompleteness of the self – but she remains as model because she guides the subject's own aspirations; without her, desire would have to be renounced. In other words, victory (in appropriation) entails defeat, as with victory comes the de-investment of the objects and the prestige of the rival who conferred on them their value. Thus, the masochist aims not exactly for his own defeat *per se*, but the model-obstacle's victory; in this way, the model – and desire itself – can be preserved. By the same token, a successfully attained object signifies only to the masochist that a more powerful rival should be sought, as this would secure the 'really' desirable, of which the acquired object has proved to be only a paltry simulation (*VS* 148/220–1). Only the victory of the rival would indicate an 'authentic deity, a mediator who is invulnerable to his own undertakings' (*DD* 176/181).

Girard sees the continual search for failure in the masochist as predicated on a certain (perverse) kind of theology; masochistic endeavours appear analogous to the search for a kind of primitive god, a far superior rival who is, for all intents and purposes, insensitive and invulnerable to the masochist's own projects and desires. The masochist seeks out only those models of desire who will deny him access to what he seeks. Desire is 'attracted to violence triumphant and strives desperately to incarnate this "irresistible" force. Desire clings to violence and stalks it like a shadow because violence is the signifier of the cherished being, the signifier of divinity' (*VS* 151/224). Like Groucho Marx, the masochist would never like to be admitted to a club where he would be accepted. In turn, the masochist then turns this judgement onto others; he will reject those who love him most (or profess to) and admire only those disgusted with him.

But Girard doesn't want to make of the masochist some kind of museum exhibit or bizarre psychological anomaly, operating in a fundamentally different way from 'normal' psychological processes. Contrary to the received interpretation, Girard argues that Dostoevsky wasn't so much interested in 'abnormal' psychological processes – merely normal ones *in extremis*. The masochistic relation merely crystallizes a far more widespread but rarely acknowledged psychological dynamic: that desire is prone to feed on those obstacles placed in its way. In fact, in terms of the realization of this dynamic, Girard suggests that the masochist possesses a lucidity that has actually drawn him very near the truth of conflictual (internally mediated) desire, while still participating in its primary delusion: the rival (competition) is everything and the *object of desire is nothing*. In this assessment, Girard seems to be very much at odds with those psychological theories – such as 'rational-

emotive' therapy – that suggest that the pathological psyche simply
needs a healthy dose of 'reality', that most psychological dysfunc-
tions are essentially *epistemological* afflictions; this kind of therapy
attempts to reveal to the patient her 'distortions' of thought
and encourages the patient to 'reorganize' her thinking patterns.
Girard would suggest that the pathological psyche has seen reality
very clearly, and any distortions are brought out, in fact, by this
realization.[25]

In 'pseudo-sadism', Girard sees the 'dialectical reversal' of
masochism. The sadist seeks to be a model for imitators for whom
she will provide obstacles, and in playing the part of mediator,
hopes to turn the adoption of her role – that of a divinity – into
reality (*DD* 184–5/188–9). Pseudo-sadism emerges at the point
when the masochist, who has worshipped violence, begins to
emulate those who have blocked his access to objects of desire:
'Tired of playing the part of the martyr, the desiring subject chooses
to become the tormentor' (*DD* 184/189). The sadist looks for imitators whom he can torture in the same way that he thought he was
tortured prior to adopting the role. Indeed, it is the sadist's prior
experience as victim that suggests the appropriate course of action.
Yet, the emergence of sadism, of this 'dialectical reversal', is by no
means the simple 'opposite' of masochism: it is, rather, the same
condition at a different moment. Nor is the movement from
masochism to sadism stable or irreversible; both masochism and
sadism are subject to the same double-imperative – of wanting to
overcome the rival and simultaneously to be overcome *by* the rival
(relating to the fact that the model underwrites the value of the
object while keeping the desiring subject from it). In *The Brothers
Karamazov*, the underground man is eventually able to attend the
school reunion, only to behave like a fool and (again) feel humili-
ated in front of his peers. This humiliation provokes a mimetic replication of the behaviour of those in front of whom he felt disgraced,
a (momentary) sadistic reversal, which ends with his torturing of
Liza, a prostitute he picks up (*DD* 185/190).

Although Girard attempts to develop and utilize notions such as
'pseudo-masochism' and 'pseudo-sadism' as accurate descriptions
of psychological realities, he is interested in these phenomena not
merely as clinical psychological or literary entities, but as realities
– both symptoms and causes – that are often rooted in far
broader social and historical shifts. We now therefore need briefly
to consider this possibility in relation to the phenomenon of
'modernity'.

Metaphysical desire and Stendhalian modernity

Although Girard has attempted to construct – or perhaps has often given the appearance of constructing – theoretical models that accurately depict the operations of human desire *per se*, free from any cultural context, his analyses are often tempered with an acute sensitivity to historical contingencies that give the expressions of such desire very different inflections. At least in part, *Deceit, Desire, and the Novel* functions as a kind of social history of mimetic desire in Europe from the sixteenth to the nineteenth centuries, as mediated through fiction; various incarnations of the modern novel, as well as political ideals and institutions, are woven together in *DD* in a field of reflection centred on mimesis. Although the work contains a theory of the novel, its concerns are characteristically trans-disciplinary. The implications of Girard's theory – as well as the reflections which lead to it – are often able to connect with and help to articulate much broader historical trends and the existence and persistence of certain social imaginaries.

One of the important secondary theses of *Deceit, Desire, and the Novel* is that internally mediated desire – and the forms of resentment and envy that invariably accompany it – is exacerbated in those cultural environments where traditional social structures have become eroded and their expression less easily able to be legitimately channelled into forms of physical violence. Needless to say, the label 'modernity' is often applied to describe such a cultural environment in relation to the history of the West since the Renaissance.[26]

Additionally, modernity's witness to a general reticence to grant any kind of deference to 'superiority' and its hostility towards traditional forms of authority finds one of its chief ethical expressions in what is often called the 'egalitarian ideal', an ethico-political imperative which rendered 'equality' the privileged yardstick for gauging the application and distribution of justice. To give this characterization a Girardian inflection, modernity offered – and continues to offer – fewer and fewer opportunities for external mediation, and, in this respect, models of desire were (and are) more likely to become, simultaneously, rivals.[27] And yet, despite this valorization of equality during modernity – or, rather, *because* of it – life quickly became a task centred upon 'distinguishing oneself', especially among the middle classes.[28] This project became increasingly common in a world where social hierarchies had become

eroded and each person was progressively subject to a kind of
romantic individualism which was predicated on the disavowal of
any kind of mediation, external or otherwise. In an insight which
finds interesting analogues in works such as Alexis de Tocqueville's
Democracy in America and key elements of Thomas Hobbes's
Leviathan, Girard argues that the emergence of increasing democra-
tization, acquisitive individualism, and (upward) social mobility
manifested especially in nineteenth-century Europe gave rise to
heightened forms of rivalry (*DD* 136–7/141–2).[29]

In the context of his discussion of *The Red and the Black*, Girard
notes the exacerbation of internal mediation attendant upon the
demise of monarchical authority during the French Revolution.
The previous acceptance of the theory of the Divine Right of Kings
structured a certain kind of transcendence that underwrote other,
derivative, forms of social differentiation; the very tangible
socio-historical presence of the king was offset by his status as a
quasi-divine figure – the instantiation of an 'immense spiritual distance' between him, his royal subjects, and the rest of the population. When this divine right was abandoned with the overthrow of
the monarchy, another, equally secular, theology took its place:
'idolatry of one person is replaced by hatred of a hundred thousand
rivals. *Men will become gods for each other*' (*DD* 119/125; 117–22/
122–7).

And indeed, one of the foci of Stendhal's work was itself the historical dimension of the egalitarianism of the nineteenth century
which allowed rivalrous relationships to proliferate. For instance,
Julien's seduction of his master's wife, or of the aristocrat Mathilde
de Mole – even being accepted as a potential son-in-law by her
father – represent key instances where the social and cultural hierarchization that would have once prevented these episodes had
eroded. In the case of Rênal and Valenod, the approximate equality
of the two men – for instance, their inhabiting of the same town,
their being of a similar social class – allows for the development of
internal mediation, which in turn exacerbates their 'equality' (that
is, identity). Neither character functions for the other as a transcendent model, but both are subject to what Girard calls 'deviated
transcendence' (*DD* 158/163). The destiny of the modern subject –
well represented by those archetypal Stendhalian *vaniteux* of *The
Red and the Black* – involves it assuming the place of divinity after
the progressive demise of transcendence, whether this 'demise' is
thought about in terms of the Nietzschean 'death of God' or that of
the overthrow of political feudalism. After such shifts, the modern

subject endeavoured to replace those transcendent forms of mediation *with itself* (and those forms of utopianism on which such humanism relies) (*DD* 158–9/164).

For Girard, again taking his lead from Stendhal – as well as from Flaubert and Proust – one symptom of this failed project correlates to the disillusionment that people feel when physical gratification doesn't equate to metaphysical fulfilment (which is the origin of such desire); this Girard labels 'ontological sickness': the kind of disappointment witnessed in *The Red and the Black*, and the felt inadequacy of the narrator in Proust's *Swann's Way*. It is not that Girard (or Stendhal or Flaubert) argues that physical gratification is somehow 'base' or unworthy of attention; it is that the more someone attempts to find ultimate (metaphysical) fulfilment in physical pleasure, the less she is able to attain *any satisfaction from physical pleasure at all* (*DD* 85–7/91–3).

For Girard, the Proustian 'snob', like the *vaniteux*, provides a highly refined – even caricatural – image of the metaphysical desire and ontological sickness rampant in late modernity. The snob, in fact, looks for no concrete pleasures at all; his desires have become *purely* metaphysical; he therefore represents the degradation of interpersonal relationships into a rivalry that is almost totally abstract. For Girard, the emergence of this literary figure (which also finds correlation in the Flaubertian 'bovarist') is contingent on those historical conditions of the nineteenth century which saw the transformation of functioning aristocracies into nominal aristocracies; with their functionality denied to them, 'leisure classes' begin to seek achievement solely through the inheritance of status or prestige. The fight for prestige literalizes the idea of 'fighting over nothing'. But this 'nothing' appears as everything to those internal to the fight (*TH* 305/328–9). It is precisely its world of dematerialized, auratic objects that gives snobbism its caricatural qualities and lends itself so well to literary representation (*DD* 220–1/222–3).[30]

We have seen how – in selected work of the novelists discussed in *Deceit, Desire, and the Novel* – Girard detects an unveiling and antidote to the romantic construal of the subject characteristic of late modernity: these authors are said to deconstruct the vanity of the romantic subject and the proclaimed but delusional primacy, autonomy, and originality which they accord to individual desires. Girard argues that certain literary works reveal that the romantic subject hasn't escaped the mediated nature of desire, but has merely allowed this mediation to become dissimulated behind the strategies of desire itself. To this, Girard adds an even more contentious claim: that this literature does not simply offer an antidote to a cultural era which dissimulates its own slavish servitude to the mediator – it is also an antidote to most of those intellectual forms which emerge with and from that dissimulation. In the next section, we will look at how psychoanalysis itself articulates in highly refined form this dissimulation and how the psychology of mimesis allows Girard to account for the phenomena Freud wished to explain without the cumbersome theoretical apparatuses he employed to service this attempt.

The engagement with psychoanalysis

Like Freud, Girard developed his understanding of desire on a detailed reading of literature. To a certain extent, this sets the theses of both thinkers apart from those approaches to human psychology whose claims of scientific status rely on the repudiation or disavowal of the theoretical, even potentially 'clinical', perspicacity of fictional works. But the parallels between these two thinkers should not be overdrawn. Girard has had a protracted and highly complex engagement with psychoanalytic theory, an engagement during which he has not been reticent to acknowledge Freud's prodigious theoretical and clinical abilities, but also one in which he has been sharply critical of certain theoretical presuppositions and conclusions of psychoanalytic thought. To date, Girard's engagement with the work of Freud has centred on three main areas: Freud's theory of the 'Oedipus complex'; the psychoanalytic notion of 'narcissism'; and the more idiosyncratic Freud of (the late works) *Totem and Taboo* and *Moses and Monotheism*. We will leave a consideration of the last of these until the second chapter.[31] For now, we turn to examine the first two: the Oedipus complex and the notion of 'narcissism', as these are taken up and developed by Freud and subsequently examined by Girard.[32]

As already discussed, Girard contests the idea that desire is primarily object-oriented – involving what psychoanalysts commonly refer to as 'cathexis' – and favours instead the notion that the mediator provides the origin of a desiring subject's impetus towards an object (*VS* 180/264–5). Given this, it is little surprise that Girard argues that Freud was mistaken in his belief that the libido was the 'sole motor and basis' of psychic processes (*TH* 345/367). Girard's theory of mimesis can therefore not avoid a confrontation with the psychoanalytic characterization of desire as fundamentally object-oriented and sexual. Let us look then at how Freud depicts desire and sexual cathexis. In his *Group Psychology and the Analysis of the Ego* (1921), Freud offers us the following, now familiar, 'family scene':

> A little boy will exhibit a special interest in his father; he would like to grow like him, and take his place everywhere. We may simply say that he takes his father as his ideal. This behaviour has nothing to do with a passive or feminine attitude towards his father (and towards males in general); it is on the contrary typically masculine.[33]

Freud argues that, through identification with his father, a boy will want to 'take his [father's] place everywhere'; but to do so would inevitably lead to conflict, as this desire would include the intimate mode of relationship that the father has with the boy's mother. (Here Freud explains that the 'little boy notices that with regard to his mother his father stands in the way.') In this particular configuration, Girard has few problems with Freud's scene; allowing for a moment its descriptive veracity – that is, without importing into it any exclusively Freudian interpretation – the relationship between the father and son can be construed like any other form of conflictual mimesis. Indeed, Girard argues that Freud came very close to the notion of mimetic desire in his notion of 'identification' in *Group Psychology*, but eventually turned from it (*VS* 170–1/ 250–1). But the mechanism that Freud eventually adopts to explain the above family scene relates not to imitated desires or the model-obstacle relationship, but to the presence of the sexual/maternal object and the emergence of the Oedipus complex.

Freud describes this mechanism in *The Ego and the Id* (1923), where he contends that the boy develops an 'object cathexis' for his mother, the maternal object, and an identification with his father. This object cathexis (for the mother) undergoes progressive intensification, at which point the father – seen with increasing 'ambivalence' by the child – is perceived as the primary obstacle to the consummation of the boy's desires. For Freud, it is this dynamic which stands at the origin of the Oedipus complex.[34] Girard points out that, in the earlier *Group Psychology and the Analysis of the Ego*, Freud depicts the boy's identification with the father as developing in a way that is seemingly independent of any sexual cathexis; it involves primarily identification with a parent, with sexual rivalry instead being a *product* of this identification. But, Girard argues, as Freud turns away from this idea in later work, towards his thesis concerning the primacy of object cathexis – of primary sexual rivalry as the causal element of 'identification' and the generative principle of all other desires – the very notion of 'identification' itself becomes an increasingly vague, problematic element of Freud's explanatory scheme.

Contesting the plausibility of the Oedipal scene – or, rather, the theoretical elaborations that Freud draws from it – Girard argues that this sexual rivalry between father and son, where this occurs, is not the result of some perennial structure, but the product of the same historical situation discussed in the above section: the dissolution of traditional structures of authority during modernity – the increasing range of internal mediation in an era which also included the diminution of a certain kind of parental authority (*VS* 188/275–6). Obviously, what is at issue between Freud and Girard is not the potential for conflict inhering in the family scene, but recourse to very different explanatory mechanisms that attempt adequately to account for this antagonism. For Girard, Freud is ultimately a 'Platonist', yet another thinker who reifies a contingent historical condition into the realm of essences (*TH* 352–6/374–8). As Girard points out, in *Oedipus the King* and *Oedipus at Colonus*, the predominant rivalry is actually that between uncle and nephew; but we would be unwise, he suggests, to conclude therefore that this gives strong evidence of some perennial 'uncle–nephew rivalry' (any more than Dostoevsky's *The Brothers Karamazov* evinces a 'father–son theme'). In the case of Sophocles' tragedy, as soon as the 'groundless suspicion' is aroused against Oedipus, Creon becomes his rival; eventually, Oedipus's two sons, Polyneices and Eteocles, join in the struggle for the crown. That is, rivalry does not necessarily divide neatly along genealogical lines – and *ad hoc* attempts by psychoanalysts to refract all rivalries through a primordial Oedipal scene are vacuous to the extent that such a refraction appears to fit all conflictual intersubjective phenomena indifferently.

Central to Freud's schema is the notion that desire is the result of the spontaneous influence of an object on a subject: and the putative spontaneity of this attraction to the (maternal) object Freud believes is directly attributable to its intrinsic desirability. With this in mind, Girard spells out exactly what is in contention between his view and the psychoanalytic perspective: 'The mimetic process detaches desire from any predetermined object, whereas the Oedipus complex fixes desire on the maternal object. The mimetic concept eliminates all conscious knowledge of patricide-incest, and even all desire for it as such; the Freudian proposition, by contrast, is based entirely on a consciousness of this desire' (*VS* 180/264).[35] It is for this reason that Girard has claimed that Dostoevsky's mature works (along with the mature works of others such as Proust and Nietzsche) supply far better frameworks for the analysis of intersubjective phenomena than Freud's to the extent that the former acutely perceive the centrality of mediation in the genesis of desire, not the intrinsic value of any particular cathected object. It is in light of this that Girard contends that Dostoevsky will furnish a more adequate explanation of so-called Freudian phenomena than psychoanalysis can offer with regard to Dostoevsky's 'fiction' (*DB* 36–60).[36]

Contra Freud, it is the father – a certain kind of father in a particular socio-historical situation: a 'Freudian father' no less – who reads into the child 'patricidal' and 'incestuous' urges. Despite his innocence, the child experiences the father's rejection and will begin to perceive the ambivalent nature of his desire. In imitating his father, the child learns and begins to inhabit his culture; but the child learns also that this imitation has particular restrictions, that in certain circumstances the model of desire may simultaneously be an obstacle to its fulfilment. Here we can see the pertinence of Freud's observations concerning the 'ambivalence' involved in identificatory relationships. For Girard, this 'ambivalence' represents nothing more than the oscillatory emotions directed at a model/obstacle – the movement of feelings from admiration to hostility and back again.[37]

For Girard, then, psychoanalysis presents a manifestly incoherent developmental sequence of psycho-sexual development: Freud offers the Oedipus complex – a rivalry devoid of originary identification – followed by the emergence of the 'superego' – identification devoid of originary rivalry (*VS* 185/271). And this characterization itself allows us to see another signal difference between the Freudian and Girardian theorizations of desire. Where psychoanalysis explains conflict as originating *within* the self – the competing demands of the id, ego, and superego – Girard's explanatory scheme inverts this: conflicts within the individual, sado-masochistic 'perversions', and feelings of 'ambivalence' originate in conflicts with others – or, rather, in conflicts located *between* subjects.

As we have seen, mimesis – especially internally mediated mimesis – is invariably not conscious. That is, the imitation of models is dissimulated behind self-representations of unique,

object-oriented desires. Although, with some metaphorical displacement, this dynamic might be said to represent a kind of
Girardian 'unconscious', it is not equivalent to the Freudian notion.
The mimetic imitation of others is *unwitting* but not (in the Freudian
sense) 'unconscious'; it is unconscious only in the sense that it is
'misrecognized' [*méconnu*] or lacks self-reflexivity.[38] Mimesis, in other
words, involves the unconscious modification of consciousness.
For Girard, the postulation of the Freudian unconscious erro-
neously individualizes intersubjective relations and thereby locates
psychological dysfunction 'inside' the subject. Where the Freudian
unconscious defines an individual repository of repressed trauma,
the Girardian subject is constitutionally imbricated in a *public field*
of misrecognized beliefs and behaviours that inheres between
individuals and which, in turn, shapes them.

A further qualification – to talk of the Girardian 'subject' or 'individual' in this way – or perhaps in any way – is misleading.[39] There
is, according to Girard, no 'subject' that is temporally (or ontologically) antecedent to intersubjective – or, as Girard says, 'interdividual' – relations. It is not merely the case that we are subject to
others' 'influence'; it is, somewhat more radically, that others come
to dwell inside us. Indeed, Girard has even gone so far as to depict
the 'self' as a convergence point in an indeterminate field of
mimetic desire, of 'the interdividual relation' [*le rapport interdi-
viduel*], which is constituted, at base, by its interactions with others.
'Individuality' then, strictly speaking, doesn't exist – it is always
already 'interdividuality' (*TH* 84–104/93–113; esp. 84–9/93–8).[40]

Here one might be tempted to see close affinities between
Girard's work and that of Jacques Lacan, whose structuralist development of Freudianism envisaged a subject constituted by the
(necessarily social) symbolic order; indeed, Lacan's 'subject' is
something of an epiphenomenon of it.[41] Now, while not for a
moment contesting the importance of the symbolic order, and language particularly, on thought or on the constitution of the subject,
Girard locates language itself as an outgrowth of the more fundamental movement of mimesis.[42] That is, mimesis not only incorporates a larger field than 'representation' – in many instances, it
actually precludes it (especially *self*-representations concerning the
fact that we are imitating: there is no need to have propositional
knowledge of *how* to imitate or *that* one is imitating in order *to*
imitate). So where the (Lacanian) Freudian unconscious is a kind
of holding bay for the storage and dispatch of representations,
Girardian mimesis is able to operate without representation.

That is, representation takes its cues from mimesis, not the other way around: representation must entail 'consciousness' at some level, but mimesis, needless to say, doesn't always operate with the intentionality of a Don Quixote and his self-reflexive imitation of Amadis.[43] Indeed, mimetic antagonists can operate as such only if their mutual imitation remains obscured from themselves; to them, 'intention' must appear as a 'revelation' originating in themselves – indeed, representation must be effaced in order that mimesis can take hold.

Just as Girard throws into question the 'essence' or 'thing-like' structure of both the Oedipal complex and the 'unconscious', the same kind of critical strategy is applied to the Freudian notion of 'narcissism'. In *On Narcissism*, Freud examines the way in which the so-called narcissistic personality inverts the standard scenario of healthy psychological development. Freudian psychoanalytic theory posits that all children are naturally narcissistic but as they develop this self-love becomes externalized by increasingly attaching itself to a sexual object (of desire). Although supposedly 'normal', according to psychoanalytic theory this process results in the (sometimes pathological) libidinal undervaluation of the ego and overvaluation of the object. In the case of the narcissist (and here, for reasons well debated by feminist scholars, Freud discusses only women), the process is markedly different. Owing to certain developments, 'woman' has been denied the kind of freedom of choice regarding the object that man has been allowed, and so retains her narcissistic outlook by virtue of the fact that her libidinal investments aren't able to find external attachments. As a result, the narcissist develops a self-sufficiency that expresses itself in the desire not to love, but to *be loved*.[44] And here, for Freud, lies the seductive powers of the narcissist. Having been able to retain what the (non-narcissistic) man has not, she – the 'eternal feminine' type (as Freud calls her) – is supremely attractive to him, reminding him of the lost paradise of childhood; she is everything the man is not: indifferent, self-sufficient, inaccessible.

With regard to his theorization of narcissism, Girard sees in Freud a certain theoretical naivety strictly commensurate with his 'Platonism': 'At no point', argues Girard, 'does Freud admit that he might not be dealing with an essence but with a *strategy*, by which he himself has been taken in' (*TH* 370–1/393–4). 'Narcissism', for Girard, is simply the Freudian mythologization of coquetry. Such autonomous 'self-love' – absolute self-sufficiency, metaphysical plenitude – is implausible, standing largely as the ideal state of being, immortalized by the endless tributes paid to it by romanticism. Girard explains 'narcissism' as another configuration of the mimetic relation; the narcissist realizes that desire attracts desire and that in order to be desired she must demonstrate self-desire. Thus, narcissists' purported self-sufficiency – their aura of indifference – is a projection, a strategy, effected in order that they be coveted (sexually or otherwise) by others. This is the means by which the 'coquette', as Girard renames Freud's narcissist, possesses the 'divine' status that is capable of attracting others to her.

By the same token, the coquette's self-desire is mediated by those attracted to her at the same moment that *their* desire is mediated by the coquette's projected self-sufficiency. This demonstrative self-desire then receives nourishment from the desire it engenders, which is how the mechanism itself is able to regenerate. There is then, strictly speaking, no true 'narcissism', if by that one means true autarky, but only 'pseudo-narcissism' (*TH* 370–1/393–4; cf. *DD* 105–6/109–11). In other words, the attribution of ontological self-sufficiency attributed to the narcissist is an illusion generated by mimetic desire itself. It is because the Other appears to desire himself that I accept him as the object-model of my own desire. This, as Henri Atlan and Jean-Pierre Dupuy indicate, is the self-referential paradox at the heart of all mimetic figures: 'the illusion of self-containment is produced by precisely that which it itself produces, i.e. the fascinated stare of men.'[45]

It is in his construal of narcissism that Freud reveals most clearly what Girard sees as his thoroughly romantic theoretical orientation. Here we see the figure of the radically independent (albeit pathological) subject, possessed of uniquely powerful, individuating desires, in a one-to-one relation with those kinds of romantic heroes, seen, for instance, in many of the characters created by Freud's beloved author Goethe. It is in light of this that Girard asserts that 'psychoanalysis has been able to grant a reprieve – even apparently to grant new life – to the myth of the individual' (*VS* 183/268).

And it is in this context, perhaps, that we can understand the American welcome – and continuing infatuation – with psychoanalysis. The appearance of Freudianism in America, that great historical experiment of democracy and social 'equality' (however well or poorly realized in actuality), correlates with a more general transition from social hierarchy and constraint, to a newer imperative of *self-constraint*. Freudian desire, as the (putative) fundamental fact of life, as the most utterly irreducible element of individuality, functioned to legitimate the realization of this social change and authorize the generalized (American) ambition of upward mobility, by reading these characteristics as if they were part and parcel of 'human nature'.[46]

This is not to say, of course, that the kinds of maladies observed by Freud are merely nominal or in some way 'unreal'; Girard is deeply appreciative of Freud's observational capacity and his ability to articulate the sufferings of the modern subject. It is rather that he sees the somewhat romantic psychological atomism present in Freud's work as both clinically impoverished as a therapeutic modality and, where 'medically' efficacious, systematically misleading about its own modest successes. Psychoanalysis carries, Girard argues, some of the signal vestiges of what he calls the 'primitive sacred' – the presence of a sacred aura surrounding the analyst which confers on him a kind of transcendent power. And the greater the asymmetry of the patient–therapist relationship, the greater the therapeutic power of analysis. Psychoanalysis represents, therefore, the resurgence of a certain kind of authority during late modernity that confers upon it a kind of religious power; as such, it is also a victim and parable of modernity and its relentless assault on transcendent authority. Psychoanalysis becomes progressively less effective as it becomes de-legitimized, and not, contrary to popular belief, the reverse – its increasingly diminished ability to sacralize the analyst and prevent a thoroughgoing modernization of the patient–analyst relation is what psychoanalysis itself recognizes as the danger of 'counter-transference' (although it certainly doesn't describe it in these terms).

It is in light of this blindness towards its own therapeutic veracity that psychiatrists and psychologists have attempted to transform and extend mimetic psychology's theoretical perspicacity into the clinical setting; but there is no room here for any sustained consideration of what has become known as 'interdividual psychology'.[47]

In those works that have provided the focus of this chapter – his studies of the novels of Dostoevsky, Proust, Cervantes, Stendhal, and Flaubert – Girard examined the dynamics of mimesis primarily at the micro-level; although these dynamics were invariably seen in the broader socio-historical contexts in which they occurred, these early studies remained largely focused on those small-scale interpersonal relations depicted in the novels under scrutiny. In subsequent work, however, beginning with *Violence and the Sacred*, Girard turned to consider the functions and generative capacity of conflictual mimesis in culture and society more broadly. For now, we must direct our attention to those aspects of Girard's work that deal with issues which link mimesis – especially conflictual mimesis – with social and cultural order. Far from representing a dramatic shift in Girard's more 'psychological' concerns, his reflections at this broader level amplify certain key dynamics already discussed; and, in turn, his theorization of culture and society sheds some new light on issues broached in this chapter.

2
Sacrificial Crisis and Surrogate Victimage

> Violent antipathies are always suspicious, and betray a secret affinity.
>
> William Hazlitt

Beginning in the early 1960s – prompted by a colleague at Johns Hopkins, the literary theorist Eugenio Donato – Girard embarked upon an intensive exploration of nineteenth- and twentieth-century anthropology and detected there what he thought to be a startling range of convergences between key findings and themes of the field and some of his own prior work on literature. As a result of this research, Girard eventually redeployed and developed some of his initial insights on mimetic desire first broached in *Deceit, Desire, and the Novel*, and derived from them a far more general theory of violence and religion – an ambitious series of connected theses that offered no less than a morphogenetic hypothesis concerning the generation of social and cultural order. After a decade of reading and research, Girard presented his ideas in his book *Violence and the Sacred* (Fr. 1972), for which he was awarded the Prix de l'Académie Française.

The task of this chapter is to explicate the main formal and substantive features of Girard's major anthropological hypothesis: the surrogate victimage mechanism. To this end, we will begin our consideration of this second phase of Girard's work – a consideration that extends into the next chapter – with the notion of the 'monstrous double', a concept central, if not always by name then certainly by implication, in his formative works.

Monstrous doubles: the sacrificial crisis

One of the key postulates of Girard's early thinking, carried through
into all subsequent work, concerns the progressive erosion of differences between mimetic antagonists. He observes that, as rivalry
and combativeness between individuals intensifies, characteristics
that had previously distinguished them begin to dissolve – the
antagonists effectively become 'doubles' of each other: 'When all
differences have been eliminated and the similarity between two
figures has been achieved, we say that the antagonists are *doubles'*
(*VS* 159/235; cf. *VS* 164–5/242–3).

In our previous discussion of the novelistic work, we outlined
Girard's contention that the antagonists depicted in those novels (in
contradistinction with their *authors*) were typically unaware of the
doubling attendant upon interpersonal rivalry, more often than not
prone to pledge loyalty to the *mensonge romantique*. For instance, in
the rivalry between Valenod and Rênal in *The Red and the Black*, both
attribute to themselves the original, 'real' desire for the services of
Julien – and both attempt to secure Julien's favour in an increasingly desperate struggle for self-differentiation. We saw that in this
scenario resides a distinctly Girardian irony: more neurotic attempts
at differentiation or 'distinction' at the interpersonal level are not
simply compatible with the effacement of all significant differences
– they are *coeval* with it. That is, the more Rênal and Valenod attempt
to *outdo* each other, the more both come to *resemble* each other –
including the resemblance of each other with respect to their
increasingly desperate attempts at differentiation.

Girard moves one step beyond this initial postulate, however,
and argues that conflict does not merely *produce* doubling (although
it does) – it actually *depends* upon it. At the beginning of *Violence and
the Sacred*, he approvingly cites the psychologist Anthony Storr,
who notes that nothing 'resembles an angry cat or man so much as
another angry cat or man' (*VS* 2/10). This endorsement of Storr is
based on the psychologist's corroboration of one of the central preoccupations of Girard's work: the pervasive symmetrical pattern-
ing evident in forms of rivalry and agonistics.[1] Girard argues that
such 'sissiparity' has been recognized and emphasized by a variety
of authors; it is conspicuously evident, for instance, in depictions of
contest in classical and Shakespearean tragedy:

> There is no aspect of the plot, form, or language of a tragedy in which
> this symmetrical pattern does not recur. . . . [T]he core of the drama

remains the tragic dialogue; that is, the fateful confrontation during which the two protagonists exchange insults and accusations with increasing earnestness and rapidity. . . . The symmetry of the tragic dialogue is perfectly mirrored by the stichomythia, in which the two protagonists address one another in alternating lines. . . . No sooner is something added to one side of the scale than its equivalent is contributed to the other. The same insults and accusations fly from one combatant to the other, as a ball flies from one player to another in tennis. The conflict stretches on interminably because between the two adversaries there is no difference whatsoever. (*VS* 44–5/71–3)

The claim that a 'conflict stretches on interminably because between the two adversaries there is *no difference* whatsoever' undoubtedly seems counter-intuitive from the perspective of many of the claims of contemporary socio-cultural theory, which tends towards explanations of the genesis of interpersonal conflict in terms of unmanageable *differences* between people rather than the *absence* of those differences.[2] But this, Girard asserts, is almost the inverse to the truth: 'Order, peace, and fecundity depend on cultural distinctions; it is not these distinctions but the loss of them that gives birth to fierce rivalries and sets members of the same family or social group at one another's throats' (*VS* 49/78). He argues that one of the central factors which has blinded anthropologists and other social and cultural theorists to the relations between undifferentiation and virulent forms of social conflict – in 'primitive' as well as 'modern' societies – is a kind of entrenched hermeneutic ethnocentrism, an unwitting imposition onto all cultures and interpretative schemes of certain egalitarian ideals originating in the West.

But a close examination of literature and myth will tend to militate against explanations predicated upon the notion of difference as the origin of socio-cultural antagonism. Girard offers, for instance, a wide array of dramatic examples in which the manifestation of conflict is inseparable from the symmetry of its form – those episodes in tragic drama, for instance, in which adversaries match each other 'blow for blow': the deadly duel between the brothers Eteocles and Polyneices in Euripides' *Phoenician Women*, who imitate each other's verbal – and eventually physical – attacks, until they die simultaneously; the fatal encounter between Heracles and Lycus in Euripides' *Heracles*; the resemblances of Oedipus and Laius in Sophocles' *Oedipus the King*; and the increasingly undifferentiated rival camps of Brutus and Cassius on the one hand, and of Octavius Caesar and Mark Antony on the other, in Shakespeare's *Julius Caesar*.

Girard calls this escalation of violence – perpetuated by, and contingent upon, the effacement of differences between antagonists – a 'sacrificial crisis'. And it is not, he contends, merely a property of certain kinds of dramatic literature; its reality and structuring effects operate in actual human communities, and evidence of its occurrence can be detected in a startling array of cultural artefacts and practices. At peak levels of intensity, the sacrificial crisis involves not merely the progressive intensification of those kinds of violent reciprocity evident at the 'micro' (interdividual) level, but a form of contagious violence that moves in the direction of undermining those systems of cultural order in which antagonists are all positioned and from which they receive their individual and collective identities.[3] The sacrificial crisis is, therefore, what Girard has often also called a 'crisis of distinctions' or a 'crisis of degree' – one affecting the whole cultural order, typified by a gradual erosion of the 'regulated system of distinctions in which the differences among individuals are used to establish their "identity" and their mutual relationships' (*VS* 49/77–8).

To put the same point slightly differently, Girard argues that culture *itself* is gradually eclipsed as a preponderance of its actors become progressively de-differentiated (*S* 14/26). One of the obvious manifestations of the kind of phenomenon to which Girard refers – to resituate this discussion from the literary to the anthropological domain – is what cultural anthropologists have called the 'blood feud': the often catastrophic escalation of violent reciprocity which generates – and in turn is generated by – an ongoing replication of the strategies, actions, and even rationale of adversaries (*VS* 13–27/26–46). In this context, the occurrence of a blood feud represents the failure of a cultural system which would otherwise prohibit certain forms of violent (and imitative) behaviour and, where such prohibitions fail, redress transgressions by directing culturally acceptable levels of violence along endorsed pathways – such as we see in phenomena like capital punishment and ritual sacrifice. In the blood feud, however, prohibitions ultimately prove ineffective for regulating behaviour and mechanisms of 'redress' fall outside their proper, religiously prescribed, channels.

At each and every stage of the blood feud warring parties strive to establish a final and decisive 'payback' for their opponent's previous transgressions, yet no 'final' or decisive retributive act is available to participants, no payback ever securely underwritten. In the blood feud, rather, every move is reciprocated with 'interest' in a desperate and paradoxical attempt to arrest violence through a frenzied administration of the same.[4] The erosion of the identities of the warring parties and the absence of a judicial or juridical power that transcends antagonists ensure that such conflicts remain autogenous, their singular gesture reiterated indefinitely. Early in *Things Hidden Since the Foundation of the World* (Fr. 1978), Girard emphasizes the paralysing monotony of such conflict and its obvious links to forms of rivalrous 'doubling':

> At the level of the blood feud, in fact, there is always only one act, murder, which is performed in the same way for the same reasons, in vengeful imitation of the preceding murder. And this imitation propagates itself by degrees. It becomes a duty for distant relatives who had nothing to do with the original act, if in fact an original act can be identified; it surpasses limits in space and time and leaves destruction everywhere in its wake; it moves from generation to generation. In such cases, in its perfection and paroxism mimesis becomes a chain reaction of vengeance, in which human beings are constrained to the monotonous repetition of homicide. Vengeance turns them into *doubles*. (TH 12/20)

Here again we note the tenor of Girard's interpretation in relation to much work done in contemporary social theory, with which it might undoubtedly seem to be at odds. Girard's point is not simply that his notion of the erosion of differences is a more adequate theoretical rendering of the forces behind social conflict and cultural disintegration than its alternative, but that – insofar as they affirm that difference *per se* is what engenders social-cultural conflict – contemporary cultural theories are prone unwittingly to replicate the actual *perspectives of antagonists in social conflicts themselves*, who are also blind to such reciprocities. (Although individual parties in a conflict *participate* in mirroring they are not able consciously to *acknowledge* it.) And, likewise, because such parties are constitutionally unaware of the mechanism that causes them to converge on the same objects, they become unwittingly implicated in conflicts whose origin they do not adequately comprehend.

The Canadian philosopher Paul Dumouchel concurs and elaborates upon this point; he suggests that one of the primary reasons that even those 'external' to a dispute (including those who are theorizing about it) are unlikely to perceive this doubling – correlative with the theoretical impositions of the egalitarian hermeneutic – is that *we often take far too seriously the words of the antagonists themselves*:

Each one claims that an absolute difference separates him from his enemy, the great Satan, the empire of evil or the imperialist powers. We should know better and see through this, for the exchange of words but mimics the exchange of blows. On both sides the utterances are identical, enemies trade insults and threats, they make sure that the exchange is fair, that no one should receive less than he has given.[5]

And just as the breakdown of cultural order characteristic of what Girard calls the 'sacrificial crisis' can be seen as the result of violent reciprocities, this corrosion itself, operating as a positive feedback loop, *further promotes such rivalries* by erasing all forms of 'external mediation', all vestiges of social, cultural, and religious transcendence – during a sacrificial crisis, no deference to 'superiority' is tolerated as competitors increasingly meet each other in the same time and on the same ground. That is, as antagonism generates doubling, this doubling itself gives rise to renewed threats of violence, violence which is able to draw in people putatively external to a dispute while at the same time obscuring *the very symmetry in evidence at the moment that they become implicated*: 'From within the system, only differences are perceived; from without, the antagonists all seem alike. From inside, sameness is not visible; from outside, differences cannot be seen' (*VS* 159/235).[6]

So Girard holds that violent social conflict is *mimetic* not simply in the sense that antagonists can be unwittingly drawn into a monotonous replication of each other's offensives, but in terms which render pellucid the very contagiousness of violence itself: violence exhibits a remarkable capacity to infect those in close proximity to it, even, perhaps especially, those ostensibly 'rational' parties who intervene in an attempt to arrest its spread (*DB* 121–35). Girard argues, then, that the social problem of human violence is not simply that there is no natural end point to it (save, perhaps, death) – there is the related and perhaps greater problem that violence, like desire, is easily 'caught' by others, such that a personal dispute may eventually threaten to engulf an entire community.[7]

Girard argues that, once the sacrificial crisis has crossed a certain threshold, social institutions are powerless to halt the escalating disorder; in these circumstances, such institutions – for instance, those that are supposed to enforce 'law and order' – begin to be perceived by members of a particular society as little more than additional parties in the same struggle, rather than as its impartial arbitrators.[8] That is, the symmetry of gesture that characterizes the antagonism of individual opponents can very easily become a characteristic of social institutions: in such a context, 'adjudication' will appear as little more than revenge, and the justice it claims to represent will be seen to be the embodiment of the most profane aggression.[9]

But here we have what might appear to be a serious problem with Girard's theoretical scheme. If one provisionally grants Girard's hypothesis that the pervasiveness of mimesis tends towards forms of interpersonal conflict and rivalry, forms of conflict that escalate both in intensity and in reach, and for which there is no natural end point, then it is exceedingly difficult to imagine just how culture or society could themselves survive for very long. Indeed, it is difficult to see how culture or society *per se* developed in the *first instance*. Tracing Girard's response to this potential dilemma will open up the key features of his theory of cultural morphogenesis and order.

The scapegoat and the surrogate victimage mechanism

Rather than introduce at this point into his depiction of human conflict some 'faculty' or biological propensity that would 'balance' or mitigate against contagious violence, Girard argues that the reintroduction of order at the social and then cultural level involves a non-conscious intensification and polarization of violence itself – an intensification and polarization directed at a randomly selected victim. That is, mimesis, which functions to divide people among themselves (while uniting them in a symmetry of opposition) can and does reunite them *in fact* at a certain point by virtue of a rapidly emerging mutually endorsed enmity directed at a common enemy: the mimetic violence that divided a community by infecting it undergoes a vertiginous transformation whereby disparate antagonisms become mimetically polarized against a single party:

> If acquisitive mimesis divides by leading two or more individuals to converge on one and the same object with a view to appropriating it, conflictual mimesis will inevitably unify by leading two or more individuals to converge on one and the same adversary that all wish to strike down. (*TH* 26/35; cf. *IS* 22–3/42–3)

Girard says of the sacrificial crisis that 'only an act of collective expulsion can bring . . . oscillation to a halt and cast violence outside the community' (*VS* 151/224). What makes cultural disorder a specifically 'sacrificial' crisis, then, is that the only thing that can stop it after a certain threshold has been crossed is the operation of a spontaneous act of collective violence. And just as the formation of desires operates mimetically, so does this violent polarization; 'mimetic' is the best adjective to describe the process of the convergence of desire onto some person or object – and it equally well designates the imitative dynamics at work in the opportunistic selection of a victim. But contrary to acquisitive mimesis, however, this second, *accusatory*, mimesis draws together those who are implicated in it, with the moral certitude of the accusation itself standing in almost exact proportion to the extent of the *esprit de corps* that it is able to produce. Such a spirit of unanimity, crystallized in the operation of scapegoating, is testament to the intense human solidarity which seems to emerge between those who take it upon themselves to fight an identical enemy together, a spirit of unanimity predicated on a kind of violent catharsis in which the tension and unrest bedevilling a community is purged, temporarily at least, by inflicting the violent rage of a mob on a victim or a group of victims (*TE* 186; *TH* 26–7/35).[10]

As we have seen, Girard characterizes the sacrificial crisis as a 'crisis of degree' or a 'crisis of distinctions', a situation in which antagonisms are typified by an easily specified formal property – the pervasive mirroring of gestures and rationale of rivals. (Indeed, Girard argues, the very interchangeability of antagonists is a prerequisite for the emergence of an arbitrary 'sacrificial substitution' (*VS* 159/235; cf. *IS* 22–3/42–3).) But it is precisely here that we must also somewhat complexify the very notion of 'doubling': although rivalry and conflict undermine those differences upon which personal identity and social hierarchy are predicated, absolute undifferentiation can be approached only asymptotically; that is, the mimetic interchangeability of antagonists constitutive of a sacrificial crisis is inherently *finite*. Even at the heights of a sacrificial crisis, figures remain who are sufficiently different from others – or at least *seem* or are *seen* to be so (which, in any case, amounts to the same thing) – to prevent the emergence of total symmetry. It is these perceived differences, Girard argues, that function as cues for victimization; as chaos threatens cultural and psychological stability, these groups or individuals perceived to be different become the increasing focus of the hostile energies of the crowd.

Girard suggests that, typically, such scapegoats have committed no crime – or at least no crime that would distinguish them from any other; their 'crime', rather, is to possess features that when seized upon by the opportunistic mob serve to differentiate them from others. That is, the selection of a scapegoat invariably takes its cues from physical, mental, or cultural markers of difference that are easily recognized and singled out during moments of extreme social disorientation, during the 'crisis of degree'. These cues or markers represent, strictly speaking, what Gregory Bateson simply called 'information': 'a difference which makes a difference'.[11] They are, of course, not difficult to imagine: physical, behavioural, and mental abnormalities such as 'madness' and sickness, as well as genetic deformities, injuries, and disabilities. (In this context, the very notion of 'disability', for instance, extends to include a whole series of banal victimary signs: 'in a boarding school for example – every individual who has difficulty adapting, someone from another country or state, an orphan, an only son, someone who is penniless, or even simply the latest arrival, is more or less inter-changeable with a cripple' (S 18/30–1).)

The putatively physical or behavioural elements typical of the victim's 'stigmata' are not, however, always easily separated from more properly *cultural* designations. That is, it is often the case that a social, cultural, or ethnic minority that is a victim of scapegoating will be *attributed* deformities or disabilities which function to reinforce polarization against its members, lending further validation for their stigmatization in the eyes their persecutors. For instance, racist cartoons and military propaganda rely either on trivial differences of target groups (such as skin colour) and work to exaggerate these; or else they actually *create* these differences in order that the victims be readily identified and rendered grotesque.[12]

Girard calls the process of violent convergence – the collective expulsion of victims – 'surrogate victimage', the adjective [Fr. '*émissaire*'] well denoting the dynamics of transference by which an individual or group bears the brunt of the aggression and violence that were previously distributed haphazardly through a body politic: 'When unappeased, violence seeks and always finds a surrogate victim. The creature that excited its fury is abruptly replaced by another, chosen only because it is vulnerable and close at hand' (VS 2/11).

Girard argues that, just as diffuse violence can turn to a single party at a whim, a redirection of that violence after the initial polarization can occur just as rapidly if the chosen victim is or becomes unavailable. He, in turn, calls this movement of displacement – both the original polarization and all subsequent ones – a 'sacrificial substitution' [*la substitution sacrificielle*], the process whereby, if unable to resolve itself, violence will find another victim on which to unleash its fury. He furnishes readers of *VS* with some vivid literary illustrations of this phenomenon, such as the case of Ajax in Homer's *Iliad*: incensed by the leaders of the Greek army who have refused to award him Achilles' weapons, Ajax – unable to vent his rage on those responsible for this decision – slaughters a herd of sheep in a deluded frenzy. In an analogous way, in Euripides' *Medea*, the heroine murders her own children in a fit of rage during which she can't find her husband Jason, the (ostensibly) real object of her hatred (*VS* 9–10/20–1).

Girard argues that the arbitrary nature of surrogate victimage, the fact that the victim is chosen merely because it is 'vulnerable and close at hand', is invariably concealed to those involved in its perpetration; scapegoats, in other words, are not seen *as* scapegoats by those involved in their expulsion – the arbitrariness of a mob's selection must be largely unwitting in order that sacrificial substitution has its socially beneficial effects (*VS* 159/235).[13] Indeed, rather than being seen as victims, scapegoats are invariably viewed as victimizers *par excellence*. We can see that, in historical episodes such as the Salem witch trials and the monotonous reiterations of anti-Semitic persecution that have occurred throughout the history of the West, persecutors often attributed to their victims remarkable – indeed, often supernatural – capacities that imbued their malevolence with extraordinary malignancy: the putative ability to cast spells, for instance, their incredible capacity for infanticide and ritual cannibalism, or their almost preternatural ability for the accumulation of wealth (*S* 12–23/23–36). Indeed, the lack of *thematization* or self-reflexivity about the arbitrariness of their own scapegoating among the members of a crowd is, in fact, what allows for the almost alchemical transformation of diffuse violence into concentrated violence at the same time that this violence does not implicate any individual perpetrators in its machinations. No single person, that is, can be blamed for the lynching or expulsion of the victim: 'Violence belongs to all men, and thus to none in particular. All the actors have the same role, with the exception of the surrogate victim. But anybody can play the part of the surrogate victim' (*VS* 257/383).

Yet, Girard admits that, although anyone *can* play the part of the victim, given the chaotic and indiscriminate oscillations of mob behaviour, it is not overly difficult to detect certain well-established patterns of persecution, at least in the modern West. He argues – as both common sense and the findings of the empirical social sciences tend to corroborate – that scapegoats or surrogate victims tend to be marginalized figures or outcasts, persons often existing on the fringes of society who, for that very reason, are especially vulnerable to the kinds of violence of which surrogate victimage is the most radical expression (*VS* 12/24). As is well known, in contemporary cultures which show even a minimal degree of cultural, ethnic, or religious diversity, minorities repeatedly become the targets of volatile masses during periods of social discontent:

> Ethnic and religious minorities tend to polarize the majorities against themselves. In this we see one of the criteria by which victims are selected, which, though relative to the individual society, is transcultural in principle. There are few societies that do not subject their minorities, all the poorly integrated or merely distinct groups, to certain forms of discrimination and even persecution. (*S* 17–18/31)

The marginal position of such minorities renders them easily identified and their presence within a broader community (despite their marginality) makes them convenient scapegoats, susceptible to blame for any problems that are, in actual fact, domestic. The primary targets of the rampant anti-Semitism of German national socialism of the 1930s, for instance, were German Jews, who were at the same time both internal to the German national community *and* marginal to it (the latter by virtue of their cultural and religious distinctiveness); that is, both 'German-ness' and 'Jewish-ness' were essential features of their emergence as scapegoats.[14] Girard suggests that it is this property of marginality that allows violence to be externalized by transforming the perception of civil (internal) strife with civil origins into internal strife with (putatively) external origins – in this case above, of civil discord putatively prompted by an alien 'race' or nation.[15]

Additionally, scapegoats must not be seen by their persecutors as an integral part of a community such that any elements of this group may, eventually, act as advocate on their behalf – otherwise, the aggression directed at them will risk reciprocation and, hence, the continuation of that very phenomenon from which surrogate victimage is ostensibly able to provide relief (*VS* 13/26–7). Similarly, the unitive consequences of the polarization against victims are effective only to the extent that this polarization is unanimous: the unanimity of the violence directed at the scapegoat is a (formal) necessity of the process of (re)structuration that Girard describes; the abstention of any participants makes such situations highly volatile by risking the perpetuation of the fracas (*VS* 100–1/150–2).

The fact of a typical victim's marginality does not require, however, that all scapegoats are to be found in the less privileged sectors of society. Following some threads of an argument first broached in J. G. Frazer's study of magic and religion, *The Golden Bough* (1890), Girard notes how royalty, and kings especially, has proved to be particularly suitable as a scapegoat for cultural orders under threat of collapse.[16] Again, these figures possess somewhat ambiguous or liminal positions in relation to the larger communities over which they preside; they are both a part of those communities *and* separated from them by virtue of their exalted status.[17] Such distinguishing features, constitutive of a certain regal 'in-betweenness', can function as privileged 'victimary stigmata' should a culture descend into violence. In *The Scapegoat*, Girard points to the example of Marie Antoinette, whose privileged status as queen and her Austrian origin made her a particularly suitable target for the Parisian mob in search of a scapegoat during the revolution of 1789 (and, interestingly enough, her ethnic origin is also repeatedly mentioned in the accusations levelled at her). Marie Antoinette was also, importantly, accused of engaging in an incestuous relationship with her son (S 20–1/33–4). Girard argues that such charges are typical of those laid at scapegoats; incest, as well as rape, bestiality, and patricide, is a crime which involves transgressions that level and confuse the identity of subjects and their relative *loci* in the social order. Scapegoats, that is, tend to be accused of exactly the kinds of acts which would contribute to the annihilation of distinctions within a community, crimes which are thought thereby to bring about the crisis of which they are accused: 'They attack the very foundation of cultural order, the family and hierarchical differences without which there would be no social order. In the sphere of individual action they correspond to the global consequences of an epidemic of the plague or any comparable disaster' (S 15/27).

For instance, the crimes typically attributed to the Christians during the early reign of the Roman empire and, in turn, crimes attributed to the Jews in Christian countries during the Middle Ages well fit this description: religious profanation, infanticide, bestiality, and incest; food and water poisoning, as well as violent attacks on prestigious or influential people (S 17/29). Girard points out that crimes such as those mentioned here fall into a broader hermeneutic taxonomy of representation, a taxonomy he labels 'stereotypes of persecution' – misrepresentations of scapegoat events that are patterned in such a way as actually to provide evidence for the historical reality of the violence they attempt either to cover up or to justify (*S* 12–23/23–36).

While the phrase 'surrogate victimage' may seem to make sense of Girard's hypothesis, as outlined above, it might seem less self-evident as to why, and in what sense, this explanation purports to name a 'mechanism' [*mécanisme*]. To begin with, we should note that one sense of that term has already been broached, albeit some-what tangentially: surrogate victimage is properly described as a mechanism insofar as the mob's polarization against the victim operates in a non-volitional, automatic way. Surrogate victimage is not, in other words, part of any explicit or tacit 'social contract' (however amoral), consciously entered into by social actors for the purposes of group cohesion. Indeed, the fact that surrogate victim-age operates unbeknown to its participants is not 'accidental' (in the Aristotelian sense of that term) – in the Girardian purview, its very operation *requires* miscomprehension.

To this clarification of surrogate victimage as a 'mechanism' we should be careful to add a further specification of the latter term, a specification that is integral to capturing one of the key epistemo-logical features of Girard's theory itself: the notion of 'mechanism' well encapsulates the intended *morphogenetic* scope of the proposed explanation. Girard's hypothesis is morphogenetic in that it attempts to furnish a hypothetical account of the *origin* of cultural forms.[18] Surrogate victimage, therefore, is not an 'institution' (politi-cal, economic, or cultural) in any sociological or anthropological sense. Rather, according to Girard, it is *temporally antecedent* to these: it is a mechanism that functions (first) to *dissolve* institutions and then to *generate* them.

The primary task of the next two sections of this chapter is to bear this claim out through an explication of how surrogate victimage structures two of those institutions that it purportedly engenders: ritual and prohibition. (The third 'institution', myth, will be covered in the next chapter.) For Girard, ritual and prohibition both func-tion to control mimesis – conflictual desire and violent reciprocity – by freezing into relatively stable cultural forms the imperfect comprehension of surrogate victimage; both are genre-specific embodiments of a simultaneous remembrance *and* misrecognition [*méconnaissance*] of the events of social disintegration and restora-tion – of the sacrificial crisis and its resolution through surrogate victimage. That is, they are institutions of recollection, but institu-tions structured, and therefore disfigured, by the operation and impact of the surrogate victimage itself.[19]

To specify this characterization further, and to put it in summary form, Girard argues that ritual has primarily a *propitiatory* function: it renews the therapeutic effects of the original mobilization of surrogate victimage by canalizing violence along sacrally endorsed channels. Prohibition, on the other hand, serves a predominantly *prophylactic* function: it incarnates social hierarchies and forms of differentiation that prevent conflictual mimesis by proscribing those behaviours that might lead, or have led in the past, to social disintegration.

It what follows, we will attempt to examine these initial, overly schematic, claims, opening our discussion with a consideration of the main features of Girard's analysis of ritual. To this end, we will restrict the following discussion of both ritual and prohibition to 'primitive' cultures; although, of course, Girard's hypothesis of surrogate victimage is by no means *itself* restricted to such an application, this focus will assist in our task of introducing some of the main features of the hypothesis without having contemporaneously to qualify, temper, and complexify them a great deal in relation to contemporary or 'modern' cultures.[20]

Ritual: re-enacting the sacred

Girard's analyses of ritual have incorporated a very broad range of phenomena and theoretical perspectives – he has considered, at one time or another, most of the signal elements of ritual, as deployed and developed in nineteenth- and twentieth-century anthropology. But, he argues, it is ritual sacrifice and those (ritual) preparations for it that provide the key means for opening up a comprehensive understanding of this area *per se*. For Girard, again to put the point somewhat summarily, ritual functions to renew the salutary unity provided by the original, spontaneous violence of surrogate victimage by a selective replaying of it (*TH* 19–30/28–39).[21] It represents, he claims, 'the proper reenactment of the surrogate victim mechanism: its function is to perpetuate or renew the effects of this mechanism; that is to keep violence outside the community' (*VS* 92/140; cf. *TE* 221). The primary function of ritual is therefore *propitiatory* – it re-enervates some of the salvific power of victimage through a controlled replaying of both the 'crisis of degree', the sacrificial crisis, and the equally violent resolution of that violence through an act of scapegoating. But where the sacrificial crisis and its resolution operate automatically, ritual functions to control retroactively all of those elements which were uncontrollable during the original chaos: the time, place, and selection of the victim (*VS* 102/154).

In *VS*, drawing on Godfrey Lienhardt's *Divinity and Experience*, Girard examines the (Sudanese) Dinka practice of animal sacrifice and the series of ritual preparations which lead up to it. He begins with the following description of the ritual scene: 'The insistent rhythm of choral incantations gradually captures the attention of a crowd of bystanders who at first appeared scattered and self-absorbed. Participants begin to brandish weapons in mock warfare. A few isolated individuals strike out at others, but without any real hostility' (*VS* 97/147). As the ritual proceeds, participants become progressively agitated (or at least appear to be), agitation manifesting through verbally and physically aggressive gestures that ritual participants direct at each other.

Increasingly, however, the hostility directed towards one another is redirected to a sacrificial cow, selected prior to the commencement of the ceremony and tied up nearby; participants gradually detach themselves from the group to strike out at or verbally abuse the animal. The ceremony concludes with a stampede towards and slaughter of the cow, after which it is ritualistically venerated (*VS* 97–8/147).

Girard argues that the series of events recounted by Lienhardt represent a ritualized re-enactment of the original, founding murder of the Dinka, and the sacrifice of the animal reiterates the essential structure and function of this act: preventing or expunging violence from the community though a selective redirection of it. The ritual, in other words, recapitulates the social salvation and cultural regeneration attendant upon the metamorphosis of reciprocal violence into unilateral violence (*VS* 97–8/147), From start to finish, Girard argues, the ritual enacts a mock mimetic crisis and its resolution – it reiterates in displaced form the collapse of distinctions and their subsequent reinstitution through the sacrifice of a scapegoat. And, although the ritual is a form of tacit gratitude directed towards the original event of social cohesion, it is not a straightforward *recollection* of it: to remember the original event clearly, Girard maintains, would effectively undermine a ritual's efficacy and threaten new violence (*VS* 134–5/201–2). (This, therefore, is why such a 'remembrance' is best figured as paradoxically both a remembering *and* a forgetting, an apprehension that doubles also as a misrecognition.) Above all, the sacrificial ritual of the Dinka, like surrogate victimage itself, doesn't *abolish* violence – rather, it keeps vengeance in check by tricking it into unleashing itself on a victim whose death will precipitate no reprisals. This, Girard argues, is the reason for the (felt) purgative effects of ritual sacrifice, which can occur either at regular intervals or during times where the social order appears to be under threat (or, indeed, at both of these times).

Far from being an exceptional instance, Girard suggests that the practice of the Dinka is homologous with a very wide range of cultural phenomena, some obvious – like, for instance, the Greek Bouphonia (*VS* 98/147–8) – and some far less obvious – like Greek tragedy (*VS* 100/150–1). Indeed, much of the analytic force of *Violence and the Sacred* is tied to Girard's capacity to show that a seemingly highly disparate assortment of cultural phenomena are generally isomorphic to ritual practices such as the Dinka's – and that ritual, in turn, shares common patterns with myth and prohibition.

And if the phenomenon of sacrifice, as Girard argues, provides a key to understanding ritual as a whole, it is the notion of *substitution* that provides a key to a proper understanding of sacrifice (*VS* 3/13). Given Girard's characterization of ritual sacrifice as a propitiatory re-enervation of surrogate victimage, sacrifice stands as a kind of 'double substitution' – a surrogation that reiterates a prior surrogation: where the surrogate victim of the original crisis substituted for the (nascent) community (original substitution), the ritual re-enactment of the crisis concludes with the substitution of a sacrificial victim, who substitutes for the original victim (double substitution) (*VS* 102/154).

Yet it is not simply the brute fact of this double substitution that interests Girard, but the formal homologies between the two acts of substitution. In both instances, the victim possesses an inherently liminal status with regard to the community that exacts violence against it. Expressed normatively, we can assert that the victim must either: come from outside the community and be capable of being integrated into it; come from inside the community and be set aside in order that some distance is instituted between that victim and the others; or come, already, from the margins of a community – neither 'inside' nor 'outside' it. If the (surrogate or sacrificial) victim comes from outside the community and no attempt is made to integrate it, then its death will not possess the requisite cathartic power to halt the sacrificial crisis; and if the victim comes from *within* the community and no attempt is made to distance them from it, then its death risks provoking reprisals and is thus likely to *precipitate*, rather than *resolve*, the crisis (*VS* 272/405–6; 269/401). The case of the Dinka is instructive here. The animal selected is never one taken straight from the herd – it undergoes a period of isolation and is provided with shelter in close proximity to human inhabitants; religious invocations are also directed at it to bring it closer to the human community for which it will surrogate. If the animal remains merely a 'common' animal taken from the herd the sacrifice will not have enough binding force; but if the victim were simply a member of the (human) community then their sacrifice would likely provoke an indeterminate chain of reprisals (*VS* 272–3/405–6).

Girard argues that sacrificial ritual is culturally and temporally antecedent to other cultural forms. This is not to say, however, that he restricts his analyses solely to this domain and merely attempts to generalize all else from it. Rather, he is interested in and attempts to show the relevance of his morphogenetic hypothesis to a wide range of phenomena – from those such as the well-known 'rain' ceremonies and (A. Van Gennep's) 'rites of passage', to the kingship rituals of sacred monarchies – and in so doing shows both their distinctiveness as well as their continuities with ritual sacrifice. Although a consideration of all of these anthropological phenomena is well beyond the size constraints of this chapter, we will now turn to consider briefly just the last of these to see the kind of interpretation that Girard brings to it, and to discern to what extent it might by seen to provide corroboration, and illustration, of some of his main theses.

Although the enstatement rituals of sacred monarchies may often not explicitly involve any animal or human sacrifice, Girard is firm in his insistence that the development of monarchical rule began as a modification – small, at first – of ritual sacrifice. In his discussion of the sacred monarchies of continental Africa (*VS* 103–10/157–65), Girard begins by noting the kinds of ritual preparation often undertaken prior to enthronement. Nascent kings, for instance, are invariably required – on the day of their enthronement and on other select occasions reserved for particular rites of renewal – to commit acts of incest, either real or symbolic. He argues that this imperative is part of a broader series of ritualistic behaviours that work to invert a king's relationship to prohibitions by actually *prescribing* forbidden or transgressive acts; for instance, the king may be required to commit explicit acts of aggression, to eat normally forbidden foods, and/or to wash in blood (*VS* 104–5/157–8).

Drawing on the anthropological work of theorists such as L. de Heusch, L. Makarius, and J. Vansina, Girard notes that after such transgressions ('obligatory crimes'), and before the enthronement

itself, the nascent king is invariably subject to insults from his subjects – the royal army may orchestrate a mock attack on the king's
bodyguard, or even the king himself. In one of the Rwandan monarchies Girard discusses, such insults and ritually delimited insur-
gencies are followed by a presentation of the king and queen with
a bull and a cow, animals which are then clubbed to death in front
of the royal couple. The king then completes this stage of the ritual
by pouring the bull's blood over himself (*VS* 104–5/158).

Girard argues that kingship rituals constitute re-enactments of
scapegoating and that the enthronement ceremony itself restages
the sacrificial crisis and its resolution: the king's (staged) crimes and
his methodical transgressions of taboos justify his persecution, and
his symbolic lynching recalls the immolation of a victim whose
death was the key factor in the foundation of the community. The
sacrifice of the bull in the Rwandan ceremony renders possible the
sacralization of the king in the blood of a sacrificial victim; the king,
at one point heavily implicated as the origin of the community's
discontent, is henceforth transformed into its saviour (*VS* 103–10/
157–65).

In corroboration of this analysis, Girard notes that kingship
rituals find strong analogues in those preparations for ritual sacrifice which habitually involve warlike games, the highly stylized
playing out of (symmetrical) antagonisms, the use of masks, and
the obligatory transgressing of taboos. It is this last feature that
proves to be a focal point for Girard's analogies – both preparation
for sacrifice and kingship rituals demand culturally prescribed
enactments of social deterioration undertaken to 'position' a particular subject in relation to the cultural/ritual order. For instance,
Girard describes how, in Alfred Métraux's accounts of the inter-
tribal conflicts of the Tupinamba (of northwest Brazil), captured
enemies are imprisoned and then slowly, ritually transformed into
sacrificial victims (*VS* 274–80/409–19). Prior to their deaths, captives are imbricated in a detailed series of ritualistic preparations
which veer unstably between torture and veneration; at times
physically and verbally abused, the captives are also substantially
integrated into the community and even held in high regard: their
sexual favour may be sought by members of the village and they
may also marry into a family. Then, prior to execution, captives are
set free before being quickly recaptured; they are denied nourishment and are thus forced to steal food to live; and they are 'allowed',
even encouraged, to commit other crimes in order to 'avenge' their
imminent demise.

Girard argues that Tupinamba prisoners are coerced into playing the role of transgressor so that their sacrifice may be rendered legitimate. In the case of sacred monarchies, however, the king's transgressions – and indeed the very permissibility of these – ends just prior to the moment of his enstatement. It is in this light that Girard interprets the process of monarchical empowerment to be a ritual homologue of sacrifice (which, as pointed out above, it actually precedes in some cultures). It is not, therefore, the case that the king transgresses taboos because such transgressions are no longer reprehensible when carried out by a king. Girard argues, to the contrary, that it is precisely *because* these acts remain reprehensible that they are selected for the king to perform (*VS* 104–5/157–8). He posits that the initial purpose of these rituals was to transform the king into the most abject of men; through the committing of the crimes required of him he came to embody impurity itself and was thus transformed into a scapegoat for those crimes.

In light of this, therefore, Girard argues that kingship is best understood as the result of a prolonged delay between the selection of a victim and their immolation. The 'king for a day' rituals common to practices of sacrifice – like the ceremonies involving the Greek *pharmakoi* or those that implicate the Tupinamba prisoners – bestow upon victims a kind of religious aura that eventually becomes a form of political power (*IS* 92/126–7). (Indeed, the study of sacred monarchies is a very important undertaking for the humanities, Girard argues, for in these he posits the origins of political power *per se*.) The 'original' sacred monarch, in other words, was probably a victim who, during sacrificial preparation, became so revered that he could no longer be killed (*TH* 51–7/59–66). The king's regal power, therefore, does not somehow stand *despite* his often awful fate – it is, rather, a *result* of it: 'The king reigns only by virtue of his future death; he is no more and no less a victim awaiting sacrifice, a condemned man about to be executed' (*VS* 107/161).[22] Girard argues, that is, that the development of monarchical power is merely a 'frozen moment' in the sacrificial process, of the 'good times' enjoyed by the sacrificial victim just prior to his or her immolation.

Kings, like priests and mythical and tragic 'heroes', are inherently ambivalent figures; they are both feared and revered, and their positions, and *lives*, are held in precarious balance. Communal perceptions of all of these, Girard notes, can shift from adoration to detestation very rapidly (*VS* 104–8/157–62). And kings – also like scapegoats and sacrificial victims – are neither quite 'inside' nor 'outside' the communities they rule. As subjects, they are, therefore, key components in the stabilization of those communities; monarchs both engender and incarnate order (regardless of their own intentions).

It is important to note, in the instances so far discussed, that the representations and treatment of surrogate victims – the Rwandan bull, the African king, and the Tupinamba prisoner – evince a paradoxical structure that renders them liable to be the objects of both cursing *and* veneration. Girard is particularly sensitive to the manifest ambiguity of such representations as well as the seeming pervasiveness of this paradox. Another particularly refined example of the same kind is present in the ancient Greek *pharmakoi*, mentioned above – those displaced persons, sometimes prisoners, that Greek cities housed and fed in order that they be later utilized for assassination during Thargelia and other Dionysian festivals. As receptacles of violence, the *pharmakoi* were ideal – victims whose deaths would elicit little or no fear of reprisal. Here, Girard elaborates on their somewhat grisly function:

> The city of Athens prudently kept on hand a number of unfortunate souls, whom it maintained at public expense, for appointed times as well as in certain emergencies. Whenever some calamity threatened – plague, famine, foreign invasion, or internal dissension – there was always a pharmakos at the disposal of the community. (*VS* 94/143)

Despite this – or, rather, *because* of it – the *pharmakoi* were also subject to veneration and had access to privileges not available to ordinary citizens; they were, in fact, objects of both scorn and veneration (*IS* 76/106). Indeed, the very term *'pharmakos'* itself gives a significant linguistic clue regarding the paradoxical construal of the archetypal scapegoat. As the French philosopher Jacques Derrida has eloquently pointed out in his extended meditation on a foundational paradox in Plato's *Phaedrus*, all attempts to render this Greek term univocal are ill-fated: it means, irreducibly, both 'poison' and 'cure'.[23]

Girard argues that the paradoxical representation of the scapegoat is attributable to the fact that his or her lynching or expulsion has the peculiar but predictable effect of producing calm and a return to order and redifferentiation – but *not for the reasons that the mob suspects*. The mob's 'explanation' to itself concerning the calm that has followed in the train of a successful persecution, that is, winds up being a post-hoc justification of the violence against the scapegoat; the re-emergence of order, in other words, *vindicates the lynching*, as the return of peace appears to give substance to the conviction that the scapegoat was, in fact, the real cause of the violence and disorder. At this point, commensurate with this fundamental misrecognition, Girard contends that a second transformation of the scapegoat is likely to take place. Staring at the victim's corpse, the astonishment of the crowd turns to awe at the realization that this death has brought about unanimity and peace:

> The experience of a supremely evil and then beneficent being, whose appearance and disappearance are punctuated by collective murder, cannot fail to be literally gripping. The community that was once so terribly stricken suddenly finds itself free of antagonism, completely delivered. (*TH* 28/36)

Because the newly found calm is the product of the mob's immolation or banishment of the victim, Girard suggests, a desire emerges for reproducing this event in a controlled and selective fashion, through ritual and myth. To consolidate the return to social order secured by the process of victimage — the real mechanics of which are not understood by its socio-cultural beneficiaries – it becomes an imperative for the community involved in the persecution to: (1) prohibit those actions thought to have led to the crisis in the first instance; and (2) (paradoxically also) *replicate* the violent events in mythical and ritual, sacrificial, form (*TH* 28/37; cf. 103/112–13).

This reproduction of the crisis through ritual, prohibition, and myth is what Girard invariably calls 'the sacred' [*le sacré*]. The 'sacred', in Girard's purview, denotes the cultural products and practices of the distorted and selective comprehension of surrogate victimage by those involved in its perpetration.[24] For Girard, the purpose of the sacred is to put an end to reciprocal violence (*VS* 55/86); as Andrew McKenna states, 'If god did not exist, man would have invented him, as Voltaire says; not in order to explain the cosmos however, for it gets along fine without us, but in order to prevent violent chaos among ourselves.'[25] In *VS*, Girard argued that, if the violence exacted on the victim was successful in bringing a sacrificial crisis to an end, this act would serve as the inaugural moment for a new cultural (that is, ritual and totemic) system.[26] It is in this sense that Girard claimed that the violence of surrogate victimage is *generative* – it functions to initiate new 'constructive' cycles of cultural renewal, marked by sacrificial rites, which serve to replicate (mimetically) both a previous crisis and the resolution that engendered it (*VS* 93–7/140–7).

Sacred renderings of (violent) events typically reverse the state of affairs that gave rise to them by a constitutive transcendental-ization of mob violence: the sacrificed victim in ritual, for instance, becomes an appeaser of the gods, rather than the actual state of affairs – of the victim/god being the *appeaser of the mob*. The primary task of the sacred, Girard argues, is to keep the preceding events at a distance by proscribing actions that are thought to have brought it about and to replicate both the (sacrificial) crisis and its resolu-tion (through surrogate victimage) in controlled, ritually legitimate ways. For Girard, sacrifice – as one of the constituent elements of the sacred – is an act of violence that minimizes the risk of vengeance; it replaces the 'impure' violence of the victim with the sacred violence and, like surrogate victimage itself, functions equally to suppress internal dissension (*VS* 13/25–6; 8/18).[27] In this sense, the sacred might be said to 'contain' violence in both mean-ings of the term: it *possesses* violence as well as being able to *control* and *curtail* it. It is, Mark Anspach reminds us, one of the central paradoxes of the sacred that it plays a 'vital role in controlling violence *without* being antithetical to it.'[28]

Girard argues that, because a community associates the cessation of social and cultural disintegration with the victim's banishment or lynching, the victim is therefore associated with being central to both the violence *and the peace that follows it*. This is the reason, there-fore, that the scapegoat is invariably subject to paradoxical repre-sentations, both malevolent and beneficent, corresponding to the way in which the violence infecting the community moved from the malevolence of all-against-all to the (social and psychological) beneficence of a united, socially cohesive violence (*VS* 251/374). Indeed, owing to their causal centrality in the alleviation of the dis-order besetting a community, the scapegoat may even be construed as a kind of saviour figure or deity. Girard labels the process which leads up to this inherently paradoxical construal of the scapegoat the 'double transference'; he observes of the scapegoat mechanism '*vox populi, vox dei*', which, he suggests, gives us a 'strict definition of the scapegoat system' (*J* 131/152; cf. *J* 18/25).[29]

(But here, an important qualification is in order. For complex historico-religious reasons related to the progressive *unveiling* of the surrogate victimage mechanism (which is the subject of chapter 4), the deification or sacralization of the victim in the strict sense detailed above is a largely pre-modern or pre-state phenomenon, occurring for the most part in the ritual and myth of primitive and ancient societies.[30] Modern persecutions, such as those mentioned previously – German national socialism and the Salem witch trials, as well as persecutions of ethnic minorities – are largely immune from the sacred pull towards a deification of victims.)[31]

But here, again, we meet a question that needs to be faced squarely if Girard's hypothesis is to remain tenable. Provisionally allowing for the cogency of the above analysis, one may wonder why it is that ritual – and, indeed, surrogate victimage itself – ever has to be *repeated* if either of these do, in fact, succeed in bringing about returns to order and peace. Why would ritual require reiteration if the original act on which it is founded secured the social and cultural stability that Girard claims for it? His answer to this is instructive, and allows us to see another key feature of his theoretical schema.

The reason for this need for repetition, Girard argues, is that the stabilization of order attained through the operations of surrogate victimage and its ritual repetition is inherently fragile, its binding power only ever temporary. The transitoriness of this stabilization is attendant upon the fact that the particular kind of selective recollection that lies at the base of ritual (and prohibition and myth) equally *prevents* a real comprehension of social crises and their resolution. And, just as surrogate victimage itself needs to be repeated periodically in order that its cathartic effects be felt anew, the very structures – including ritual structures – which this mechanism produces are just as likely to have their binding power exhausted over time. This, needless to say, is the necessary condition for a replaying of surrogate victimage and the origin of a new 'community' and totemic system. And of the binding force of ritual itself, much the same could be said. Although ritual, under normal circumstances, is strictly regulated by cultural mores and norms, it is also capable of overstepping its boundaries and becoming extremely threatening. Indeed, the often maximally charged nature of ritual behaviour opens the distinct possibility that the attempted deflections of violence that lie as its core will provoke counter-violence in turn, and thus effect a reproduction of the original crisis that it functions to replicate in controlled fashion.

This observation, in turn, leads us to an important qualification about the operations of surrogate victimage: although the way in which victimage has been presented thus far has tended to imply a very neat formal distinction between it and its (ritual) repetition, Girard argues that there are a host of intermediate forms between these two poles – cultural events that stand somewhere between originary violence and its controlled reiteration (*VS* 113/170). The image of the 'festival gone wrong', well depicted by Euripides in

The Bacchae, finds numerous literary, filmic, and anthropological analogues, from those dramatic events which take place in Federico Fellini's films, to Jules Henry's anthropological accounts of the 'festivals' of the Kaingang people of Santa Katarina in Brazil (*VS* 125–7/188–91; cf. *VS* 260–2/388–91).

If ritual, however, *is* successful – if its performance does not somehow go awry – the distribution of power and the cultural order that is contemporaneous with it will prevent, for a time at least, con-flictual mimesis. For Girard, it is sacral prohibitions that function to thwart mimetic rivalry and control appropriation in the most endemic fashion. Such prohibitions, for instance, typically proscribe the acquisition of certain sacred objects, objects that were previously contested – that is, served as pretexts for conflictual mimesis (*TH* 10–19/18–28; 76–7/85). In other words, culture, through prohibi-tions, canalizes desire. It is to this sacred institution – and to some broader reflections concerning the relationship between the social and the sacred – that we will devote the discussion of the next section of this chapter.

Prohibition: proscribing the sacred

One of the strengths of Girard's theory of sacrifice would seem to be that he neither treats sacrifice as if it were an ontological 'given' – somehow a part of 'human nature' or 'nature' in a wider, more inclusive sense – nor figures it as a product of more powerful or pervasive institutions (about which the same question of genesis would emerge).[32] To put it another way, one of the chief virtues of Girard's theory of ritual sacrifice is that it is *not simply a theory of ritual sacrifice*. Although it is a key element in his analysis, Girard argues that it is but one institution of the sacred, generated by a more fundamental, self-regulating system of cultural morphogene-sis: the surrogate victimage mechanism.

Girard argues that, just as sacrifice *prescribes* (in somewhat dis-placed form) the sacrificial crisis and the action that ended it, pro-hibition represents the concerted effort to *prevent* that same crisis from repeating itself. Prohibition, for instance, invariably involves rendering taboo those kinds of behaviour associated with the sac-rificial crisis; it consists of rules that govern the use of objects – decrees which regulate their exchange and acquisition – as well as regimes of purification enacted to protect those who *are* able to make use of them.

Consistent with the hypothesis of surrogate victimage, Girard argues that prohibitions function to avert a (non-ritual) repetition of the crisis through countering possible instances of conflictual mimesis. Incest taboos, for instance, involve distancing siblings in order to control mimetic rivalry; these regulations put into effect the imperative that generations must leave their families – the 'proper' place for sexual relations, in other words, is with *others*. Through this imperative, such taboos establish protocols for the correct proximity of potential rivals. For Girard, prohibitions reflect the supposition that the victim/god has not simply controlled the violence and the peace that followed in its train – they also reign over the law; the god/victim legitimates and becomes the signifier of all prohibitions. Invariably, therefore, the primary proscription against appropriation involves the god itself – the divinity is not to be possessed, touched, or, sometimes, even approached. Girard argues that the first prohibition and the first distinction are homologous: the distinction between the sacred and the profane is strictly equivalent to the separation between the god/victim and the community.

While a broadly 'functionalist' approach such as this will make sense of some prohibitions, Girard supplements this with a complementary insight – prohibition functions to prevent or canalize violence by proscribing those *signs* of imitative behaviour associated with it. He suggests that what has prevented anthropologists from seeing this is that intellectual frameworks which have originated in Western societies have typically bestowed upon violence a degree of conceptual specificity or autonomy unknown in primitive and ancient societies. But, far from being the outcome of violence 'itself', such a construal is the result of certain contingent sociohistorical and institutional conditions; what allows, in fact, modern societies to construe violence in the way that they do is the presence of judicial institutions that (ostensibly) transcend antagonists (or parties of antagonists), and so are able to halt violent reciprocity by undermining the symmetry of antagonism. But equally, if the transcendent (judicial) institution is no longer there – or becomes incapable of commanding respect – the repetitious, mimetic character of violence becomes manifest once again, regardless of the particular society in which it manifests itself (*TH* 11–12/20).

It is within this interpretative frame that Girard suggests we can make sense of common, albeit seemingly perplexing, laws such as those which prescribe the compulsory killing of twins at birth, those laws which strictly delimit the use of mirrors to certain persons and times, and those other, general laws which proscribe imitative behaviour (the last of these often associated with the dangers of what is called in the anthropological literature 'imitative magic') (*VS* 56–8/88–92; *TH* 14/22–3). Girard holds that all of these can best be understood as cultural codifications – or, rather, mythic translations – of the fear of the emergence of doubles, the erasure of differences or transgressions of culturally inscribed hierarchies. In short, Girard argues, the most salient feature of prohibitions is their rigorously anti-mimetic character (*TH* 10–19/18–28).[33]

The connections that Girard draws between surrogate victimage and prohibition on the one hand, and these to ritual on the other, demonstrate one aspect of the hermeneutic and heuristic strength of his hypothesis. Girard's theory provides a cogent solution to a puzzle raised repeatedly by anthropologists throughout the nineteenth and twentieth centuries: that ritual behaviour appears systematically to *reverse* the prohibitions that constitute, at all other times, the most central normative elements of a culture. Why is it that within a single culture the strict and programmatic upholding of taboos gives way to their equally strict and programmatic transgression? Where the first presents a strongly hierarchical social/sacred order, the second stages a concerted inversion and then effacement of hierarchies; order gives way to all of those Bacchanalian excesses well analysed by Mikhail Bakhtin, who talked of carnivalesque transitions, of metamorphoses, of 'the violation of natural boundaries'.[34]

Girard answers this conundrum – of the paradoxical double-imperative presented by ritual and prohibition – by positing a single generative mechanism that engenders both. Rather than resort to what Michel Serres has dubbed a 'thermodynamic' hermeneutic of socio-psychological phenomena[35] – something like two (biologized) 'drives', instincts, or appetites which get 'stored' and require discrete 'outlets' – Girard suggests that ritual and prohibition are both forms of remembrance, each of which is a specific temporal transposition of distinct moments within the process of surrogate victimage – of the sacrificial crisis and its violent resolution. Where ritual reiterates in muted form the sacrificial crisis and its resolution through surrogate victimage, prohibition incarnates a detemporalized 'result' of this process. It is, in fact, the *continuity* of these forms that accounts for the fact that, where prohibition proscribes any behaviour reminiscent of the sacrificial crisis, ritual actively reiterates it. Where prohibition derives its impetus from limiting mimetic rivalry, ritual initially *replays* that rivalry within a rigorously delimited spatial and temporal sphere, and concludes with a return to order brought about by ritual sacrifice.

Concluding short excursus on the social and the sacred

As institutions of the sacred, we have seen how both prohibition and ritual represent religious translations of inherently social events. It is in this light that we can best see Girard's self-professed 'Durkheimianism': his endorsement of the thesis which affirms the coevalness of the social and the sacred – that religion, in fact, stands as a society's primary expression of order.[36] Girard, like the early twentieth-century French anthropologist Émile Durkheim, sees 'the sacred' as the transcendentalized or displaced representation of social formation; the sacred, in other words, is not something 'added to' society after it gets going, but that which arises with and is integral to society and social order. Girard admits that he pursues a certain Durkheimian intuition concerning the 'identity of the social and religious domains, which means, ultimately, the chrono-logical precedence of religious expression over any sociological conception' (*TH* 82/90; cf. *TH* 70/78; *IS* 88–9/122–3).

What Girard sees as inherently valuable about the tradition of which Durkheim is the key proponent is its rigorous rejection of both the liberal-individualist construal of society – of which the self-interested individual is the basic constituent and agent, and the attitudes and actions of which the social order is merely an epiphe-nomenon – and the Enlightenment theory of religion, perhaps best encapsulated by the views of Voltaire, who thought that religion was little over and above a 'conspiracy of priests', an inherently dangerous collective of clerics who at some point deigned them-selves fit to 'take advantage of natural institutions' (*TH* 63/71–2; 70/78).[37] To the contrary, for Girard, as for Durkheim, even puta-tively 'biological' realities, far from being brute givens which are then interpreted religiously, are 'always-already' sacred ideas; the cadaver, for instance, is never simply a physical or chemical mass – even in supposedly atheistic or materialistic metaphysical schemes – but a 'talisman', 'a bearer of life and fertility' (*TH* 80–3/88–92).

But while Girard does little, in itself, to contest such conclusions, he argues that this Durkheimian insight does not somehow *solve* the problem of relating religion and society; rather, the question remains as to *what the origin of the sacred is itself*. In 1899, Henri Hubert and (Durkheim's nephew) Marcel Mauss offered a substantial refinement of their predecessor's theses in their book *Sacrifice: Its Nature and Function,* by putting sacrifice at the very centre of religion and, hence, society. While Durkheim had been satisfied to assert that the sacred held the pre-eminent forms of social representation, and that totemism was the pre-eminent form of the collective self-representation of the sacred, Hubert and Mauss attempted to locate the origins of the sacred and totemism themselves in sacrifice.

Girard remains deeply impressed with Hubert and Mauss's attempt, as well as the intuition that sustained it – but it is also, for him, as theoretically stultifying as Durkheim's attempt at the same. While Girard agrees with a substantial number of Hubert and Mauss's findings, he is ultimately frustrated by their implicit endorsement of the view that one cannot move further in analysis than comparison – Hubert and Mauss, like Durkheim before them, seem to equate analysis with *comparativism.* So while Hubert and Mauss figure sacrifice as an erstwhile 'origin of religion', they seem simply to treat the former as a cultural given, raising it almost to the level of a metaphysical absolute. This being the case, Girard argues that ultimately, therefore, Hubert and Mauss will not be able to tell us about the *origin* of sacrifice itself (*VS* 89/136). Girard believes very firmly that theory is obliged to move beyond mere analogies, or patterns of correspondence, that hold between social patterns and religious patterns: it needs, rather, to ask *how these institutions and correspondences are themselves generated.*

And here Girard is not reticent to point out what he sees as a (Durkheimian, Maussian, Hubertian) functionalist mistake: they mistake their (sound) intuition concerning the identity of the social and the sacred as a solution to the problem of the formation of social and cultural order rather than a refined *articulation* of the same. Functionalism offers almost nothing in the shape of a morphogenetic account of the way in which the sacred – and the social – is engendered. In response, Girard proposes the hypothesis of surrogate victimage, which figures violence itself as the heart and soul of the sacred. The sacred, that is, arises because human beings perennially figure their own violence as having independent being; the sacred is testament to a recognition that the individual is transcended, but misconstrues this transcendence by attributing it to something other than the social (*VS* 31/51; 42–3/50–1).

For Girard, the real extra-social, transcendent origin of social and cultural order is the surrogate victim; the sacred, in other words, effectively transcendentalizes mimetic conflict itself by transfiguring the manifest aggression of interpersonal relations and the scapegoating that this produces by representing this human propensity as expressing the anger of the gods (*TH* 14/22). The sacred, then, is that 'sum of human assumptions' predicated on the foundational misprision of the cause of social unanimity (*TH* 42/50–1); violence – and the reification of this violence – is its lifeblood (*VS* 31/51). Indeed, for Girard, surrogate victimage penetrates all ritual and myth, and is also at the heart of metaphysics and world-modelling (*VS* 96/147; 113/170; 297–306/444–59).

In the last section of this chapter we have considered the idea that, in communities or societies which evince a relatively stable social order, what interrupts processes of hostility and violent reciprocity is, to put it simply, 'culture': those ostensibly legitimate hierarchies of power and social stratification that regulate relationships, direct violence into 'appropriate' channels, and redress transgressions through controlled retributive (or other) means. Girard believes, however, that any putatively complete explanation of social and cultural order among humans will also need to account for the emergence of human culture *per se* and, hence, for the origin of the human. Any hypothesis, that is, concerning the transition from animal to human cannot refer to a pre-existing 'culture' through which the origin of the human can be thought, as the birth of the human *is* the birth of culture. In the transition from the proto-human to the human, no culture existed ready-made; culture, therefore, must be thought of as the *institutionalization of a solution, not the solution itself*. Again, the invocation of the domain or even the term 'culture' in theory, as Girard suggests, invariably merely *situates* a problematic: it does not provide for a resolution (*TH* 88/97). Given this state of affairs, Girard wants to know: *What is the birth of culture?* It is this question that we will now need to take up.

3

Myth, Tragedy, History

History is what hurts.
> Frederic Jameson, *The Political Unconscious*

The unconscious is structured like a lynching.
> Philippe Sollers, 'Is God Dead?'

We concluded the previous chapter with a question pertaining to the origin of culture *per se*. As radically unfashionable as it may be to reflect on such issues – especially within the purview of the overriding trends and preoccupations of the current humanities and social sciences academy – Girard believes it to be an essential task for those who would seriously undertake the study of culture. To this end, he attempts to provide a kind of *tertium quid* between the human and the natural sciences, between positive, empirical anthropology and cultural anthropology – between, in other words, ethnology and ethology. Girard argues that, where much contemporary cultural theory is prone to pay little or no heed to the biological basis of human interaction, empirical anthropologists (particularly sociobiologists and evolutionary psychologists) are equally prone to read human culture almost straight off animal behaviour. For Girard, neither of these approaches is adequate to its object.

He argues, in the first instance, that ethnologists are correct to reject the overly simplistic theoretical tendencies of ethologists when and where the latter ignore the genuine discontinuities between animal and human societies. Here one can appreciate the appositeness of the remark of Jacob Bronowski, who claimed that, as valuable as ethological approaches to the study of humans are, 'they cannot tell us everything. There must be something unique about man because, otherwise, evidently, the ducks would be lecturing about Konrad Lorenz and the rats would be writing papers about B. F. Skinner.'[1] By the same token, however, Girard argues that ethologists are to be praised for their efforts at elucidating the indubitable homologues between animal and human sociality; and these are also right to admonish structuralist ethnology – and much other humanistic cultural and social theory – for its insularity, for its 'absolute refusal to resituate human culture in nature, and to the wholly metaphysical conception of symbolic structures' (*TH* 91/100–1).

We begin this chapter, therefore, with a consideration of how Girard has proposed to resolve the question of the origin of language and culture, with 'hominization' – the birth of the human. We will then turn our attention to the last of the major institutions of the sacred, myth, before placing the deliberations of this and the previous chapter in a wider context by enlarging our discussion such as to take in a consideration of tragedy, on the one hand, and what Girard calls 'texts of persecution', on the other.

Hominization: the birth of the human

As already alluded to, Girard is somewhat antipathetic to the widespread pessimism regarding the possibility of theorizing the origin of human culture and language within the disciplinary purview of the humanities. Such pessimism is well captured in the figure of the French psychoanalyst Jacques Lacan, who held that any speculation on the origin of language and the symbolic – on human culture, in other words – cannot be adequately undertaken, as 'we find it absolutely impossible to speculate on what preceded it other than by symbols.'[2]

Yet, by itself, it is difficult to see exactly why the paradox that Lacan points to somehow constitutes a decisive *a priori* refutation of any hypothetical explanation of the origin of culture. The paradox the psychoanalyst indicates is undoubtedly present in any systematic reflection on such origins – there is indeed a circularity about theorizing the origin of language within the domain of language itself – but there seems to be little reason for seeing this circularity as (epistemically) vicious. To the contrary, *all* reflection about language – even structuralist and psychoanalytic reflection –

must take place within (a) language, just as all speculation on the evolutionary history of the species must necessarily take place within that history. There seems to be little reason, however, in either case, to suspect that this paradox – the imbrication of a reflection within the process of which it speaks – somehow entails the *incoherence* or 'impossibility' of that reflection. (Of course, neither does this highly schematic defence of the possibility of theories of cultural origin somehow entail their *a priori* legitimacy. Perhaps our riposte of Lacan here simply attests to the fact that the problems that any such hypotheses must face are not necessarily *a priori* at all.)

Girard locates his own reflections on the process of hominization [*le processus de hominisation*] within the problematic of surrogate victimage. As was noted in the first chapter, Girard is not averse to pointing out that certain kinds of imitative behaviour are also conspicuously present in other animals, especially the higher primates (as, for instance, the very name 'ape' tends to suggest) (*TH* 90/99). Additionally, animal mimicry, like human mimesis, can certainly be acquisitive and rivalrous. (It is important to note then that, in this sense at least, Girard's notion of mimesis is not, or not only, 'philosophical' in its orientation; it is rooted, ultimately, in *phylogeny*.)[3]

But what also seems clear, however – given the preponderance of evidence from ethology – is that animal species invariably have instinctual protection from the mimetic sort of collective or 'mob' violence to which humans are prone. What ethologists have usually referred to in the (English-language) literature as 'dominance patterns' or 'dominance hierarchies' function as a bulwark against the total effacement of social hierarchies to which human conflicts are susceptible. The auto-appearance of those kinds of dominance patterns common to higher primates (and a variety of other animals) is the basis of animal sociality and functions to establish and maintain hierarchies in intraspecific groups and so prevent conflict – or at least institute highly specific limits on conflict and its possible outcomes. Dominance hierarchies, for instance, function to solve attempts at appropriation by regulating access to certain 'goods' (including sexual partners); additionally, such hierarchies allow for imitation to exist between dominant and submissive animals – but only in non-acquisitive areas of social life (*TH* 90–1/99–100). And where intraspecific conflicts between (non-human) animals *do* eventuate – conflicts involving a contestation of 'pack order' – these invariably occur on a one-on-one basis. The outcome of such intraspecific conflicts will result either in a slight reordering of the hierarchy or a reiteration of the old one; in either case, however, the outcome of the conflict will serve as a relatively secure template for future social relations (otherwise, the very idea of an animal 'sociality' or 'society' would be, *ipso facto*, nonsensical).

But this is precisely what does *not* occur at the human level; to say that conflict is truly mimetic at the level of the human is to say that the outcome of an encounter will not necessarily be sustained, that it will not become a pattern of behaviour between antagonists. Humans, as a result, have depended on another mechanism for the prevention and cessation of intraspecific conflict: culture. Culture reintroduces, through social differentiation and hierarchization, those relations of subordination that reinstitute the 'order of nature' – both in the sense that these differentiations are subsequently 'naturalized' by culture, and in the way in which culture itself surrogates for those relations of subordination integral to animal hierarchies. It would appear to follow, then, that the transition from animal to human is predicated on a weakening – if not a complete dissolution – of those biologically circumscribed hierarchies for which social and cultural structures substitute in human communities (*TH* 90–1/100).

Girard argues that concomitant with an increased capacity for imitation among animals *is* such a weakening of instinctual mechanisms. For instance, some kinds of birdsong rely on an imitative transmission of melody between adults and the young; the song of a species is underdetermined, in other words, by instinct, and is 'supplemented', instead, by imitative capacity – or what might be said in this context to equate roughly with 'social knowledge' or even 'culture'. It is, needless to say, among the higher primates that imitative abilities reach their (sub-human) pinnacle. In recognition of this fact, and drawing partly on the work of the evolutionary biologist Jacques Monod – who posits that the 'simulative function' of the human brain is what distinguishes it from other animal brains – Girard argues that, beyond a certain threshold of mimesis, animal societies are no longer possible.[4] As the propensity to imitate one's social peers increases – especially in their choice of objects – animal dominance patterns become slowly destabilized. In short, the proto-human had, Girard suggests, become 'too mimetic' to remain an animal (*TH* 94–5/103–4).

So although Girard is quick to emphasize the continuities between animal and human mimesis, as well as the vastly enhanced capacity for imitation common to higher primates and humans, he is not content to assert that human sociality *per se* develops directly

out of this capacity. While Girard is deeply appreciative of studies
of animal societies, a crucial difference between his own thinking
and those readings of human culture common to sociobiology and
'evolutionary psychology' is apparent: while dominance patterns
might tell us something about animal societies, they don't appear –
in any straightforward sense – to be properly 'human'. To begin
with, humans don't exhibit the general repugnance to intraspecific
killing that animal dominance patterns typically ensure. Even
where contesting for dominance in animal groups involves fights to
the death (such as is sometimes seen in wild cattle and deer) such
fighting is never a 'group' phenomenon; animal groups display
neither forms of collective dominance nor collective violence. Additionally, seeming 'instinctual' restraints (such as those against
intrafamilial murder) are constantly overridden in human society
(*TH* 86–7/95–6). Rather than 'instinctual' restraint, what prevents
human conflict from descending into death is extremely powerful
symbolic frameworks (*TH* 93/102).

As such, Girard suggests that, for hominization to occur, mimesis
requires the intermediation provided by surrogate victimage (*TH*
93/103). Although imitative abilities in animals are sufficient to
produce some degree of intraspecific conflict via a mimesis of
appropriation, Girard argues that the threshold of hominization is
reached only when the contested *object* of the nascent human community 'disappears' as a result of a frenzied escalation of acquisitive mimesis and is replaced by the *surrogate victim*. The transfer of
violence to a single individual through a process of mutual imitation is, formally speaking, the re-emergence of the object, now as
something to be *annihilated* rather than *appropriated*. Girard puts it
this way:

> At the point when mimetic conflict becomes sufficiently intense to
> prohibit the direct solutions that give rise to the forms of animal
> sociality, the first 'crisis' or series of crises would then occur as the
> mechanism that produces the differentiated, symbolic, and human
> forms of culture. (*TH* 94/103)

The awe produced by the sudden transformation brought about by
the death of the victim brings about a new form of attention,
directed at the cadaver, who is now the source of meaning (*TH*
99–100/109–10). What constitutes the human community, therefore,
is not ultimately the convergence upon the victim by virtue of a
single distinguishing trait, but the *corpse* of that victim, which pro-

vides the nascent human community with its first truly non-instinctual form of attention (*TH* 99/109).[5] In his discussion with Girard and Guy Lefort in *TH*, Jean-Michel Oughourlian offers the following summation of Girard's theses concerning the structuring effects of surrogate victimage in the genesis of culture:

> [T]he disorder of the pre-cultural and pre-sacrificial stage possesses its own structure, which is exactly defined and is based, paradoxically, on the principle of absolute symmetry. It is this mimetic symmetry – which generates disorder and violence, and is in a perpetual disequilibrium – that is stabilized by the scapegoat mechanism: the zero hour of culture and the zero degree of structure. The culture produced by this differentiating mechanism will possess a structure based upon asymmetry and difference. And, this asymmetry and the differences associated with it form what we call the cultural order. (*TH* 312/336)

But herein lies a further implication of Girard's thesis: to claim that the hypothesis of surrogate victimage is capable of accounting for social and cultural order is simultaneously to assert that it also provides an explanation for the origin of *signifying systems* – the reason being that a necessary element of human social and cultural frameworks is provided by systems of *representations*. To put the same point slightly differently, human social and cultural systems are constituted in large part *by* representations (*TH* 92/101). In the first chapter, we indicated much the same in relation to human *desire* – that biological need or appetite is not a sufficient condition for the appearance of desire, which invests itself in cultural signifiers that direct how and what an individual may pursue. Animal mimesis, on the other hand, remains anchored in the object, not in its aura or 'prestige'. As such, Girard utilizes the explanatory hypothesis of victimage mechanism to explain how both that investment and the symbolic system on which it is predicated (and subsequently canalized) originate.[6]

So here we can see that Girard is interested not simply in the operation of human signifying systems, but with their *origin* (*TH* 6–7/14). For Girard, the victim is the originary 'it', the original sign – the 'transcendental signifier' – for the human group (and, subsequently, any new social formation) (*TH* 100–4/109–13). He or she is the origin of all consequent differentiation/categorization, in which the victim and the mob represent the two originary poles of signification.[7] Girard's theory of language – and sign systems in general

– therefore incorporates the central structuralist insight that language primarily involves semiotic differentiation;[8] but he does not,
by contrast, consider this an insight somehow complete in itself.
One might say that Girard's theory moves away from the somewhat
idealistic tendencies of structuralism while not contesting its central
insights: he maintains that differentiated thought and representation, being coeval, are defining characteristics of the human, of all
conceptual thought and cultural differentiation. But he is not
content to remain within that system of differences, to replicate the
structure that anthropology sees before it by merely translating that
differential structure into a theoretical lexicon. For Girard, an adequate theory of sign systems, of 'symbolicity' [*le symbolique*], will
also attempt to describe the conditions of possibility for the *emergence* of this semiotic property. He calls his own hypothetical genetic
account of this development, described above, '*le modèle de l'exception en cours d'émergence*' [the model of the exception in the process
of emerging] (*TH* 100/110).

One of the advantages of Girard's model of hominization is that
it allows us to make adequate sense of the commonplace notion that
the function of tropes – indeed, of language-in-general – is *substitution*: the former with a figure of speech for a 'literal' meaning, the
latter with the more general surrogation for the thing to which it
refers. Metaphor, synecdoche, metonym are secondary substitutions that build on the more formative substitutions that characterize language and sign systems more generally. The sign is defined
traditionally as *aliquid stat pro aliquo*: something that stands (in) for
something else; it is, in other words, a semantic 'proxy'.[9] The victim
provides a good hypothetical origin for the creation of sign systems
because 'the ritual imperative consists in a demand for substitute
victims, thus introducing the practice of substitution that is the basis
for all symbolization.'[10]

In his laudatory gloss on Girard's theses on violence and the
sacred, Philippe Sollers lucidly captures the trajectory of this
thought, including its implications for semiotics:

> His interpretation reveals the connections between murder and the
> sacred, the sacred being maintained at all costs by murder. . . . It
> appears that every culture emerges through a tomb and that conse-
> quently every culture exposes and hides a cadaver. The series of eva-
> sions in relation to this question are successions of (neurotic)
> compromises regarding the signifier taken at the letter, which is the
> cadaver.[11]

One of the tasks of the previous chapter was to discuss two of the institutional forms of those 'series of evasions' – ritual and prohibition. The primary task of the next section is to consider how Girard proposes that surrogate victimage engenders and structures the last of these institutions of the sacred: myth. We have already discussed how Girard figures these institutions in the most general terms: they function to control and canalize mimesis; and they embody a reification of a (structurally necessary) incomplete comprehension of surrogate victimage: they are cultural forms that double as both recollections and misrecognitions of victimage. Where we argued that ritual's function is primarily *propitiatory* and prohibition's is primarily *prophylactic*, we will see how myth reiterates both prohibition and ritual in narrative form and in so doing serves as a justification for and explanation of those institutions, their origins, their strictures, and, in a limited sense, their 'rationale'.[12] While doing this, we shall deem it necessary to extend some of the cursory reflections on structuralism entertained above, as Girard's theory of mythology is itself worked out in close proximity and dialogue with the work of Claude Lévi-Strauss, the most influential structuralist anthropologist of the twentieth century.[13]

Myth: narrating the sacred

In *Myth and Society in Ancient Greece*, Jean-Pierre Vernant makes the point that any contemporary academic consideration of myth must acknowledge that the vast bulk of the Western intellectual tradition, at least since the Greeks, has positioned myth as both irrational and fictitious.[14] In the twentieth century, however, this tradition struggled with a variety of challenges to its legitimacy: from those provided by Vernant himself, through to figures such as Kenneth Burke, who argued for the absolute 'inescapability' of myth, and the psychoanalyst Carl Jung, who went further, advocating for myth's epistemological acuity and even ontological supremacy over other forms of thought and knowledge.[15]

   Although he has distinct sympathies with both the charge of myth as irrational and false *and* those claims made on behalf of its coherence and perspicacity, Girard does not ultimately endorse either. He affirms the idea that myths cannot be read as simple referential truths – or even great religious or symbolic truths – but he does not figure them simply as flights of fancy, 'pure' fictions. Rather, he suggests, myth possesses elements integral to both of these characterizations and yet is not quite reducible to either. Girard argues that myths stand as partial representations *and* partial obfuscations of mimetic violence, and operate primarily via (specifiable) processes of narrative transformation;[16] myths, in other words – like ritual and prohibition – recall something they don't clearly *comprehend*.

Like Freud's figuration of myth, therefore, Girard's construal suggests a certain 'return of the repressed'; however, contra Freud, he argues that it is not 'suppressed desire' that is at the heart of mythology, but the terror of violence. Philippe Sollers further elucidates this understanding of Girard by offering a (peculiarly Girardian) reformulation of Lacan: 'the unconscious is structured like a lynching.'[17] Myth is the narrative reiteration of the surrogate victimage mechanism from the perspective of its beneficiaries; it represents, Girard argues, a 'retrospective transfiguration of sacrificial crises, the reinterpretation of these crises in light of the cultural order that has arisen from them' (*VS* 64/100). The ultimate task of myth, then – and the origin of *mythopoeia* – is to recall both the chaos and the founding murder, that sequence of events which constitute the breakdown and reconstitution of the cultural order (*TH* 120/ 129). Girard sees myth, therefore, as a narrative form which has its roots in actual acts of violence against real victims (*S* 24–5/37–8); it is, he suggests, 'part of the process by which man conceals from himself the human origin of his own violence, by attributing it to the gods' (*VS* 161/237). Girard's view of myth is therefore (like J. G. Frazer's and Freud's) 'euhemeristic' – it involves, at least in part, the deification of actual historical figures (however distorted these may seem).[18]

In *The Scapegoat*, Girard examines the legend of Romulus and Remus, the founding narrative of the city of Rome (*S* 89–94/ 128–35). For Girard, this myth is highly suggestive of an act (or a number of acts) of collective violence, and he examines two accounts provided by Livy (59 BC–AD 17) in his *History of Rome*. In the first, better-known, version, Romulus kills his twin brother in anger when Remus jumps over the map outline of Rome which the former had drawn in the dirt. The lesser-known version of the myth, however, contains a scene of collective violence. In this scenario, the brothers argue over which one of them will lead Rome; and, when the religious officials and prophets are unable to resolve this dispute, the two brothers – and eventually their followers – become embroiled in an increasingly violent feud during which Remus is killed. In this second version, Girard detects a number of mythemes which, he suggests, represent narrative transfigurations and obfuscations of violent reciprocity and its resolution through surrogate victimage: twin brothers who covet the same object; the progressive intensification of this rivalry, which eventually sweeps through a community; and, finally, the resolution of the crisis through murder.

Girard makes similar points concerning accounts given of the death of Romulus. Plutarch (AD 46–120) furnishes us with several versions of this death, and, of these, three detail collective murder: 'According to one, Romulus was suffocated in his bed by his enemies; according to another, he was torn to pieces by the senators in the temple of Vulcan. In still another version, the murder took place in the Goat Marsh, during a great storm' (S 89/128). Girard argues that the differences between accounts of the death of Romulus reflect the chronological development of the myth whereby the explicit and collective violence of earlier versions is progressively effaced through a series of narrative transformations that function to obscure the violent origins of the account and to sacralize the victim. This process of narrative transformation, the displacement and/or effacement of violent elements, is what Girard calls 'mythic crystallization'. Where early accounts give every indication that Romulus was killed at the hands of a mob, later ones decidedly move in the direction of mythologizing his death. One of Livy's accounts, contained in his *History of Rome*, even describes Romulus disappearing in a thick cloud which hovers above the Roman assembly – after this remarkable departure, he is proclaimed a god.

But it is now worth pausing for a moment to reflect on some of the issues broached above. It could be objected that Girard seems merely to be pushing whatever textual evidence he can through his preferred theoretical lens, that the interpretations he proffers suggest not so much valid extrapolations from the data but the deployment of considerable theoretical acumen and creativity in the service of an *idée fixe*. What, we might ask, are the hermeneutic tools Girard draws on for such interpretations? And what are his reasons for employing these? Although an adequate exploration of these questions cannot properly be undertaken until the concluding section of this chapter (developed more substantially in the final chapter), it is worth pointing out at this stage that Girard has, in fact, been very clear about both what kind of typology he employs to read myth and why he believes this typology justified. Setting aside – for the moment at least – issues pertaining to the latter issue, we will now undertake an examination of the former.

Girard argues that a number of themes or motifs occur in myths which give textual evidence of the sacrificial crisis and surrogate victimage: (1) a theme of disorder or undifferentiation; (2) the presence of an individual who has committed some kind of transgression (and who is thus responsible for this state of undifferentiation); (3) the presence of certain stigmata or 'victimary signs' on the responsible party; (4) a description of the killing or expulsion of the culprit; and (5) the regeneration or return of order (*GR* 119; cf. *TH* 119/128).

Let us now consider each of these in more detail before turning to apply them to some further actual examples of myth:

1   *A theme of disorder or undifferentiation:* Girard argues that, because they are generated by scenes of collective violence against innocent victims, the beginnings of myths often depict states of undifferentiation that correspond with the way in which intense mimetic rivalry and the resulting sacrificial crisis progressively erode all meaningful (cultural) distinctions: 'Day and night are confused; heaven and earth communicate; gods move among men and men among gods. Among god, man, and beast there is little distinction. Sun and moon are twins; they fight constantly and cannot be distinguished from each other' (*S* 30/47). The beginnings of these myths, therefore, represent the crisis of degree, 'the recollection of which is systematically distorted by the successful scapegoat effect that concludes it' (*TE* 221).

Most creation myths, for instance, begin with a depiction of a state of the 'world' as an undifferentiated mass or an original chaos. Girard suggests that this theme can also be found in mythical accounts of cosmic catastrophes, fires, floods, droughts, pestilence, and fights between people (especially twins). Girard argues that references to plagues, for instance – very common in certain kinds of mythological literature – invariably represent displaced depictions of the process of undifferentiation, the annihilation of specificities symptomatic of a sacrificial crisis (*DB* 136–54).[19] (In this sense, the 'plague' is a coded representation of the undifferentiation besetting a community, rooted in violence and social decay.)

2   *An individual who has committed some transgression (and who is thus responsible for the state of undifferentiation):* Myths often portray particular individuals as being, in significant respects, culpable for the disorder besetting communities – culpability taken, by the myths, as incontestable fact. The accusations typically directed at these victims in mythology (which justify their lynching or banishment)

implicate them in crimes that represent an erosion or even inversion of those kinds of distinctions that stabilize (a) culture: parricide, incest, and totemic theft, for instance. Alternatively, the transgressions of which these characters are guilty need be little more than unintended *faux pas*. In either case (grave or seemingly trivial offence), however, the utter seriousness of the crimes is indicated by their gravely serious *consequences*.

3 *The presence of certain stigmata or 'victimary signs' on the responsible party:* Girard points out that the central figures of mythology are invariably remarkable characters: highly unusual humans, aliens, monstrous creatures or gods; these all bear obvious signs of physical or moral exceptionality: '[World] mythology swarms with the lame, the blind, and the crippled or abounds with people stricken by the plague. As well as heroes in disgrace there are those who are exceptionally beautiful and free of all blemish' (*S* 31–2/49). Girard indicates a number of ways in which the presence of these preferential signs of victimage on central figures points to those minor differences that function to canalize the hostilities of a crowd. And that these exceptional beings are often depicted as heterogeneous mixtures of god, human, and animal is also indicative of that effacement of distinctions and those distortions brought about by acceleration of 'conflictual reciprocity' (*GR* 119; cf. *TH* 120–3/130–3):

> As the rate of conflictual reciprocity accelerates, it not only gives the impression of identical behavior among the antagonists but it also disintegrates perception, as it becomes dizzying. Monsters are surely the result of a fragmentation of perception and of a decomposition followed by a recombination that does not take natural specificity into account. (*S* 33/51)

4 *A description of the killing or expulsion of the culprit:* Myths detail events whereby a guilty party is killed or driven away, either by the whole community acting as one, or by one person who acts for the whole community. For Girard, this signifies the scapegoating act *stricto sensu*, 'the fruit of the mimetic polarization triggered by the mimetic crisis' (*GR* 119; cf. *IS* 83/115). It is this killing that constitutes a community or polity, a killing that the religious studies scholar Mircea Eliade has referred to as the '*meutre créateur*' [creative murder].[20]

5 *The regeneration or return of order:* The killing or banishment referred to above has the effect of engendering peace and a return

to order (which is often narratively presented, in fact, as the *genesis* of order). Simultaneously, the victims represented in myths are invariably sacralized or venerated – given the features and even the moral profile of saviour figures – owing to the way in which they have transformed the crises and 'saved' the communities under threat. It is this double transference that accounts for the kinds of idealization (for instance, through the attribution of physical prowess or beauty) which invariably characterizes mythical heroes. Drawing links between ritual sacrifice, kingship, and surrogate victimage, Girard supplies an interesting solution to questions regarding the oft-noted paradoxical nature of primitive divinities, who are presented as simultaneously malevolent and benevolent (*VS* 251/375). The unstable alternation to which the victim is subject, the sometimes disorienting oscillation between scorn and adulation, recapitulates the same double transference of the original sacrificial victim whose violent death made communal order possible (*VS* 274–6/410–13).

In *Things Hidden*, Girard examines two myths recounted and discussed by Claude Lévi-Strauss in his *Totemism* (1962) – the first from the Ojibwa indians of North America and the second from the Tikopia people of the Pacific (*TH* 105–25/114–35).[21] This allows Girard not only to interpret and discuss the myths, but to engage with Lévi-Strauss – and indeed structuralist analysis itself – in more general terms. We will now take up the first of these issues, beginning with synopses of the myths under discussion.

The first of the myths depicts the origin of the five Ojibwa clans from six anthropomorphic supernatural beings who came from the ocean to mix with humans. Initially, one of the six beings covered his eyes and refused to look at the humans. His curiosity, however, eventually got the better of him, and – lifting a corner of the veil covering his eyes – his gaze fell upon an Ojibwan man, who was killed instantly. Although he was possessed of no malicious intent, the other supernatural beings persuaded the godly being with the deadly gaze to return to the water. The five remaining beings continued to dwell among the humans and became a great blessing to them. From these remaining five came the five great totems or clans (*TH* 105–6/115).

The second myth, of the Tikopia, tells of how at one time the gods were little different from mortal beings and even served as representatives for the various clans. It happened one day that a foreign god named Tikarau came to visit; the local gods prepared a feast for the visitor and organized some competitive 'trials of speed and strength' to see whether they or their guest would triumph. During one of the races the visitor slipped and claimed to be injured; in a flash, however, he stopped limping and bolted towards the food prepared for the feast, gathered it all up and dashed away in the direction of the hills. The local gods set out after him and Tikarau slipped and fell again, enabling his pursuers to retrieve some of the stolen food: a coconut, a taro, a yam, and a breadfruit. Although the thief was successful in escaping with most of the food that he had gathered up, the four vegetables retrieved were saved for the humans – these fruits became the basis of the totem system (*TH* 106/115).

Girard points out the means by which these myths can be interpreted utilizing the five-element typology detailed above. The beginning of both myths involves a depiction of an undifferentiated state – the confusion of human and divine, the mixing of heterogeneous elements – which, Girard argues, is homologous to the violent destructuring characteristic of a sacrificial crisis. The state of conflictual mimesis is further alluded to, Girard argues, by reference to the 'trials of speed and strength' arranged by the 'humano-divine consortium' subsequent to Tikarau's arrival. In both myths, certain noxious effects – the only 'bad' elements in otherwise peaceful narrations – are attributed to individual culprits, transgressors whose guilt is (taken by the myth as) incontestable. In the first case the culprit is the Ojibwa god who possesses the deadly gaze, and, in the second, a visitor who turns out to want to steal, in effect, a whole cultural system (*TH* 106–7/115–16).

Both of the culprits also bear certain distinguishing marks, the stigmata of scapegoats; and, in both cases, these signs constitute an integral part of their (respective) nefarious behaviours. The Ojibwa god possesses the 'evil eye', which differentiates him from other gods and humans; it also serves as the modality through which his crime is perpetrated. In addition, considered more broadly, it is a typical (even banal) accusation directed at scapegoats. Although attributions of the 'evil eye' are often seen by folklorists as little more than a harmless vestige of pre-scientific beliefs, Girard points out that accusations of this type invariably result in the persecution of those singled out (*TH* 116/126).[22] And Tikarau, like Oedipus, possesses a limp, which is the result of a fall during the 'trials of speed and strength'; but it is also integral to his guilt – he exploits it as a strategy to 'sucker' his opponents and so to aid his theft. Lastly, in both instances the expelled god is not part of an 'original' totality, but instead originates from an 'outside', either emerging from the sea or from another, foreign, land.

Girard argues that the expulsions detailed in each instance are explicitly depicted as collective acts. Further, he draws attention to the fact that there are renderings of both myths discussed that add considerable support to the hypothesis of surrogate victimage. For instance, the anthropologist Raymond Firth's account of the Tikopia myth in his *Tikopia Ritual and Belief* provides a more substantial elaboration of the final stages of the narrative; in this version, the god is pursued until both the god and the pursuers reach the edge of a cliff where Tikarau escapes by flying away. Again, although this version of events does not explicitly detail an act of sacrificial violence against a victim, it is even more suggestive of collective violence than Lévi-Strauss's account. Girard points out how, in societies which lack an elaborate legal or judicial system, the event 'not quite described but indubitably referred to' by the 'flight' of Tikarau constitutes a favoured mode of capital punishment (given suitable geographical conditions):

> The prisoner is led up the slopes that lead to the cliff, and the community, forming an arc, advances slowly, blocking any path of escape except of course for the one leading to the cliff edge. Nine times out of ten, panic will probably force the unfortunate to throw himself off the cliff without it being necessary to lay a hand on him. The famous Tarpean Rock is only one example among others of the same custom. The advantage of the procedure, in the religious sense, is that the entire community participates in the execution and no one is exposed to the 'pollution' or contact with the victim. This same advantage figures in other types of capital execution in archaic societies. (*TH* 107–8/116–17)

Finally, in both cases, the expulsion produces a return to order. In the Ojibwa myth, the five sea gods who banish the transgressing god back to the ocean become 'pillars' of the community, the original founding gods of the five clans or totems. And, in the second case, the 'family of gods' who chase away Tikarau are construed as beneficiaries of the fruit he drops accidentally; the food left forms the basis of the Tikopia totemic system.

Short excursus on Lévi-Strauss and structuralism

For both Girard and Lévi-Strauss, these two myths chart the movement from an undifferentiated state to a differentiated state via an expulsion or occlusion of a 'foreign element' through which (differential) meaning is established. At the start of both myths the gods mix with the humans; there are no apparent distinctions between humanity and divinity. This scenario is disrupted by one of the gods' transgressions; the offending party is then eliminated and this elimination has several effects, chief of which is differentiation. In the Ojibwa myth, the five gods who chase the god with the deadly stare back into the ocean henceforth live among the humans, originating the five clans or totems. In the Tikopia myth, the food left by Tikarau also functions to differentiate, forming the basis of the totemic system.

Reflecting on structuralist analysis in the context of a discussion of the above myths, Girard points out that, despite his reservations, Lévi-Strauss's method – and structuralism more generally – has much to commend it: 'Structural analysis cannot deal with everything', he admits, 'but within its limits it is highly satisfactory' (*VS* 241). Indeed, Girard's own work remains true to structuralism in several respects, not least insofar as both affirm the idea that there are generative structures which lie beneath the surface of texts that supplant authorial intention and 'direct' the action of the narrative in the absence of the subject's conscious collaboration. Additionally, Girard agrees with Lévi-Strauss that mythology is a particularly apt embodiment of differential thought, of a narrative form of symbolic differentiation achieved by a 'driving out' or expulsion of a foreign element (*TH* 109). For Girard, Lévi-Strauss remains important as a theorist of myth, as he is perhaps the first to appreciate the centrality of differentiation and undifferentiation in analysing the symbolic structures of mythology.

But equally, Girard indicates what he considers to be an unusual, and ultimately unfortunate, feature of Lévi-Strauss's account: while Lévi-Strauss points to the 'all-against-one' structure of both myths – and even furnishes his readers with further examples of it – he assumes that this structure has no autonomous meaning, possesses no sense outside the logico-semantic world of myth itself. For Lévi-Strauss, it is simply the case that the narrative expulsions or occlusions that he describes are necessary conditions for the generation of meaning. Therefore, the structuralist interprets the expulsions as exemplifying a *logic* of exclusion or elimination, which, in its execution, frees the mind from a certain perceptual or conceptual congestion. Lévi-Strauss, in other words, treats mythic motifs as atemporal structural patterns somehow inhering in the human mind; as Girard says, for structuralism, the problem of 'sense' [*sens*] is, at base, a purely *logical* problem, 'an act of symbolic mediation' (*VS* 244/362).

And it is here that Girard finds fault with Lévi-Strauss's analyses, contending that he can offer no adequate explanation of the actual structural commonalities that he has found, instead having to treat these – no matter how pervasive – as always simply fortuitous (*TH* 114–15/124). Girard argues, that is, that Lévi-Strauss is able to delimit the *significance* of the structures he finds only by avoiding their substantive *content* – he limits their meaning to their abstract structures, that is, by ignoring *how* the differentiation he details is established. The difference is that, for Girard, this elimination is not merely an abstract operation that somehow makes conceptualization possible, but a historically based event, or series of events, that provides the impetus for the generation of the narratives. Far from being merely a conceptual grounding for a community, myths – including those of the Ojibwa and Tikopia – are transformed accounts of acts of real violence which work (partially) to conceal their origins. Girard contends, in other words, that the elimination of the gods in both myths suggests communal acts of violence directed at victims.

By raising differentiation itself to the level of what he calls a 'metaphysical absolute', Girard argues that Lévi-Strauss fails to take advantage of his own insight by treating this (differentiation) as an end unto itself, by simply equating 'differentiation in myth with the process of "human thinking"' (*DB* 163). The structuralist confuses, in other words, a logical with a substantial or 'historical' process. But it is not through some ill-defined philosophical commitment to an extra-textual generative mechanism that motivates Girard's claim regarding the putative insufficiency of Lévi-Strauss's reading, but what he sees as the hermeneutic and heuristic inefficacy of the structuralist account itself. Nothing in Lévi-Strauss's account, Girard suggests, goes any way towards explaining the conjunction of the chief elements in the actual structure the former describes: (1) why the eliminated fragment has a negative connotation (as exemplified by the Oedipal limp of Tikarau or the 'evil eye' of the Ojibwa god); (2) why these (differentiated) features implicate the eliminated element in a crime; (3) why the eliminated fragment (and the elimination itself) is also given positive connotations, and; (4) why the elimination – if merely the generation of innocuous (conceptual) differentiation – is invariably represented (and described, by Lévi-Strauss and others) as both violent and collective (*TH* 105–25).[23]

Girard argues that structuralism, as applied to anthropological and mythological texts – from Lévi-Strauss through to contemporary theorists such as Jean-Pierre Vernant, Luc de Heusch, and Marcel Detienne – is constitutionally unable to get behind the structures it describes. It needs, rather, always to assume that the binary oppositions it uncovers are never *generated* for them but are somehow 'always already' there; the mediation of conflictual polarities always takes place through transformations in the system itself. But if the insight of structuralist theories of myth ultimately boils down to the assertion that these narratives are simply the result of the human need to 'distinguish things', then *what exactly does this hypothesis suppose to 'explain'?*[24] Resolving all issues of sense in terms of transformations in a system disallows from the start asking the (legitimate) question of what *engenders* these systems. And if structuralism suggests that symbolic systems disencumber congested perceptual fields and mediate perceptual and conceptual polarities, it then leaves unaccounted *how* this disencumbering or mediation is accomplished.

So, Girard argues that, although structuralism is correct both to warn of confusing representations with referents and to assert that mythology represents the birth of human thought, it errs in determining this birth as an 'immaculate conception' (*TH* 120). Structuralism provides a non-genetic account of sign systems that must always assume that 'In the beginning was difference'; and herein lies its blind-spot: 'The issue that structuralism will never be able to work out', Girard contends, 'is the reciprocal dependence between the differential principle and the undifferentiated symmetries in the relationship between doubles, the "zero degree" of structure' (*TH* 402). He concedes that, *within* the realm of the symbolic, structure reigns supreme – but it is the sacred, Girard argues, that reigns over structure itself (*VS* 242).

We can see, therefore, that, although Girard has no problem with Lévi-Straussian structuralism at a certain stage of analysis, he wants to posit a hypothetical mechanism that is able to account for the generation of these structural patterns by taking more seriously the narrative elements (and structures) than does Lévi-Strauss himself. This is the reason why it is best to characterize Girard's work not as 'anti-structuralist' but as 'astructuralist'. There is reason to believe, Jean-Pierre Dupuy argues, that Girard's approach 'brings forth what structuralism carried within itself, but was prevented by its very method from delivering.'[25] Ultimately, Girard contests the idea – best encapsulated by Lévi-Strauss's metatheoretical dictates in *Anthropologie structurale I* – that synchronic structures cannot yield diachronic knowledge. So, while he is happy to concede the structuralist's notion that the meaning of any symbolic set is a product of differences between symbols, he is not content to foreclose the question of the origin of representation *a priori*. Girard's method of reading myths is based on structuralist inferences, therefore, but does not allow the metatheoretical dictates of structuralism to proscribe the possibility of all morphogenetic hypotheses.[26]

So, for Girard, Lévi-Strauss – and structuralism more generally – remains over-infatuated with his own discovery, by the structural patterns he reveals, which are somehow seen to be sufficient, in themselves, to provide for their own explanation. Therefore ultimately, structuralism – like functionalism before it – 'succumbs to the same kind of error – it mistakes the stating of the problem for its resolution' (*TH* 75). It is, Girard argues, limited by its being seduced by a kind of transcendental (synchronic) idealism that puts language in the place of the idea (or rather, collapses the latter into the former). Structuralism, Girard argues – considerably more provocatively – is the latest incarnation of Platonic essentialism, of Cartesian 'clear and distinct' ideas (*J* 95):

> From Aristotle to structuralism, all ideas of static classification are the late products of a ritual mentality. The recent insistence on differential linguistics is merely another recipe for the perpetuation of this immense tradition, behind which there is always essentialism, the fundamental Platonism of a philosophy which, throughout history, remains true to the great trends of ritual inspiration. (*J* 98)

Part of the appeal of Girard's thinking is that it is capable of being faithful to the considerable insights of structuralism by plotting structural homologies over a broad range of cultural institutions, practices, and texts, while at the same time not resting content with these homologies, refusing to see in these complete 'explanations'. For instance, the ambiguity with which ritual holds its sacrificial victims and myth holds its heroes is amenable to a more satisfying explanation if one can actually explain – and not merely articulate – these correspondences by appeal to a single generative mechanism that engenders both ritual and myth.

We will have cause to examine further some of the epistemological principles at work in Girard's hypothesis of surrogate victimage in the concluding chapter. For now, we will turn to consider his elucidation of two other kinds of cultural texts: firstly, Greek and

Shakespearean tragedy, and then 'texts of persecution', the second of these constituting perhaps the most crucial kind of evidence for Girard's euhemeristic interpretations of cultural texts and phenomena.

Tragedy: surrogate victimage
'through a glass darkly'

In tragedy we can see evidence of a variety of narrative elements that have already been highlighted in our consideration of ritual and myth; for instance, here again we witness the existence of the 'double transference': tragic heroes – like mythical heroes and sacrificial victims – very often undergo apotheoses whereby their reviled status is transformed into a kind of valorization virtually indistinguishable from religious awe. The reiteration of certain structural features of mythical narratives in tragic literature is what Northrop Frye, in his *Anatomy of Criticism*, called 'displacement' – the pervasive socio historical processes by which certain mythemes become the images, conventions, and structures of drama.[27] While certainly not buying into the questionable veracity of Frye's schematization of the 'Ur Drama', it seems uncontentious that dramatic literature has often involved the explicit adaptation of mythical narratives and themes. But such displacements, Girard argues, by no means make the two functionally equivalent. Turning our attention to tragedy will help clarify and elaborate certain issues of Girard's examination of myth and extend this discussion into new territory.

Despite its often explicit utilization of mythic themes and structures, Girard argues that tragedy is distinct from myth insofar as the tragic vision is more explicit in its preservation, its presentation, of the sacrificial crisis and surrogate victimage. In Greek tragedy he sees a partial uncovering of the workings of the victimage mechanism; and although it does not completely render explicit the workings of violence which give rise to it, it does not disguise its operations as completely as myth (*J* 45).[28] For Girard, tragedians saw the sacrificial reality upon which their culture was founded, albeit 'through a glass darkly', yet had no religiously significant possibilities for ordering their lives otherwise. Gil Bailie elaborates: 'The insight of the Greek tragedians rises like a plaintive cry only to be absorbed again into the mythological thought from which it was never able to fully extricate itself.'[29] To see the means by which

Girard pursues this unique reading of tragedy, we begin with an overview of his discussion of Sophocles' *Theban Plays*, a dramatic trilogy, the first two plays of which he has regularly returned to reflect upon (*VS* 68–88/105–34; *S* 25–44/37–67; *IS* 107–14/146–54).[30]

In the figure of Oedipus, Girard sees the distinctive marks of a scapegoat/king; he draws out what he sees as the manifest parallels between this tragic hero and the Greek *pharmakos* (*VS* 94–5/143–4). Here is Girard's own summation of his reading of the first play, placing the action of the tragic drama in a somewhat broader context, thereby rendering his interpretation of Oedipus (-the-scapegoat) explicit:

> Harvests are bad, the cows give birth to dead calves; no one is on good terms with anyone else. It is as if a spell has been cast on the village. Clearly, it is the cripple who is the cause. He arrived one fine morning, no one knows from where, and made himself at home. He even took the liberty of marrying the most obvious heiress in the village and had two children by her. All sorts of things seemed to take place in their house. The stranger was suspected of having killed his wife's former husband, a sort of local potentate, who disappeared under mysterious circumstances and was rather too quickly replaced by the newcomer. One day the fellows in the village had enough; they took their pitchforks and forced the disturbing character to clear out. (*S* 29/45–6)

Although Girard is not the first to pursue a reading in which Oedipus is figured as a scapegoat/king, he is the first to embed this reading in the comprehensive anthropological framework that such a reading would seem to demand.

Oedipus the King opens with a depiction of a plague that has been infecting the city of Thebes. (We have already had occasion to discuss the Girardian contextualization of references to the 'plague' and its putative correspondence to the state of undifferentiation correlative of a sacrificial crisis, of how the designation 'plague' allows for a convenient externalization, and divinization, of human violence.) The contagious undifferentiation which Sophocles depicts as sweeping through Thebes manifests at the most local levels of interpersonal relations, best typified through that series of altercations which take place between Oedipus, his brother-in-law, Creon, and the prophet Tiresias.[31] All three men judge themselves fit to mediate and, if necessary, adjudicate the ongoing fracas between the other two; each sees himself as somehow external to the heated exchanges of the other parties, and so uniquely capable of putting an end to these. Yet, as witnesses to the action, we are well aware that each ultimately proves to be thoroughly imbricated in the struggle that they aim (and proclaim) to moderate. Indeed, it would be more accurate to assert that the struggle between the three *originates* in the fact that each imagines himself capable of quelling the violence – that each alone considers himself external to the structure of violent reciprocity readily detected in the other two. All parties in this infernal struggle come initially from some ostensible 'outside' but mistake, Girard suggests, 'this positional and temporary advantage for a permanent and fundamental superiority' (*VS* 69/107). Oedipus accuses Tiresias and then Creon of causing the crisis, whereupon these then reciprocate, charging Oedipus with the same. And, as is to be expected, this exchange of accusations in which each attempts to differentiate himself from the others produces a startling erasure of differences; each, in turn, becomes a violent double of his antagonists.[32]

Correlative to this interpersonal conflict is the generalized and progressive erosion of cultural order and identity that the conflict both evinces and engenders. Tiresias's accusations against Oedipus do not simply represent phases in an altercation that can be exhaustively understood at the psychological level; rather, his charges are directed at the most esteemed member of his community, Oedipus the *king*, of which he suspects the most terrible of crimes. And when Creon challenges Oedipus's goodness and wisdom, the hierarchical superiority attendant upon the king's royal status is further undermined.

Ultimately, we know that it is, in fact, Oedipus who is found responsible for the plague, who is, Girard contends, the unwitting victim of a hunt for a culprit that he himself initiated. (At the play's opening, Oedipus states that he will find the individual responsible for the death of King Laius – the one whom the Oracle claims is responsible for the plague and the calamitous state in which Thebes finds itself. For Girard, this declaration by Oedipus signifies the *search for a scapegoat*.) The conclusion of the first play of the trilogy, *King Oedipus*, sees the condemnation of Oedipus himself for the murder of Laius. And yet, despite this condemnation, Girard reminds us that no indubitable evidence is actually brought against him; the herdsman, who saw the said regicide, did not indicate whether one person or many murdered Laius. There is reasonable doubt, in other words, whether Oedipus is actually the murderer. Girard also draws our attention to the fact that the crimes attributed to Oedipus are levelled at him only *after the fact* – subsequent to his designation as scapegoat – which, he argues, are exacted in this manner so as to justify his expulsion. Oedipus is, in other words, the scapegoat of Thebes.

Girard points to how his reading confers sense upon and is, in turn, corroborated by the archetypal 'victimary signs' of the king: by his kingly position in the first instance; by his physical deformity (the swollen foot); and by his status as foreigner in Thebes. It well correlates, also, to the crimes attributed to the hero. The charges of incest, regicide, and parricide are those kinds of transgressions which so strongly implicate the accused in the erosion of social and cultural identities; they are, in short, the (putative) crimes of a scapegoat:

> We must return once again to the so-called crimes of the son of Laius. The act of regicide is the exact equivalent, vis-à-vis the polis, of the act of parricide vis-à-vis the family. In both cases the criminal strikes at the most fundamental, essential, and inviolable distinction within the group. He becomes, literally, the slayer of distinctions. (*VS* 74/114)

At the conclusion of *King Oedipus* the tragic hero indeed admits his culpability for the crimes of which he is accused; he plucks out his eyes and demands his own expulsion. He adopts, Girard argues, the perspective of his persecutors, succumbing, like them, to the mimetic pull of the mob by endorsing its condemnation of him. Oedipus accedes to what Job (in the Hebrew Bible) resists: the condemnation of 'friends' who attribute the existence of terrible misfortune to the sins of the one accused (*J* 111–12/129–30). This accession of the scapegoat to the verdict of his or her accusers creates a situation in which no persons remain to argue against the crowd's version of events, and, as a result, the scapegoating itself – which both precedes and follows the accusation – recedes from view. Girard argues that it is for this reason – Oedipus's own accession – that readers of the tragedy have been unable to recognize in Oedipus a scapegoat, and have, instead, figuratively joined Oedipus's persecutors in viewing him as actually perpetrating the horrendous crimes of which he is accused (regardless of whether they see Oedipus's perpetration of those crimes as, in some way, unwitting).

Girard extends this reading to the events of *Oedipus at Colonus*, the second play of the trilogy. It is here, the play which details the final days of the scapegoat/king, that Girard detects the final stage of surrogate victimage and its structuring effects. Early in the play, Oedipus is considered the same accursed, polluted figure whom the Thebans had rightfully charged and expelled. But a transformation occurs during the course of the action, and by the conclusion of the drama the citizens of Thebes and Colonus come into conflict with each other over the rights of the possession of the deceased king's corpse. This valorization of Oedipus, the sacralization of his body, is consistent with the double transference of the sacrificial victim, who is transformed from criminal to revered figure after the resolution of the crisis (*VS* 85/130–1).

Girard's engagement with *The Theban Plays* is important not simply as a demonstration of the fecundity of Girardian hermeneutics as applied to tragic drama, but because this specific engagement enables him to contest the conceptual machinery of psychoanalysis at the point of its inaugural scene. We have, however, already considered Girard's critique of psychoanalysis. Needless to say, he has limited his reading of tragedy to neither Oedipus nor Sophocles.

Another of Girard's readings of tragedy (especially germane to a discussion of the work of Friedrich Nietzsche and the notion of 'the Dionysian' – issues taken up in the next chapter) is that of Euripides' *The Bacchae*, a play far more explicit than *The Theban Plays* in its vivid depictions of the machinations of mob violence and mimetic doubling. The drama opens with a depiction of the 'bacchanal', a Dionysian festival that – as Nietzsche saw clearly in the nineteenth century – provides an ideal site for the violent regeneration of culture through a series of reversals and ritual celebrations that end in bloodshed. *The Bacchae* takes as its subject matter a festival that goes wrong; what starts as an 'idyllic' ritual celebration by the women of Thebes turns into a nightmare that progressively envelops the whole city in an orgiastic frenzy of violence and excess (*VS* 126–7/190–1). The Dionysian celebration depicted in the play initially unfolds in such a way as to correspond to those anthropological studies of carnival and festival itself: the suspension or inversion of hierarchies of social role and status, of age, professional, and gender identities.[33]

But in *The Bacchae*, this levelling and mock inversion of hierarchies takes a deadly turn and descends into violent reciprocity. In the throes of a sacrificial crisis, all meaningful social structure erodes; even the distinction between human and divine is erased, as Pentheus, King of Thebes, and the namesake of the festival,

Dionysus, become mimetic doubles, impossible to distinguish. For Girard, Euripides' drama underscores the 'destruction of distinctions as the god sweeps away all the barriers that usually divide mortals'; it 'perpetuates an essential aspect of the sacrificial crisis: the destruction of differences. Beginning as a gesture of harmony, the Dionysiac elimination of distinctions rapidly degenerates into a particularly virulent form of violent nondifferentiation' (*VS* 126–7/190–1). In a terrifying encounter between Dionysus and Pentheus that occurs shortly before Pentheus is murdered, the two have the following exchange:

> *Pentheus*: I seem to see two suns, two Thebes, with two times seven gates. And you, you are a bull walking before me, with two horns sprouting from your head.
> *Dionysus*: You see what you ought to see. (cited in *VS* 162/239)

This (quite literal) instance of 'seeing double' is what Girard calls 'Dionysiac vertigo' (*VS* 162/239), a hallucination which corresponds to a violent reassertion of mimetic reciprocity, occurring in 'the most disquieting and grotesque form available' (*VS* 160/237).[34] As Dionysus possesses Pentheus, all distinctions are effaced – sensible phenomena become radically interchangeable, amenable to continuous substitution. And the most portentous instantiation of this interchangeability of phenomena is the effacement of distinctions between Dionysus and Pentheus themselves. Girard argues that the symbolic import of this last doubling operates by virtue of the fact that Pentheus is presented initially as an outsider, a conservative defender of the order of the city; but he too becomes part of the violent throng when he disguises himself as a Bacchant. It is only when Pentheus is quite literally torn to pieces by the Bacchants that the sacrificial crisis is resolved, that the 'strange illness', which Pentheus himself observed had afflicted the city, abates.

Girard argues that, despite its drawing near to an explicit thematization of sacrificial violence, *The Bacchae* – like tragedy more generally – eventually backs away from its partial revelation: rather than pointing to the human origins of the violent chaos it depicts, rather than directly indicating the arbitrariness of the selection of Pentheus as the victim who would bring the delirium to an end, the play *rehabilitates* the god Dionysus, a divinity figured as exacting harsh but legitimate revenge on a community that has failed to honour him appropriately. For Girard, then, Euripides ultimately sacralizes (the human origins of) the violence which he has allowed

us to glimpse, however furtively, and in so doing transcendentalizes and legitimates this violence by projecting it onto a deity.

Girard's assessment of what he sees as the ambiguous moral and
epistemological accomplishment of the Greek tragedians may seem
overly harsh to contemporary ears. But this judgement needs to be
read in terms of the broader cultural theory he has constructed, in
the context of the kind of cultural dynamics that he has theorized
in more general terms. Moreover, one should be clear that Girard
does not reserve such judgement simply for the playwrights, but
for literary theory itself, insofar as the latter derives its conceptual
resources from Aristotelian aesthetics. He contends that the Aristotelian proclivity to define tragedy in terms of the possession of a
'tragic flaw' [*hamartia*] by one of its central characters (*Poetics* 1453a,
5–15) works to *reinstate the mythic vision itself* (S 81/117–18). Girard
points out, to the contrary, that a character like Oedipus is no
more obviously 'flawed' than those who oppose him; even his oft
remarked-upon temper could not prove to be 'tragic' if that flaw
were not reciprocated in kind by others. (An important conclusion
of Girard's reading of *The Theban Plays* therefore is not to declare
Oedipus's 'innocence' but, rather, to see his guilt as unexceptional.)
Girard's point here is therefore that the flaw attributed to protagonists such as Oedipus by literary theorists does not so much
explain as *justify* their tragic end (*VS* 68–9/105–7). Indeed, it is for
this reason, Girard argues, that in this sense at least the tragedians
show a degree of perspicuity superior to that evinced by their
critics.

While in terms of its aesthetic theory the Aristotelian tradition
may be seen as a force of mythologization, its notion of the 'tragic
flaw' equally points in a direction which invites a recognition of one
of the central accomplishments of Greek tragedy – the inherent
moral ambiguity of its central protagonists. For the most part, we
witness in Greek tragedy iterations of a generic scenario: a community is threatened, heroes emerge to set things right, but are soon
seduced by violence and themselves plunged into the chaos that
they initially thought themselves to be capable of arresting. The
machinery of victimage, in other words, resists intervention from
those who can no more transcend this violence than their own frail
humanity: 'The tragedians portray men and women caught up in a
form of violence too impersonal in its working, too brutal in
its results, to allow any sort of value judgement, any sort of distinction, subtle or simplistic, to be drawn between "good" and
"wicked" characters' (*VS* 47/75).[35] Indeed, we can clearly see such

ambiguity in a character like Oedipus, who is both somebody with no malicious intent *and* the most heinous of criminals; both utterly guiltless and the most abject of subjects; he is alternately calm and reasonable, and then enraged and irrational. In *Oedipus the King*, Creon is the archetypal wise prince; in *Oedipus at Colonus*, he is both a criminal and a liar.

But although the portrayal of the moral ambiguity of its central characters reveals a certain acuity on the part of the tragedians that amounts to a partial demythologization, this demythologization is not sustained. For Girard, tragedy opens with myth, demythologizes its violence in part, and then, ultimately, remythologizes it. Tragedy represents therefore, as he puts it, a 'desymbolism' rather than merely 'symbolism'; but it represents an incomplete process of desymbolization, one that remains imbricated in what it furtively exposes (*VS* 65–6/101–2; *VS* 136–7/203–5).

Girard, perhaps needless to say, has neither limited his analysis of drama to tragedy nor limited his discussion of tragedy to the Greeks. Although much of his attention to tragedy *has* centred on Greek works, he has also discussed the major figures of the neo-classical French theatre – Corneille, Racine, and Molière; and he has made more partial and somewhat haphazard attempts to think about the work of twentieth-century playwrights such as Edward Albee and Samuel Beckett. But, without a doubt, the playwright who has engaged Girard's attention more than any other is William Shakespeare, with most of his substantial reflections on Shakespeare released by Oxford University Press in 1991 in a collection of essays entitled *A Theater of Envy*.

Although his sustained reflection on the work of Shakespeare makes Girard's theory of tragedy more notionally 'complete', it also complicates it significantly. Girard maintains that Shakespeare's dramatic work comes closer than any other to a radical demythologization of conflictual mimesis and surrogate victimage. Shakespeare, Girard contends, does not force us to go very far to decipher these themes in his work – he invariably thematizes these phenomena himself: 'With Shakespeare we never need to formulate the really important mimetic points; he always does it for us, writing our conclusion' (*TE* 193–4). We will defer for a moment consideration of the historical and cultural conditions which Girard argues are inseparable from this superior perspective, and turn instead to examine one of his analyses of Shakespearean drama itself. One of the tragedies that Girard discusses at some length in *TE* is *Julius Caesar*, which, from the perspective of what Girard sees as the 'most fundamental aspect' of Shakespearean dramaturgy – 'conflictual undifferentiation' – is 'the essential and indispensable work' (*TE* 197; 185).

Taking issue with those literary and cultural theorists for whom the play is primarily a 'political drama' – perhaps even a *pièce de thèses* – Girard suggests that the actual subject of the play is the cultural disintegration brought about by rivalrous desire and the socially unifying dynamics of collective violence.[36] Rome's real problem, as presented in the drama, is a crisis of distinctions, and only the violent death of a powerful figure promises to bring peace to the *polis*, a death which seemingly inaugurates a new sociopolitical order (*TE* 198; 201). But holding to this assessment of the play is not equivalent to maintaining that Girard's reading is ultimately *a*political; indeed, the play's very real capacity to reveal political issues is strictly commensurate with its capacity to reveal anthropological structures that both incorporate and generate 'the political':

> The unexplored depth of Julius Caesar lies in the unbroken continuity between an institution most of our social scientists regard as merely 'irrational' and 'superstitious' – sacrifice – and the supposedly transparent rationality of what we call 'politics'; the strength of Julius Caesar, then, is its ability to show religious anthropologists and political scientists that their 'two disciplines are really one'. (*TE* 219)

That Rome is suffering a crisis of undifferentiation is made clear in the opening scene; the populace turns up to the forum and is roundly rebuked by the two tribunes for not displaying the markers of their professions. This lack of appropriate attire serves to de-differentiate them; they are less an orderly citizenry than something approaching an indistinguishable throng. Other confusions of order then become apparent: they are dressed in attire appropriate for a holiday but it isn't a holiday; and they come to applaud Caesar's 'triumph' when there should be mourning. They are, in other words, 'in the wrong place, at the wrong time, for the wrong reason, doing what they should not do.'[37]

Shakespeare effectively interprets this scenario for us and provides more than a simple allusion to the idea that the key element that has precipitated this state of affairs is the 'political' ambitions of Cassius and Brutus, two men who have conspired to kill Caesar in order to assume his place. But, as Shakespeare – and Girard, following the playwright's lead – makes clear, the ambition of these men is neither self-contained nor autogenous; they are able to draw on models of desire and can appropriate plans for carrying their assassination out (*TE* 203). Ultimately, Cassius and Brutus are not propelled into action by virtue of an irresistible lure radiating outwards from some intrinsically desirable object; rather, they derive their impetus from *each other's* desire to kill Caesar and by a *ressentiment* born of envy (*TE* 187). For Brutus, Caesar is the archetypal model-obstacle, an ambivalent figure who is the object of both admiration and hatred (a pattern in Shakespeare that, Girard suggests, is well exemplified in a wide range of characters and plays – for instance, in Aufidius's relationship with Coriolanus, in that of Antony with Octavius, of Proteus with Valentine, and of Helena with Hermia) (*TE* 188–9):

> To a Roman with political ambition – and Brutus's ambition is great, being patterned on Caesar's – Caesar has become an insurmountable obstacle, the *skandalon* of mimetic rivalry. He is both the hated rival and the beloved model, the incomparable guide, the unsurpassable teacher. The more Brutus reveres Caesar the more he hates him as well; his political grievance and his mimetic rivalry are one and the same, most logically so. As a leader of his party, Brutus resembles his model more and more; he grows increasingly majestic and authoritarian; before and after the murder, he rejects all suggestions and decides everything all by himself. To Cassius, his equal, the man who recruited him into the conspiracy, he says: 'I will give you audience.' (*TE* 189)

As a lightning rod for others' *ressentiment*, Caesar has some physical features worthy of our attention. Shakespeare's Caesar – substantially derived from descriptions provided by Plutarch – possesses tell-tale victimary signs; he exhibits a host of infirmities, including epilepsy, a bad ear, and a general physical frailty: 'Everything that Caesar does, everything that we learn about him as a public or a private individual, including the sterility of his wife – which the popular mind readily attributes to a husband's evil eye – makes him look like a man earmarked for victimization' (*TE* 205). These infirmities and weaknesses, of course, are not lost on his would-be assassins, who refer to them repeatedly throughout the play. But, for Girard, the final indication of Caesar's status as a scapegoat in the tragedy is his innocence or, rather, again, the unexceptionality of his guilt; although those plotting his murder assert that his death is necessitated by virtue of his being a manifest threat to the Republic, Brutus concedes, in fact, that Caesar has done nothing to deserve his fate.

And yet die he must. When Brutus eventually declares that Caesar should be 'sacrificed' for the sake of the Republic, he betrays a comprehension of the socially unifying and purgative functions of violence. He well understands that the violence to be perpetrated against Caesar must be sufficiently differentiated from the violence which it is set to conquer – the 'homeopathic' efficacy of sacred violence depends on the success of an intrinsically fraught operation which requires that the violence exacted to produce the necessary *esprit de corps* must be separated from the violence which precedes it. Brutus is well aware of the extreme delicacy of the plotted assassination and so warns his co-conspirators that they should be acting as 'sacrificers', 'subtle masters', 'purgers' – that they should 'carve' their victim up as a 'dish fit for the gods'. If they fail to do this, Brutus warns, the violence exacted against Caesar will not have the desired effect. If the would-be assassins become 'butchers' or 'murderers' who 'hack the limbs' off their victim – that is, if the violence carried out is decidedly not the *other* of that which it is employed to arrest – they will perpetuate, indeed *exacerbate*, what it was engineered to avert (*TE* 211; 213; 216).

Yet, despite Brutus's words of caution, when the time arrives for the deed to be done, the murderers are unable to effect this operation, to separate the poison from its remedy; Brutus *himself* fails to uphold the kind of demeanour which he previously demanded. Indeed, at the suggestion of Brutus – who, Girard says, loses his 'sangfroid in the hot blood of his victim' – the killers cover themselves in Caesar's blood, contaminating themselves with the violence that they had sought to overcome (*TE* 194). Although Brutus's 'sacrificial strategy is excellent', Girard declares (perhaps calling to mind a certain pattern of revolutionary political plans more generally), 'its implementation is a disaster' (*TE* 219). This mistake, however seemingly grave, might still have been able to avert the looming crisis if the crowd at the forum – following the speeches of Brutus and Mark Antony – had chosen to endorse the crime, effectively rendering the killing a *collective* murder; were this to have happened, the violence could well have been rendered sacred and the victim's death could have resolved the crisis.

But this too fails, and the conspiracy falters because Rome is not united around the murder (*TE* 211). The gathered crowd vehemently rejects Brutus's plea for sacralizing the killing and, as a result, Caesar's death is rendered simply another act of profane violence, with Brutus merely now another party to an inescapably domestic fracas:

> Brutus wants to save the Republic, but the Republic does not want
> to be saved. When the crowd is still listening to him . . . a shout rises
> from its midst: 'Let him be Caesar.' From now on, whoever prevails
> against Caesar must be another Caesar. The cry from the member of
> the crowd is ambiguous: does it implore those gathered to support
> Brutus? Or is it declaring that Brutus, like Caesar, should be killed?
> Either way – which in any case may amount to the same thing – the
> new model for the crowd is the murder of Caesar itself, and the new
> phase of violence that occurs as a result of this allegiance first takes
> its toll on the poet Cinna, an innocent bystander who is singled out
> by the mob and killed. (*TE* 194–5)

After this tumultuous event, secondary conspiracies proliferate with alarming rapidity such that the very term 'conspiracy' does little to capture the generalized enmity and violence which subsequently envelops the city. These wildly contagious fractures and rents, however, become distilled such that finally all are polarized into just two rival groups – one clustered behind the figures of Brutus and Cassius, and the other behind Mark Antony and Octavius Caesar. Girard draws our attention to the fact that these collectives are *themselves* violent doubles, and Shakespeare's treatment of the subsequent battle (of Philippi) is not presented by the playwright as a 'banal military encounter but as the collective epiphany of the mimetic crisis, the final explosion of the mob' (*TE* 196).

Brutus eventually commits suicide, whereupon he is posthumously eulogized, even deified, by his former enemy, Octavius Caesar. Along with Julius Caesar, Brutus becomes one half of what Girard calls a 'two-headed god', both of these men having been sacrificed for the sake of *Pax Romana*; it is around these two that the citizenry reunites and out of whose deaths a new order sees light of day. Although perhaps Brutus remains the smaller element of this 'divine' team, he is essential to it, his death necessary for the establishment of the new order (*TE* 200–1). Of course, the order that is re-created is an order against which Brutus pitted himself; indeed, Brutus's apotheosis, Girard notes, would have seemed to him the ultimate betrayal, since it made him the junior partner in the same monarchical business that he was trying to subvert. But this 'real' Brutus is no longer relevant; a mythical figure has risen to take his place, whose death, combined with Caesar's, serves as the foundational violence of this new phase of the Roman empire (*TE* 201).

As a play, *Julius Caesar* shares some key elements with the Greek tragedy: a *polis* plagued by violence and disorder overcomes its problems through the immolation of a victim (or victims), a victim who is fated not because of his crimes but because of those features that single him out. And following this death, the victim – once considered base and monstrous – undergoes a wholesale apotheosis and divinization. But while allowing these parallels, Girard argues that Shakespeare's *Julius Caesar* differs from the two Greek tragedies previously discussed insofar as the playwright endows Brutus with a far greater comprehension of the scapegoat mechanism than the Greek tragic heroes themselves possess. Indeed, we see that Brutus believes that he is able, in fact, to deliberately *to utilize this mechanism for his own ends.*

The difference between ancient Greek tragedy and Shakespearean tragedy, Girard believes, cannot be accounted for simply in terms of a greater 'aestheticism' or Shakespeare's ability for far more complex 'psychological profiling'. The necessary condition for the creation of Shakespeare's dramatic works resides, rather, in a cultural unveiling set in motion by the ancient Hebrews more than three thousand years before Shakespeare's birth, an unveiling so thoroughly interwoven with the moral sensibility and epistemological veracity of Shakespeare's thought that this Hebraic rupture itself needs to be considered in some detail; that, however, is the task of the next chapter.

For now, we will conclude this chapter by examining a kind of text whose existence and form are directly attributable to the same formidable cultural impact of the unveiling mentioned above – the 'text of persecution'. Such texts occupy a moral and epistemological space located somewhere between myth and history. As such, they are a kind of 'test case' for Girard's reading of myth and tragedy, and provide a unique opportunity for a corroboration of the interpretations of cultural phenomena that we have examined both in this and in the previous chapter (*IS* 73–5/101–5).

Between myth and history: texts of persecution

Girard's seemingly perverse insistence – perverse at least in relation to widespread conventions and pervasive tacit axioms of contemporary scholarship in the humanities – that myths (as well as rituals and prohibitions) have their origins in real acts of persecution would seem to require a strong case be made on its behalf. One could very easily be prompted to ask whether Girard's positing of actual historical events justifies the interpretation he gives the (textual) data.[38] To pose the same issue in somewhat more pointed fashion, one might ask how it is that Girard can posit historically based 'persecution events' if these events have necessarily been obscured by the interpretation of them given by their witnesses – and if there is no documentary evidence in existence to corroborate Girard's interpretation. Why, in other words, does Girard claim that all of these cultural texts exhibit 'real facts', if these facts – almost by definition – *escape representation*?

The answer to that question, and, indeed, one's assessment of the veracity of Girard's hermeneutics more generally, will rely substantially upon the adequacy of his analysis of what he calls 'texts of persecution', narratives which occupy a mid-point between archaic mythical representations and radical demystifications of collective violence. These sit somewhere, Girard contends, between history and myth and so evince properties of both. Examples of such texts of persecution include written accounts of the medieval persecutions of Jews, of the Salem witch trials, and of the lynchings of African-Americans in the (post-Civil War) United States.

Having been provided by persecutors rather than their victims, all of these accounts contain characteristic distortions of the persecuted; yet, despite these distortions, we are still able to discern actual historical events behind the skewed accounts. Girard notes the very uncontentiousness of this conclusion – of our willingness to assert the reality of the victimization portrayed in these texts – but he wants to open up the question as to *why* we so readily accept the presence of real events behind texts which contain spurious elements such as proclamations concerning the guilt of the accused (and sometimes even their preternatural capacities). Why, for instance, do we possess unshakeable belief in the actual execution of witches when the accounts provided by those who persecuted them are so notoriously unreliable in a variety of ways? Girard does not ask such questions in order to promote or provoke scepticism about our normal conclusions, but rather to draw out more fully some implications regarding these.

Girard's contention is that texts of persecution are myths that have simply gone through an additional phase of demythologization. This does not mean, of course, that 'texts of persecution' are therefore somehow unreal or fanciful, but that myths themselves are texts of persecution that are more efficient in their effacement of textual traces of collective violence than the latter. Where the myth effectively sacralizes the violence that engenders it so successfully that this violence itself increasingly recedes from view, the text of persecution is a 'myth that fails' – it is a kind of textual witness to a violence that was not sacralized (*DB* 212). Where, in the case of myth, the victim/god is typically apotheosized or divinized, in texts of persecution, such a double transference does not take place.

Girard begins *The Scapegoat* with an analysis of a text written by the fourteenth-century French poet Guillaume de Machaut – the *Judgement of the King of Navarre* (S 1–11/7–21).[39] In the text, Guillaume recounts his participation in an amazing and bizarre series of events that conclude with his being confined to his house, waiting nervously – either for his premature demise or the end of the terrible 'ordeal'. The poet depicts the presence of a pervasive crisis, of widespread death and destruction, of 'signs' in the sky, of people felled by the hailing of stones, of cities being annihilated by lightning. Guillaume attributes the cause of this collection of supernatural calamities to the wickedness of the *Jews* – as well as those Christians who provided them with assistance – who poisoned the drinking water. The author tells us, however, that cosmic balance was eventually restored when '[h]eaven-sent justice righted these wrongs by making the evildoers known to the population, who massacred them all' (cited in S 1/7).

At first, Girard argues that the status of *Judgement of the King of Navarre* as a historical document seems highly problematic. Most of the events Guillaume refers to seem, in the very least, enormously improbable; and yet, even contemporary readers who are well accustomed to regarding the referential aspects of texts with sophisticated scepticism will find it difficult to avoid the conclusion that the 'ordeal' to which the poet refers has some relation, however problematic, to certain historical events. The signs in the sky, the hailing of stones, the destruction of whole cities by lightning, and the manifest guilt of the accused – one would suspect that none of these elements strike contemporary readers as remotely plausible. And yet, the same readers would be equally reticent to allow these implausible elements to serve as justification for the idea that the *whole text* is somehow pure fiction; we easily entertain the prospect, that is, that not all of the incredible events reported by the author are *of the same kind*, or can be interpreted in precisely the same way. Nor does the seeming gullibility of the author in believing in the veracity of his own account undermine this reading. Girard explains:

> Guillaume did not invent a single thing. He is credulous, admittedly, and he reflects the hysteria of public opinion. The innumerable deaths he tallys are nonetheless real, caused presumably by the famous Black Death, which ravaged the north of France between 1349 and 1350. Similarly, the massacre of the Jews was real. In the eyes of the massacrers the deed was justified by the rumors of poisoning in circulation everywhere. (S 2/8)

Girard wants to draw out the implications of our selective endorsement of the veridicality of the narrative by indicating how, in fact, the spurious elements of the text and the credulousness of its author actually *corroborate* the positing of a historical reality behind the textual distortions.

We now know, for instance, that many medieval communities (like Guillaume's) were so terrified of the plague that they avoided even mentioning it. And we are also aware that the theodicy which accompanied this illness often figured the plague as a form of divine punishment visited upon a community, the responsibility for which was not equally shared. Thus, these communities often sought to deal with the threat posed by the disease by selecting a scapegoat whose putative evil deeds were thought to have incurred the wrath of God. According to the historians Girard cites, Jews were often seen as responsible for the plague when it visited particular areas and were sometimes even massacred as a *preventative* measure, at the merest mention that the plague may soon be upon their community. Additionally, the massacre of the Jews described in the poet's account occurred before the height of the epidemic in the area and would be consistent with the occurrence of a few isolated cases that could be taken as poisonings. So, Girard argues, there is no reason to disbelieve Guillaume's reporting of a number of deaths. What the contemporary reader is prone to do, in fact, is accept the deaths that the author reports but *reject the meaning he attributes to them*. Guillaume, that is, furnishes us with some details of a historical event despite not perceiving the event adequately himself; he attributes the plague to the Jews, but we are aware of their innocence – and we are equally aware of the violence exacted against them (S 2–6/8–17).

The ultimate question is not, therefore, '*Are* we aware of the Jews' innocence?', but '*How* are we aware of this?' The most immediate response may be that substantial historical work has been done to justify this conclusion. But this, for Girard, is not where the real significance of this second question lies; it is not simply the presence of concrete historical work on the subject of anti-Semitic persecution in the Middle Ages that allows us to discern the credible from the less credible aspects of *Judgement of the King of Navarre*. Of course, contemporary readers accept that the poisonings could not have taken place, in part, because we know of no poison of that era capable of inflicting such carnage. But, Girard argues, we also suspect Guillaume's account *on the basis of his obvious hatred of the accused*. And yet, he states, 'these two types of characteristics cannot be recognized without at least implicitly acknowledging that they interact with each other' (S 6/14). Herein lies a crucial issue in the interpretation of this text: if there really was an epidemic, then it might have worked to stir up latent persecutory tendencies; by the same token, such persecution might be comprehensible if the accusations against the Jews were 'proven' to be correct.

It is at this juncture that we can best provide a response to both Bruno Latour's and Roberto Calasso's allied criticisms of Girard's theory of surrogate victimage. Both, in some way, accuse Girard of not taking physical phenomena seriously; for Girard, Calasso complains, 'it is as though the sun, the moon, fire, plague, and wind existed only as a cover for social tension' – Girard's 'victim', Calasso suggests, 'is silent nonhuman reality.'[40] Similarly, Bruno Latour charges Girard with a similar violence against this reality: 'he accuses objects of not really counting.'[41] But it is in relation to his discussion of texts of persecution that we can see how these criticisms actually misconstrue Girard's work in very important ways.

To talk, for instance, of 'plagues' in the way in which Girard does in no way mitigates the immense biomedical impact that actual plagues have on human communities. He does *not* argue that all references to plagues in literature and myth are invariably displaced or 'naturalized' depictions of purely 'social phenomena' (although this may *sometimes* be the case). Rather, Girard attempts to theorize how biomedical and social phenomena *interact* – how, for instance, actual physical plagues have precipitated various kinds of social and cultural collapses and so spread their 'undifferentiating effects' via non-biological means. Further, he argues that the reciprocal affinity between the biological/medical aspects and the social aspects of a plague are invariably collapsed in myth; indeed, this lack of differentiation between social and material causation – of, for instance, attributing the origin of a physical plague to moral decrepitude – is itself a constitutive factor of mythical narratives and part of the way in which they obscure their own violent origins (*DB* 138). It is not, therefore, Girard's theory but *myth itself* that tends to conflate moral and physical causality; when the mythical mind looks for a reason for suffering endured, it is invariably not satisfied with natural causes; explanations at the level of physical causality will not, Girard suggests, usually quell moral disquietude (*S* 53). The fact that Oedipus is blamed for the plague ravaging Thebes – a conclusion which the playwright shares (*J* 45/55) – does not somehow undermine the existence of a real physical or bio-medical phenomenon; but it does show the ways in which physical events are susceptible to cultural or moral interpretation. That is, a 'real' plague is likely to precipitate social crisis in societies where the distinction between efficient causation and causation at the level of social relations is either not present or has become effaced.

So the plague that Guillaume recounts is not, according to Girard, merely a convenient label, a metaphorized translation of social decay, but a real physical event that mythological thought believes to be amenable to effective intervention at the level of social relations. Indeed, the mutual textual intertwining of efficient (physical) and social causation at the level of social relations in myth is one of the key factors that prompts Girard to discard the rule that a text be considered reliable only to the level of its most dubious aspect. Here he elaborates further on the criteria by which this reliability may be established:

> If the text describes circumstances favorable to persecution, if it pre-sents us with victims of the type that persecutors usually choose, and if, in addition, it represents these victims as guilty of the type of crimes which persecutors normally attribute to their victims, then it is very likely that the persecution is real. (*S* 6–7/15)

The conclusion we might draw from this is that, in the case of a text like Guillaume's, if one attends to the perspective of the persecu-tors, the actual *unreliability* of their accusations against victims works to *validate* rather than *undermine* the informational value of the account – if only in terms of the violence that it depicts: 'If Guillaume had added stories of ritual infanticide to the episodes of poisoning, his account would be even more improbable without, however, in the least diminishing the accuracy of the massacres it reports' (*S* 7/15). That is, the more seemingly spurious the accusa-tions, the more probable the actual mob violence reported. The important point here is that it is not simply a text's inaccuracies that prompt such a conclusion, but the very *nature* of those inaccuracies.

To the example already cited we could, of course, add countless others (such as the aforementioned witch trials and race-motivated lynchings). What is common to all of these texts of persecution, Girard argues, is that they possess a specifiable *interaction* of probable and improbable elements that are suggestive of actual persecutions: 'the mind of a persecutor creates a certain type of illusion and the traces of his illusion confirm rather than invalidate the existence of a certain kind of event, the persecution itself in which the witch is put to death' (S 11/20). Accounts such as *Judgement of the King of Navarre* are narratives, therefore, of actual violence subject to the characteristic distortions attendant upon their being recounted from the perspective of persecutors.

It is here that we find one of the central epistemological bases for the claims of historical reality that Girard argues lies behind myth. He has been at pains to indicate ways in which texts of persecution share key structural features with a variety of mythological and dramatic texts. In the putatively 'fictional' texts, Girard finds the same features ('stereotypes') that constitute texts of persecution, such as the depiction of a cultural and social crisis typified by the loss of differences (S 12–14/23–6); the description of crimes that work towards or precipitate the cultural and social crisis (S 15–17/26–9); and the presence of 'victimary signs' on the accused (S 17–21/29–34) – all of these have been discussed above in relation to myth and tragedy.

For Girard, therefore, the evident homologies between mythological texts and texts of persecution show strong evidence of actual historically based lynchings and banishments. The kinds of events detailed in texts of persecution involve charges levelled at the accused that no contemporary reader would consider even remotely plausible – but such readers are not hesitant to conclude that the persecutions depicted in these accounts are real. And yet, strangely, despite the very striking structural homologies that Girard shows between those texts and mythological works, those same readers are usually confident that no reality whatsoever – or no reality beyond a conceptual or 'imaginative' one – lies behind them: 'Standing before the myths, we remain the dupes of transformations that are no longer capable of fooling us in the case of the witch hunt' (*IS* 73/102).

Girard argues that the contemporary tendency in theory towards a romantic valorization of the 'surface effects' of texts and their intrinsic non-referentiality finds its epistemological test-case in the instance of texts of persecution, where many, even most, of such surface claims *are* dismissed. But, despite the pervasiveness and the extent of this dismissal, and even though the accused – like some witches, like Oedipus – go so far as to concede their guilt, we are not even prone to *believe* in their guilt (and even, sometimes, in the crimes which they have supposedly committed). Needless to say, far from being something to lament, this tendency, Girard asserts, is something about which we should be profoundly relieved; we should be grateful that historians

> continue to affirm the actual existence of the victims massacred by medieval mobs: lepers, Jews, foreigners, women, those who are disabled, marginal persons of every sort. We would not be only naïve but guilty if we tried to deny the reality of these victims under the pretext that all such stories are obviously 'imaginary', that in any case the 'truth' as such does not exist. (*IS* 75)

What we possess in Girard's analysis of 'texts of persecution' opens interesting possibilities for the interpretation of cultural phenomena through his detailed theoretical elaboration of truths that, viewed in isolation, are almost banal: the Jews did not cause the plague or eat Christian children; witches did not place curses on people that were metaphysically efficacious; and so on. But merely making claims concerning the 'obviousness' of such conclusions is hermeneutically insufficient if the bases for these are not clearly formulated and their (putative) veracity left underspecified. To this end, Girard tries to draw out exactly *how* and *why* we (think we) know such things, and *what this means* for interpretation more generally.

We are now in a position to answer that question with which we began this section: Why does Girard claim that the kinds of cultural texts discussed in this and the previous chapter exhibit 'real facts' if these facts, almost by definition, *escape representation*? The answer is that the (hypothetical) 'facts' account for the nature and organization of mythemes and 'ritemes' in a way that positing these as explanatory 'fictions' or 'principles' *does not* (*DB* 210–11). Girard's insistence on the referentiality of the texts that he examines is not, therefore, the result of some *a priori* philosophical commitment to realism; it is merely that he sees referentiality as more adequate to the range of evidence that he examines – it is part of the hypothesis, therefore, not an assumption that precedes it: the representation of violence in myth requires the inference of its referential nature, 'because only that inference can illuminate myth as a whole and in all its details' (*TH* 119).

Through the theoretical efforts of sub-disciplines of the humanities such as 'postcolonial studies', we have become very used to the idea that the victimization of certain peoples goes hand in hand with an economy of representational distortions that 'justify' their persecution. About this, Girard is in profound agreement; and he maintains that one of the most valuable lessons that structuralism has taught is '*not to confuse representations with their referents*' (*TH* 119). 'Texts of persecution' are certainly unreliable texts, if nothing else. But far more can be said than simply this; they are, in fact, *systematically*, 'reliably' unreliable: they are unreliable in highly patterned ways, patterns which show, in turn, that their very unreliability has limits. Girard argues that, in fact, we tacitly recognize this by our acceptance of the historical reality of persecutions even where we do not always possess corroborating historical documentation that exists 'outside' or independently of these regimes of representation. Conclusions upholding the historical reality of witch burnings (or of Christian persecutions of Jews in the Middle Ages) are based on textual evidence, no doubt, but of textual evidence invariably immanent to texts of persecution themselves. The interpretation that Girard adopts reveals the structuring power of the blindness of persecutors. The reason that Girard utilizes texts of persecution is not that he believes that most theorists would dismiss their violence as fictional; but he wants to ask why it is that we are *already* credulous about some elements of these narratives and not others. One of his tasks, in other words, is to specify clearly this relation of incredulity to credulity in the reception of persecution texts.

But the question as to *how* we know what we know in the case of texts of persecution is not identical to those *reasons we give* for knowing it. The epistemological justification – of 'reasons' for knowing the innocence of accused parties in texts of persecution – has now been outlined. But to frame the issue solely in this way, as simply an epistemological issue, is not sufficient for an adequate consideration of this area more generally, because such a framing is devoid of any consideration of the cultural or historical conditions for the emergence of this interpretive frame itself. If one follows Girard in asserting that texts of persecution represent a certain 'degradation' of mythical obfuscation, then it is equally important to ask what the historical *sources* of this degradation are. What are, in other words, the cultural conditions that engender resistance to seeing the structural patterns which join texts of persecution to myth? For Girard, the answer to this question lies in the radically destructuring effects of the Judeo-Christian texts and the cultural legacy that this tradition has bequeathed to Western civilization. It is to that provocative thesis that we will now turn our attention.

4

Non-Sacrificial Violence: The Judeo-Christian Scriptures

The Gospel is the only 'twilight of the gods'.
Henri de Lubac, *The Discovery of God*

In his laudatory review of *Violence and the Sacred*, published in 1972 in *Le Monde*, G. H. de Radkowski asserted that Girard's book didn't simply represent an enormous intellectual achievement – it was also for him a highly *unique* one. The book, he asserted, offered the '"première théorie" réellement athée du religieux et du sacré' [first authentically atheistic theory of religion and the sacred].[1] In the light of many of the theses of *Violence and the Sacred*, such a reading would seem well founded; but, as an analysis of the trajectory of Girard's work more broadly, it is – in the very least – highly misleading. Regardless, my own experiences in discussing Girard's work with other academics convinces me that de Radkowski's interpretation of that work is far from atypical. Moreover, such readings would seem amply justified given the main contentions of the above book: that the social and the sacred are coeval; that violence lies at the heart of the sacred; and that institutions of the sacred give concrete cultural form to the misrecognition and transcendentalization of human violence. Indeed, if *VS* did not represent an 'atheistic theory of religion and the sacred', then one would be given to wonder as to what exactly it *did* represent.

And yet, while such a reading was certainly understandable, some anomalies remained. Towards the end of that book, Girard had made the surprising claim that the 'sacrificial system is virtually worn out' – and then, to abet (or perhaps add to) confusion about what this might mean, he claimed that this did 'not mean that violence is no longer a threat; quite the contrary' (*VS* 295/441). These somewhat quixotic assertions came quite late, however, and seemed to raise more questions than they resolved: In *what way* was this 'sacrificial system' 'worn out'? How, if true, had this wearing out happened and what were its manifestations? And why, above all, should this wearing out *give rise to more violence*?

These questions, left hanging, were fortified by what seemed to be an obvious gap in *VS*, an omission that rendered its discussion glaringly incomplete: in a book about religion, violence, and social order, Girard dealt with the Judeo-Christian texts very rarely and, when he did, did so in what appeared to be little more than brief, albeit suggestive, asides. Whatever the possible reasons readers may have attributed to this conspicuous omission in analysis, Girard was certainly conscious of it and promised that he would turn his attention to the Judeo-Christian texts in the near future (*VS* 309/463).

The appearance of *Des choses cachées depuis la fondation du monde* [*Things Hidden Since the Foundation of the World*] in France in 1978, six years after *VS*, made good this promise. *Things Hidden* contained not only a comprehensive overview of Girard's work up to that time, but a very substantial reflection on the Judeo-Christian texts. As part of a lead-in to the middle section of the book – a section entitled 'L'Écriture Judéo-Chrétienne' – Girard made the following, somewhat startling, claim about the general degradation of myth during modernity:[2]

> The most *improbable* source of our demythologizing is religion itself, and in our world, more particularly, it would appear to be the religious tradition proper to it, the one it has adhered to blindly and is particularly incapable of subjecting to criticism. I propose that if today we are capable of breaking down and analysing cultural mechanisms, it is because of the indirect and unperceived but formidably constraining influence of the Judeo-Christian scriptures. (*TH* 138/161)

What Girard was claiming was that the historico-religious condition of the possibility of the degradation of myth (and, indeed, of any conceptual interpretation of religion at all) was the intellectual and cultural legacy initiated by the Hebrew Bible and the New Testament – a legacy predicated on this tradition's capacity to destabilize and de-constitute communities and cultures founded on sacrificial violence. Where it had long been an intellectual commonplace – at least within the history and philosophy of science – to note the dependency of the development of Western scientific thought on the cosmology of biblical religion,[3] Girard was here making the analogous claim that much the same could be said to be true of *humanistic* thought.

Girard argues, that is, that the traditions that most 'educated' minds regard as supernatural fantasy – Judaism and Christianity – tell us much more about the 'natural' paroxysms of violence found in the modern world than the social sciences to which they claim undying allegiance. The biblical texts, he suggests, are the pre-condition for reading myth and other cultural mechanisms (*TH* 138/161–2). Historically, these are the necessary conditions for anthropology and the social sciences themselves; these disciplines represent a continuation of the cultural decoding that the biblical text initiates (although scholars in the humanities have rarely been able to see this link and, so, the anthropological significance of their own texts).

In *TH*, Girard argued that what was distinctive about the Judeo-Christian scriptures – beginning with the story of Abraham and Isaac and culminating in the crucifixion of Jesus – was that the violent (generative) structures of culture were progressively unveiled, revealed for their arbitrariness and horror, and, finally, utterly repudiated. To this end, he engaged in an intricate series of readings of biblical texts and related these to his previous hypotheses on violence and the sacred. His conclusion? The Bible was the sole textual mechanism to enact a complete exposé of the victimage mechanism, whose mission it was to alert us to this seemingly perennial cycle of the restoration of order engendered by conflictual desire and violence – an exposé undertaken in order that humanity refuse it without remainder.

Despite the book being dropped into the lap of an academy renowned to be fiercely (and, no doubt, legitimately) protective of its secularity, *Des choses* became a national bestseller in France and provoked intense (and often heated) discussion in the upper echelons of the French academy. Theorists such as Michel Serres, Paul Ricoeur, and Philippe Sollers were all admirers of the work, and, later, other theorists such as the renowned Italian philosopher Gianni Vattimo and the Canadian social and political theorist Charles Taylor expressed – and, indeed, continue to express – more than a token admiration for Girard's project. Of these, it was perhaps the endorsement of Sollers that would seem, even now, the most confounding. This esteemed scholar of Georges Bataille, perennial stalwart of radical aesthetics and politics, novelist and founder of *Tel Quel* – the cornerstone of the French literary avant garde – wrote a review where he proclaimed that, 'on the question of religion, René Girard's book, *Des choses cachées depuis la fondation du monde*, is in my opinion decisive. What interests me in this book is the importance accorded, against an entire tired scientific tradition, to Judeo-Christian writings, that is, to the Bible and the Gospels.'[4]

As admittedly 'tired' as such a tradition may have been in the late 1970s, it was almost certainly *not* looking to orthodox religion for rejuvenation. Regardless, Girard persistently argued that the uniqueness of the Bible was that it effectively enacted a subversion of the sacred from *within*. Just as sacred myth was 'part of the process by which man conceals from himself the human origin of his own violence, by attributing it to the gods' (*VS* 161/237), the Bible, he suggested, *reversed* this process by proclaiming the innocence of the victims of violence, beginning with Abel and Joseph, continuing through to prophets such as Jeremiah and Zechariah and the singers of the penitential psalms, concluding, finally, with Jesus Christ. As a cultural text, Girard maintained that the Bible was unique in its disclosure of the victimage mechanism both through its thematization of the generative effects of violence at the human level and through the narrative identification of God with the victims of such violence.

What Girard suggested that biblical monotheism offered, then, was not simply an 'ethics' or a 'morality' – as modern readings of this tradition have been prone to conclude, at least since Kant – but a substantive *epistemology*, a form of knowledge correlative of one of the deepest (anthropological) senses of what commonly goes under the name 'revelation' – a cognitive insight which offers humanity the possibility of 'redemption' from the violent structures which it ceaselessly reiterates. Girard asserted, and has continued to assert since, that the Judeo-Christian scriptures represent an unequalled unveiling and trenchant critique of the victimage mechanism, substituting the promotion of an ethic of love and forgiveness, of 'pacific mimesis' – a textual unveiling that allows humanity to loosen its hold on the seemingly ineluctable necessity of scapegoating: 'We can see that the significance of the Kingdom of God is completely clear. It is always a matter of bringing together the warring brothers, of putting an end to the mimetic crisis by a universal renunciation of violence' (*TH* 197/220) (cf. Matt. 5: 9, 5: 38–48; Mark 12: 28–34).

One of the ways by which Girard pursued – and has continued to pursue – this analysis was by means of an unusual *continuation* of Friedrich Nietzsche's critique of nineteenth-century anthropology *and* Judeo-Christian morality. Nietzsche's assault on the cultural anthropology of his generation consisted in challenging a deeply held assumption concerning what he held to be a thesis asserting the 'positivistic equivalence' of all religious traditions: the notion that the texts of the biblical tradition merely offered reiterations of a generic range of mythemes found in innumerable other eras and primitive traditions. For instance, the Passion of Christ was assimilated, by British anthropology especially, to the well-known structures and motifs of the 'death and resurrection' cult. Beginning with some social or cosmic crisis which culminates in the suffering and death of a mysterious victim – often at the hands of a violent mob – such myths invariably conclude with the glorious return of the victim, who is thereby revealed to be divine. In the light of this, Jesus's life, death, and resurrection were seen to reiterate a well-established pattern, typified by the amply stocked range of fictitious *personae* of myth and legend, from figures such as Dionysus, Osiris, and Orpheus, to Heracles, Theseus, Adonis, and Attis.[5] This thesis (of 'positivistic equivalence') in fact originated with the pagan apologists of the Roman empire and has since been reiterated ceaselessly throughout the modern era by theorists as diverse as James George Frazer, Freud, and Marcel Mauss, and, in the twentieth century, by figures such as Carl Jung and Joseph Campbell (as well as their seemingly innumerable proselytes). It is with a further examination of this argument – as well as Nietzsche's critique of it – that we will delve more deeply into Girard's ideas concerning the legacy of the biblical tradition; later, we will have to return our attention to Nietzsche, in order to examine more fully his contentions regarding the figures of 'Dionysus' and 'the Crucified'.

The Bible and world myth

In *The Masks of God*, the popular American mythologist Joseph Campbell gives one of the most forthright articulations of the line of thinking that Nietzsche had pilloried in the nineteenth century. Campbell describes Christianity as 'a popular, non-esoteric, politically manageable, state-supported variant' of a death and resurrection cult. To add a little more pungency to this critique, he even goes so far as to say that, as such, Christianity is not even a particularly *good* variant of these, largely by virtue of its bizarre historical fixations (fixations presumably inherited from Judaism) and its pervasive 'non-anagogical' symbolism.[6] Perhaps surprisingly, Girard has considerable sympathies with Campbell's critique – both his point concerning the continuity of Christianity with death and resurrection myths, *and* his assertion regarding its somewhat degraded status as such.[7]

Regarding the first of these claims, Girard has argued repeatedly that an adequate understanding of the religious heritage of the Judeo-Christian tradition cannot be arrived at by a process of minimizing or evading the similarities between its own narratives and those of other traditions and eras. Rather, a proper understanding should be *based on these similarities*. Therefore, Girard repeatedly emphasizes these, not simply because he doesn't want to 'wish them away' (*TH* 144/168), but because he believes that one can come to appreciate the distinguishing characteristics of biblical monotheism only if this tradition is seen in *continuity* with the mythological tradition from which it gradually became detached.

To this end, Girard has repeatedly offered detailed structural comparisons between biblical episodes and a wide range of myths from an equally wide variety of cultural traditions, critical readings in which he has repeatedly pointed out the manifest similarities between biblical accounts and others. He traces, for instance, the theme of the 'cosmic crisis' and the dissolution of differences as evinced in the stories of the Tower of Babel, of Sodom and Gomorrah, and in the Ten Plagues of Egypt. He also points to the pervasive motif of warring brothers: of Cain and Abel, of Jacob and Esau, and of Joseph and his brothers. He points to the theme of expulsion or violent murder as the means by which cultural order is generated or restored; he directs our attention, for instance, to the expulsion of Adam and Eve from the Garden of Eden, the founding of the Cainite community with the spilt blood of Abel, and the reiterated instantiations and development of interdictions and rituals which come in the wake of crises (seen, for example, in the Covenant which is instantiated after the great flood) (*TH* 141–4/165–8). And, of course, as did the pagan apologists and British anthropologists (and Joseph Campbell), he compares the Passion of Christ to the well-known structures and motifs of death and resurrection cults.

And just as the similarities between biblical stories and other religious narratives must not be evaded, Girard argues that neither can the biblical text's incredible portrayals of *violence* be overlooked. Indeed, it is a book – or rather, collection of books – that is *filled* with violence, perhaps even obsessed with it: 'The representation of violence in the Bible is enormous and more vivid, more evocative, than in mythology and even Greek tragedy. If we compare Judaic texts to pagan ones, we find that the amount of represented violence is greater in the first than in the second.'[8] Indeed, Raymund Schwager asserts that violence is easily the most repeated theme in the Bible, its most pressing preoccupation; he points out that there are over six hundred passages detailing specific violence in the Hebrew Bible. There are approximately one thousand verses where God's acts of punishment are detailed, and around one hundred passages where God demands that people kill in his name.[9]

To return to the first point raised above: Girard's thesis is that the Bible does, in fact, represent a most persistent reiteration of mythological themes and structures, but it is a reiteration constituted in large part by a *reworking* of those themes and structures. He holds that the very nature of this reworking is such that it takes myths and then subverts them from within by renarrating them from the standpoint of the *victims* of violence – by rendering explicit, by *thematizing*, the links between civilization, murder, and sacrifice, and by enacting a (prophetic) moral repudiation of the sacrificial scaffolding of traditional culture. The biblical God, Girard argues, is '*le Dieu des victimes*' [the God of (the) victims]; unlike mythological deities, He shares the lot of the downtrodden, the innocent, and the oppressed. But even so, Girard maintains that this 'revelation', to qualify *as* such, is not a purely ethical or 'moralistic' one (as Nietzsche and Kant seemed to believe) – it is an *epistemological* one: it has to do with the uncovering of the *truth* of cultural violence, and not simply its moral censoriousness. The Bible, therefore, does not simply demand that we take pity on victims – it uncovers the machinations of collective violence and the role it has in the establishment and regeneration of social and cultural order (*J* 120–1; cf. *DB* x–xi). And here we can begin to appreciate the immense role accorded to violence in the Bible, a thematic privileging that should by no means embarrass monotheists – indeed, in biblical violence, in its preponderance, its scale, and its very explicitness, we witness necessary preconditions for the gradual realization of its meaning.[10] Overall, it is for these reasons that Andrew McKenna has remarked that Girard's according of importance of the biblical texts relates primarily to their *hermeneutic* rather than their *hieratic* value, for their *theoretic* rather than their *theological* significance.[11]

And it is in light of these points that we can best see Girard's qualified agreement with Campbell's assessment of the Bible as a kind of 'degraded myth'. Campbell's charges of 'non-anagogical symbolism' and 'historical fixations' are precisely those features that for Girard reveal the particular strengths of biblical monotheism.[12] If myth, at its core, functions to obscure its own violent origins, then any movement towards historicization equates with a movement towards a *de*mythification of those violent origins. To put it another way, if one endorses the connections Girard draws between myth and 'texts of persecution' (examined in the previous chapter), then one might well wonder what could possibly be gained by reading *non-historically fixated* accounts of the Salem witch trials. Or what might the hermeneutic (or ethical) pay-offs be for reading de Machaut's depiction of the crisis he lived through as a series of 'anagogic metaphors', a non- or a-historical narrative whose 'reality' should be restricted solely to its *psychic* significance?[13]

But such a response to Campbell's charge is largely a pragmatic one; and, put in this way, may appear as little more than an attempt to 'shame' the mythologist by means of moral bullying, by pre-suming to call him to some sense of ethical sobriety and into adopt-ing a more adequate view of 'referentiality' on ethical grounds. As such, the response should properly come after an analysis of the biblical tradition has been effected, not before. To this end, we will now look at some of the evidence for the large claims made so far, starting with Girard's readings of the book of Genesis.[14]

Girard begins his analyses of biblical texts in *TH* with the story of Cain and Abel, from Genesis (4: 1–26), the first part of the first book of Moses (*TH* 144–9/168–72). The story tells of Cain, who, inflamed by jealousy of his younger brother Abel, murders him. Cain, however, is confronted by Yahweh and admonished for his actions: ' "What have you done?" Yahweh asks. "Listen to the sound of your brother's blood, crying out to me from the ground" ' (Gen. 4: 10). Banished from God's presence and forced to wander the earth, Cain realizes the danger he is in and the likelihood of his own violent behaviour returning on him in kind: 'Now that I've killed my brother, anyone will kill me at sight' (Gen. 4: 14). But God pro-tects Cain from those who would try to kill him by bestowing upon him a mark which warns of sevenfold vengeance against anyone who would attempt to harm him. Subsequently, Cain moves to and settles in a land east of Eden and establishes the Cainite community.

Girard points out that the story of Cain and Abel takes up the theme of 'warring brothers', one of whose deaths inaugurates the first human city. It provides a biblical analogue for the disputes such as that told of in the story of Romulus and Remus and provides a biblical meditation on the foundation of the earthly *polis* through fratricide, the *meutre créateur*; just as the differentiating violence of the death of Remus is the necessary condition of the foundation of Rome, so is the death of Abel foundational to the Cainite community (Gen. 4: 17) (*IS* 83/115).

But, Girard argues, the obvious similarities between the stories should not blind us to their real differences; rather, careful attention to structural similarities between these and other 'warring brothers' stories allows us to situate those differences and to see them with additional clarity. The biblical account contains an identical mythological acknowledgement of generative violence as its non-biblical analogue, but, in the purview of the former, the violence portrayed in both is roundly *condemned*: in both accounts the founding of the *polis* is associated with a murdered brother, but in the biblical account this murder is correlative to Cain's *taking leave* of God, of exacting violence unambiguously *denounced* by that God. In the best-known version of the Roman myth, Remus offends his brother by jumping across the diagram of the city drawn on the ground; and, while this renders his grisly fate somewhat *regrettable*, it remains something for which Remus himself is ultimately responsible. The biblical story, on the other hand, presents the victim of generative violence as innocent of any crime.

So where Romulus henceforth becomes a 'sacrificer and High priest', Girard suggests, who 'incarnates Roman power under all its forms at one and the same time' (*TH* 146–7/170), Cain is never divinized for his actions and so remains, simply, a murderer. The fact that his murder is, like the same in the Roman myth, foundational for a community – signifying the first cultural development – does nothing to expiate his guilt. Yahweh's reaction to Cain's murder of Abel is to forbid all murder by placing on Cain a mark which indicates that events initiated in the spirit of violence will return there in non-linear (geometric) fashion – that 'the culture born of violence must return to violence' (*TH* 148/172).

Girard argues that both stories (Romulus/Remus and Cain/Abel) are parables of human society *per se*, and not merely parables of *particular* societies (*GR* 250–1). Ultimately, however, he maintains that the story of Cain and Abel desacralizes the violent origins of cultural formation through its revelation of the innocent victim; additionally, the biblical account warns that such violence cannot ultimately be used to control itself but merely puts on temporary hold its even more momentous return. This pattern, of the unveiling of the violence at the heart of cultural formation and the vindication of victims, is a recurrent theme of biblical texts and not their mythical analogues – although such a theme can be located in non-biblical texts, these texts do not *themselves thematize it*. In the story of Cain and Abel, therefore, Girard suggests that we witness not so much a myth as a subversion of myth from within, less a 'foundation myth' than a biblical *interpretation* of founding myths (*IS* 83/115). This is the reason for Girard's contention that the biblical tradition is the precondition of any reading of myth, whether this is acknowledged or not; all forms of secular 'demythologization' are the unwitting (and invariably unwilling) heirs to the biblical tradition.

After Cain and Abel, the next example Girard turns to in *TH* (149–54/173–7) is the story of Joseph and his brothers (Gen. 37–50). Like the previous story, the story of Joseph offers a lucid account of conflict between brothers, conflict that is, again, engendered by envy. Unlike the former, however, the narrative of Joseph and his brothers deals not with a single act of violence, but a collective one: he is the victim of his eleven brothers who together conspire against him. Comparing this episode to Greek myths such as Oedipus, Phaedra, and Hippolytus, Girard points out that the story of Joseph and his brothers is, again, an account of a foundational act of violence that has undergone a significant degree of demythologization. In a recent book, *Je vois Satan tomber comme l'éclair* (1999) [*I See Satan Fall Like Lightning*], Girard pursues more systematically the range of structural analogues between the stories of Oedipus and Joseph (*IS* 107–17/146–58). He points to the following narrative features: (1) both begin with accounts of the childhoods of their central protagonists; (2) both characters are accused of incest – or what, in Joseph's case with regard to Potiphar's wife, amounts to much the same thing; (3) both detail how the crises afflicting their families are (temporarily) resolved through the expulsion of the child to a foreign land; (4) in both cases, the ability of the expelled to survive in exile is contingent on their (almost Faustian) capacity to provide 'answers to riddles'; and (5) in both narratives, the strangers ascend the social hierarchy of the foreign towns in which they are exiled.

Girard again maintains, however, that these homologies should not obscure the equally crucial differences between the story of Joseph and mythological narratives, differences that again do not militate against or negate the obvious similarities, but actually give meaning to them. Girard puts to us the sum of these differences: 'The same question underlies both narratives: does the hero deserve to be expelled? The myth answers at every point "yes", and the Bible answers "no", "no", and "no"' (*IS* 110/149). Here we can see one of the central emphases of the Girardian account; that the 'central truth' of the Joseph story resides 'not in its possible correspondence to facts outside the text, but in its critique of mythic expulsions' (*IS* 113/154). It is important to note, however, that by claiming this Girard is not asserting – which, in any case, would be contrary to the whole trajectory of his work – that the biblical story is somehow purely 'imaginary' or 'fictional', but rather that the importance of its truth *exceeds issues concerning its putative referentiality*. As much as the story of Joseph and his brothers may refer to an actual, ostensibly historical, episode, its real significance can only be seen in relation to the discourse it dismantles, in its capacity to 'desymbolize' the mythological perspective. Without this desymbolization, Girard argues, the story would surely conclude by portraying Joseph's brothers as the victims of this 'malevolent hero' who would then benefit from his violent death or sacrifice, a death which would function to divinize or sacralize him along with the violence that accompanied it. But, as it stands, the story of Joseph and his brothers

> involves inverting the relationship between the victim and the persecuting community. From the mythological perspective, the eleven brothers would appear first of all as the passive objects of the violence inflicted by a malevolent hero, then as recipients of the benefits conferred by this same hero after he has been victimized and deified. (*TH* 151–2/175)

Girard, in other words, brackets – temporarily at least – the 'historicity' of the select biblical narratives by giving them a structural reading. This is not to say that he doesn't affirm their historical reality; it is, rather, that he doesn't affirm their historical reality in order to demonstrate their non-mythological basis, but rather the other way round: it is their non-mythological features which point towards their historicity.

Although the inversion of which Girard speaks is evident in the biblical stories discussed so far, the episode that he believes brings to the fore the said inversion in perhaps the most lucid way of all in the Hebrew Bible occurs in the book of Job. This book tells the story of a righteous and esteemed man, a wealthy but generous landholder, whose life is subject to a plethora of misfortunes of such persistence and magnitude that he is all but reduced to destitution by them. We are told, however, that, despite this manifest suffering, Job's proclaimed 'friends' – Eliphaz, Bildad, and Zophar – show him little compassion. Irrespective of his continual protests of innocence and his utter bewilderment at his misfortunes, they all suggest to him that he must be somehow *deserving* of his fate by having offended against God by virtue of his own sinfulness. Indeed, the very scale and seriousness of his misfortune leads his 'friends' to conclude that the gravity of the sins committed by Job must be commensurate with his pitiful predicament.

Girard's reading of this story, pursued at greatest length in his book *Job, the Victim of his People*, is that Job is the scapegoat of his community, a community which has turned on him with alarming rapidity. Girard labels the book an *'immense psaume'* [extended psalm], insofar as it works to depict the dogged persistence of an accused party justifiably asserting their innocence (*IS* 117–18/158–9; *J* 8/14). Again, Girard pursues this reading by a series of structural comparisons between the biblical story and (other) myths and then works to contextualize these by situating them in a broader anthropological framework. He discusses, for instance, the way in which Job is subject to much the same kind of metamorphoses common to sacred kings – with whom he shares analogous prestige and power – in his transition from object of veneration to the most abject of men (*J* 84–5/100–1). He argues that Job's privileged status makes him easily targeted as a scapegoat, and that mimetic contagion provides a suitable explanation for this transition; in terms of individual psychology, Job has moved from being a model to his community to being its pre-eminent model-obstacle.

The narrative suggests that, although Job has not, in fact, done anything wrong, his 'friends' and 'comforters' insist that his misfortune can only be explained through his manifest sinfulness. Job's protests of innocence do little to shake this well-entrenched conviction. As with all scapegoats, Job's putative sins are what Girard calls 'obligatory crimes'; rather than conforming their accusations to the demands of evidence, the friends are convinced of the veracity of their charges simply by virtue of a felt unanimity – in this way, the accusers' hostility constitutes *for itself* irrefutable proof of the guilt of the accused and the necessity of their confession (*IS*

117/158). Indeed, as Girard points out, at times Job *does* accede to the pressure of the victimizers and doubts his innocence. But such accessions are only temporary; ultimately, Job insists on his innocence and so the persecutors' perspective – the 'editorial stance' of myth – does not have the final word (*J* 125–32/145–52). These accessions do, however, attest to the propensity for victims to be ensnared by the same mimetic contagion in which their persecutors are caught. Job's resistance to their efforts, halted only by short episodes of self-doubt, mitigates and eventually undermines the omnipotence of the persecutor's perspective and so goes a considerable way in preventing his final immolation or expulsion.

For Girard, what is ultimately at stake in the book of Job is not merely a decipherment of mimetic contagion and scapegoating, but an extended contestation between different conceptions of divinity. There is the God of Job's persecutors: a charlatan, a bully, a tyrant; and the God of the book itself, revealed with startling clarity in the dialogues: *le Dieu des victimes*. Girard argues that the significance of the book of Job is that it ultimately 'wrests the deity out of the process of persecution' to envision him instead as the God of the oppressed and the downtrodden (Job 16: 19–21; 19: 25–7) (*IS* 117/158; *J* 138–45/158–65).[15] Despite even the *writer* of this book – especially in moments of the divine speeches – getting snared by the lure of the mythological deity, the God of Job is eventually the God of victims; the origin of Job's misery, therefore, is not divine but *human*. His suffering cannot be attributed to God (or the 'Devil' for that matter) but to his *community*, which has turned him into a scapegoat during a period in which it is experiencing social unrest.

That the narrator of the book of Job himself occasionally succumbs to the persecutionary tendencies of the crowd highlights another important idea in Girard's interpretation of the Judeo-Christian texts.[16] These texts narrate an ongoing *relationship* of a people with God, and, in so doing, exact not simply a critique or desymbolization of myth, but an ongoing process of *auto-critique*. The biblical texts themselves show a gradual transition and refiguring of divinity – one which moves from the image of a God who will exact revenge against humans, or who will do the same on their behalf, to a stark repudiation of the very idea of divine violence. In this sense, the Bible is an ambiguous text. To put this point slightly more provocatively, one might say that the 'God of the Bible' isn't always synonymous with the *biblical God*. Although the Judeo-Christian scriptures represent a long, slow, and eventually triumphant exodus from sacred violence – the emergence of the God of victims – it is an exodus beset by reversals and shortfalls, reversals and shortfalls that don't, in fact, undermine this exodus but that are integral parts of the voyage.[17]

Perhaps more radically, for Girard, the Hebrew Bible's progressive undertaking of the demythologization or desymbolization of sacrificial violence is one which is not unambiguously 'completed' within its confines; its destination is not reached by the end of the books of Haggai, Zechariah, or Malachi. Even here, it is 'a process under way, a text in travail'.[18] Girard maintains that, despite the presence of this movement towards desymbolization operating from the very first stories of the Bible, Yahweh nonetheless remains a somewhat ambiguous figure. Even though he appears in 'less and less violent form, and becomes more and more benevolent, Yahweh is still the god to whom vengeance belongs. The notion of divine retribution is still alive' (*TH* 158/181). It is Girard's contention that the progressive undermining of sacred violence undertaken in the Hebrew Bible is brought to completion in the Gospels.

Dionysus versus the Crucified

At one level, Girard's contention regarding the 'victim-centric' perspective of biblical monotheism has numerous theoretical precedents and contemporary corroborations. For instance, in *Ancient Judaism*, Max Weber – who was by no means attempting any sort of biblical apologetic – emphasized repeatedly that the authors of the Hebrew Bible took the side of victims.[19] Reiterating this thesis in terms of the New Testament, Eric Gans, who professes no biblical faith, has stated that 'Christianity's impact on the West is a tribute to the power of its basic conception, which is the absolute centrality of the position of the victim.'[20]

It is, however, in the work of Friedrich Nietzsche that Girard finds the most unabashed and sophisticated elucidation of this signal insight; indeed, it is in Nietzsche's work – as surprising as this may seem at first – that Girard believes we are capable of locating the best resources for theorizing the profound anthropological legacy of Judaism and Christianity. Nietzsche was a thinker who was at least as convinced as Girard that the God of Jews and Christians is the God of victims *per se*. Despite the nineteenth-century philologist and philosopher being the staunchest enemy of this tradition, indeed a self-proclaimed 'Anti-Christ', Girard believes Nietzsche to be without doubt the most profound religious thinker of modernity, at least in one important respect – it was he, Girard argues, who provided the 'anthropological key' to Christianity (*IS* 171/222).

It is perhaps still widely known that what Nietzsche saw in Christianity was the culmination of Jewish 'slave morality', a morality that the philosopher thought to represent, in displaced form, a most thoroughgoing cultural ennoblement of revenge fantasies against the victors of history, carried out by those who consider themselves its victims. In other words, for Nietzsche, Christian morality was predicated on *ressentiment*. Based initially on some cursory (and, no doubt, insufficiently theorized) reflections which led him to observe that the earliest Christians invariably came from the poorest and most disenfranchised sectors of Jewish society, Nietzsche's tracing of the psychological and moral lineage of the Judeo-Christian tradition – his now infamous 'genealogy of morals' – concluded by proclaiming that Christian virtues such as 'pity' or sympathy merely represented base radicalizations of the extant Jewish resentment of pagan aristocracy. The Judeo-Christian tradition was, for Nietzsche, a kind of revenge fantasy played out largely in axiological form, one that somehow became irremediably entrenched in Western institutions and the European psyche – a fantasy which eventually emerged to be the most powerful force in human history. Needless to say, far from endorsing this tradition or vision, Nietzsche became its fiercest critic. Indeed, the philosopher's own 'solutions' to Judeo-Christian *ressentiment* involved both ethical reform and an ontological call to arms; he demanded equally a moral revolution predicated on a so-called transvaluation of all values and the emergence of a superior kind of human being – *der Übermensch* [the overman/superman] – whose unabashed 'will to power' was not engendered or sustained by *ressentiment*.

The broader context in which Nietzsche's prognosis of Judeo-Christian *ressentiment* finds its footing is in the purview of his larger critique – located primarily in *The Anti-Christ* and *The Will to Power* – of the (aforementioned thesis) of the 'positivistic equivalence' of all religious traditions.[21] Nietzsche claimed that his training as a philologist prevented him from somehow lazily assimilating the signal narrative themes and figures of the Judeo-Christian corpus to the seemingly innumerable pagan cults detailed in anthologies of myths and legends or in the dense fieldwork reports of empirical anthropologists. The latter (pagan) cults he framed with a single symbol: 'the Dionysian', which he placed in opposition to 'the Christian'. In asserting that Christianity was simply a politically opportune reheating of pagan religion, Nietzsche claimed that anthropologists and philologists missed the fact that, unlike the pagan/Dionysian vision, Christianity in fact *stifled* life by its relentless promotion of resentment and its 'morality of the slaves'. Indeed, Nietzsche held that Christianity's lamentable doctrines which affirm the 'equality of all souls before God' and the 'sacredness of the human' merely function to repress both the most powerful members and the most powerful generative dynamics of culture.[22] Christianity stood, therefore, not as a rehashing of the Dionysian, but as its chief *antithesis*, which – against biblical religion – upheld an unreserved affirmation of the will to destroy and celebrate life in all of its 'violent intensity'.

No doubt, Nietzsche saw, just as anthropologists of the nineteenth century saw, that the collective murder and 'resurrection' of a god was not unique to Christianity; it was also a central element of a seemingly immeasurable number of Greek and Indo-European cults and their mythical correlates. As such, he argued that the *death* of Dionysus at the hands of the Titans and the Passion of Jesus were similar enough to be regarded as equivalent at least in terms of their '*martyrdom*' (*GR* 248). Nonetheless, Nietzsche claimed that this ostensible similarity, if carefully attended to, made all the more obvious a radical and quite crucial *difference* between the two:

> Dionysus versus the Crucified: there you have the antithesis. It is *not* a difference in regard to their martyrdom. It is a difference in the meaning of it. Life itself, its eternal fruitfulness and recurrence creates torment, destruction, the will to annihilate. In the other case, suffering – the 'Crucified as the innocent one' – counts as an objection to this life, as a formula for its condemnation.... The god on the cross is a curse on life, a signpost to seek redemption from life; Dionysus cut to pieces is a *promise* of life: it will be eternally reborn and reborn and return again from destruction.[23]

Girard notes the significance and striking atypicality of Nietzsche's condemnation of Christianity, one based on the fact that Christianity *rejects* suffering: 'The habitual criticism is that Christianity encourages suffering. Nietzsche saw clearly that Jesus died not as a sacrificial victim of the Dionysian type, but against all such sacrifices' (*GR* 250). It is this (Girardian) comprehension of Nietzsche that makes sense of the philosopher's assertion that the Passion is 'an objection to life' or 'a formula for its condemnation'. And if one begins to suspect that Girard is here prone to be taking interpretative liberties with the now-deceased Anti-Christ, Nietzsche himself should leave us with little doubt:

> Through Christianity, the individual was made so important, so absolute, that he could no longer be sacrificed: but the species endures only through human sacrifice. . . . Genuine charity demands sacrifice for the good of the species – it is hard, it is full of self-overcoming, because it needs human sacrifice. And this pseudo-humaneness called Christianity wants it established that no one should be sacrificed.[24]

At the base of Nietzsche's accusation of Christianity's *ressentiment* was his recognition that the biblical tradition, culminating in Christianity, decisively reveals the injustice which the Dionysian willingly celebrates. 'He singled out', explains Girard, 'the biblical and the Christian not because Jesus' martyrdom is different but because it is not' (*GR* 250). Indeed, as Nietzsche recognized, the deaths of the two *need* to be sufficiently similar for the Passion of Christ to subvert the foundational myth(s) of pagan religions.

Nietzsche's (characteristically immodest) claim to have 'uncovered Christian morality', a discovery which he believed set him 'apart from the whole rest of humanity',[25] was predicated on his construal of Christianity as the religion which concerned itself with the weak and innocent, for whom 'pity' was a cardinal virtue (the latter being a moral correlate of the Christian 'interpretation' of martyrdom). In Dionysian myths, killings are regarded as legitimate, even necessary. And this view, which affirms the putative 'natural necessity' of murder, appears also in dramatic tragedy. For his contempt of the god, Pentheus, for instance, is 'legitimately' slain by his sisters and mother. And although we are aware that Oedipus is not guilty of knowingly committing his crimes, he commits them, and his expulsion stands as more than merely a justified response – it is, in fact, a *sacred duty*.[26] So even when the tragic or mythic vision seems to uphold the idea that its victims are not guilty of committing a crime – at least in the modern sense of 'guilt' – their deaths are nonetheless figured as necessary, irremediably inscribed into 'destiny' or the 'order of things'.

In Christianity, however, Jesus – just like Abel, Joseph, and Job before him – is figured as an innocent victim, a figuration that the New Testament itself initiates and sustains. Just as Pilate, of all people, proclaims of Jesus 'I find no crime in him', we are told in Luke's Gospel that the sudden realization of the Roman centurion – that 'surely this man was innocent' – well captured, in fact, the

sentiment of *all* witnesses to Christ's crucifixion (Luke 23: 47–8).
And the profoundly anti-Dionysian valences of this interpretation
of a violent death itself manage to recapitulate what had preceded
it, both in the earlier events of the Gospels (such as the death of
John), and in the descriptions of the manifold deaths of other innocent prophets in the Hebrew Bible. Indeed, Jesus explicitly supplies
for us the appropriate context in which we are to interpret his death:
he asserts that it will be akin to the deaths of the Hebrew prophets,
whose blood has been shed 'since the foundation of the world'
(Luke 11: 50–1) (*GR* 251; *S* 117/169).

The Passion of Christ, therefore, repeats what has preceded it in
the Bible: it vindicates a slain prophet. But it does this more completely by *universalizing* this vindication, by drawing our attention
to the pervasiveness of Passion-like murders that have taken place,
and continue to do so, all over the world:

> From the anthropological perspective the essential characteristic of
> the revelation is the crisis it provokes in every representation of
> persecution from the standpoint of the persecutor. There is nothing
> unique about the persecution in the story of the Passion. The coali-
> tion of all the worldly powers is not unique. This coalition is found
> at the origin of all myths. What is astonishing about the Gospels is
> that the unanimity is not emphasized in order to bow before, or
> submit to, its verdict as in all the mythological, political, and even
> philosophical texts, but to denounce its total mistake, its perfect
> example of nontruth. (*S* 114–15/166)

It is in light of this that Girard presents Christ as the last and greatest of the prophets, because with Christ sacrificial violence is left
behind *completely* for the first time. Although in profound continuity with the Hebrew prophets that preceded him, Christ is the point
at which the revelation of the violent machinery of culture is fully
laid bare and repudiated (*TH* 200/223–4). Affirming Nietzsche's
point about Christianity's impact upon victimage, Girard asserts
that the Christ of the Gospels 'dies against sacrifice, and through
his death, he reveals its nature and origin by making sacrifice
unworkable, at least in the long run, and bringing sacrificial culture
to an end' (*GR* 18).

But it is also here where we might best see Girard's equally powerful critique of Nietzsche's contention that Christianity is a religion
born of a deep radicalization of Jewish *ressentiment*. Although
Nietzsche's analysis is based on a profound intuition, it cannot help
but eventually misconstrue its object. For Girard, the real target of

ressentiment is ultimately *ressentiment* itself – it is, in other words, its own reflection, disguised such that it can no longer recognize itself. *Ressentiment*, that is, represents a thoroughgoing *interiorization* of vengeance, of a *weakening* of vengeance engendered by the Judeo-Christian revelation. Girard elaborates:

> *Ressentiment* is the product of a world in which Dionysian vengeance has been gradually eroded by the biblical revelation, and rendered vengeance *spiritual*; Christianity is the precondition of the *ressentiment* that characterizes modernity, not because it *originates* in Christianity, but because Christianity is *antithetical to any form of vengeance*. *Ressentiment*, in other words, is a sign of the weakening of vengeance under the sway of the biblical tradition; it represents the survival of vengeance under the impact of the biblical tradition, which then is far too prone to enlist that very tradition to put to use for its own ends. (*GR* 252)[27]

Nietzsche is correct, therefore, to see *ressentiment* as a child of Christianity – but he is quite mistaken to see it also as its *father*. For Nietzsche, living in his time and culture, *ressentiment* seemed to be a state worse than the violent form of physical reprisal that it superseded – or, rather, that it *intercepted*.[28] For Girard, this is a highly gilded, perhaps even bourgeois, theorization of modernity, one that takes insufficient account of its geographical and historical privileges. Needless to say, however, 'sincere prayers are never in vain, and the prayers of those who desired the return of vengeance have finally been heard' (*GR* 253). The mass violence of the twentieth century (and, sadly, what seems – even at this early stage – to be the violence of the twenty-first) also places into stark relief the manifest tension between Nietzsche's self-proclaimed 'individualism' on the one hand and his celebration of the Dionysian on the other, the latter of which must surely represent one of the most rabidly de-individuating forms of human behaviour conceivable (*IS* 173/224).

Despite these important reservations, Girard holds that Nietzsche is extremely important as a thinker on account of his being the first: adequately to comprehend the collective violence that lay behind ritual and myth; to see the similarity between the death of Dionysus and the death of Christ; and to give a highly decisive articulation of the gulf between the biblical tradition and other religions – one might even be tempted to say religion 'itself' (the *martyrdom* is the same, Nietzsche affirms: the *interpretation* is not) (*IS* 171–3/222–4).[29] Aware that his endorsement of the German philosopher may raise more than a few eyebrows, Girard draws our attention to an important distinction between our appreciation of Nietzsche's anthropological perspicacity and any ostensible support of his axiological schema:

> We do not have to share Nietzsche's value judgement to appreciate his understanding of the irreconcilable opposition between the Bible and mythology, his disgust with the bland eclecticism that dissolves all sharp issues and dominates the atheism of our time, as well as its vague and shapeless religiosity. Nietzsche is a marvelous antidote to all fundamentally anti-biblical efforts to turn mythology into a kind of Bible, and that is the enterprise of all the Jungians in the world, or to dissolve the Bible into mythology, and that is the enterprise of more or less everybody else. (*GR* 251)

The return of the repressed: things hidden since the foundation of the world

Philippe Sollers tells us that the 'cornerstone expelled from the religious or sacred question is the corporeal journey of Christ, a word cast out *a priori* from the social fact itself.'[30] And if, indeed, 'the unconscious is structured like a lynching', then we might be forced to conclude that the Gospels themselves represent something of a 'return of the repressed' – or, perhaps more accurately, a *return* of the return of the repressed. The 'all against one' structure evident in the Passion is presaged right throughout the Hebrew Bible and even earlier on in the New Testament – from the violence shown to Joseph by his brothers, to that which forms against Jeremiah and Job; from the narrators of the penitential psalms and the suffering servant in Isaiah, up to and including the murder of John the Baptist by Herod's guests.

And this structural reiteration of the 'all against one' dynamic through the Hebrew Bible and New Testament, Girard argues, goes hand in hand with a relentless thematization of mob violence – a narrative incorporation of explicit statements specifically addressing the function of sacrifice for generating social cohesion. For Girard, this constitutes an indispensable element of the biblical resistance to the mythologization of generative violence. Indeed, the presence of the scapegoat theme or motif, is, in fact, *only* a property of biblical texts and post-biblical literature. One can, of course, locate scapegoats in other stories, but one will not locate their *thematization* as *scapegoats*.[31] Where surrogate victimage structures the semantics of the thematic level of mythological texts (and texts of persecution) – of their style, logic, motifs, genre – Girard argues that the Bible actually enacts an opening of the generative mechanism as a *text itself* by introducing a semantic level prior to the thematic.

For instance, in de Machaut's *Judgement of the King of Navarre*, the scapegoat structures the themes that appear, but the scapegoat as such – as *scapegoat* – *does not* appear. It is up to the reader to examine the text and see the function of the Jews in the story owing to Guillaume's inability to do so himself. In the Gospels, however, Jesus's innocence and the brutality of the system that puts him to death are explicitly thematized; the systematic (although unconscious) misrepresentation of violence that takes place in mythological texts is laid bare. As Richard Golsan notes in relation to the Gospels, the 'text, in effect, interprets itself, and it is no longer up to the reader to disengage the scapegoat from the textual distortions that disguise him.'[32] One can see this biblical thematization, for instance, in Caiaphas's attempt to prevent retaliation by the Romans against Israel, one which he thinks may be provoked by Jesus's popularity. Indeed, Caiaphas renders the sacrificial logic of Jesus's death explicit by articulating very clearly the key principle of surrogate victimage: that it is, in other words, 'better that one man die for the people than that the whole nation perish' (John 11: 50) (*S* 112–13/163–4). And Luke notes with regard to the crucifixion that 'Herod and Pilate became friends with each other that very day, for before this they had been at enmity with each other' (Luke 23: 12).

The New Testament makes clear that the reconciliation here engendered did not, in fact, even require of Pilate any entrenched belief in the guilt of the accused; he is, in other words, shown to be merely subject to the violent whim of the mob insofar as he reiterates their bloodlust (and vice versa). Although Pilate is, officially speaking, the most powerful subject involved in the condemnation of Jesus, he too is easily overpowered and subject to the volatile convulsions of the crowd around him (*S* 106/154–5). But rather than turn Pilate himself into a scapegoat – which would rely on a simplistic moral dichotomy between a 'baddie' like Pilate and some 'goodies' (whoever they might be) – the New Testament goes on to demonstrate that even Jesus's *apostles* are not immune from the movements of mimesis when it comes to his condemnation by the crowd (*S* 105/153–4). When Jesus is taken to the High Priest and the Sanhedrin, for instance, Peter follows the party at a distance, eventually joining the guards outside Caiaphas's residence. And when a servant girl recognizes Peter and accuses him of being a disciple, he repeatedly denies this. Girard argues that Peter has, in other words, become subject to the persecutory tendencies of those around him, and is perhaps even partially swayed by their conviction of Jesus's guilt; the apostle occupies, albeit momentarily, part of the same mimetic continuum as do Herod and Pilate. Similarly, we learn that the mob that kills Jesus is the very same one that had welcomed him into Jerusalem only a few days earlier. The text, therefore, would tend to suggest that the patent instability of their relationship to Jesus exemplifies not their deep and abiding hatred for the man, or – in some peculiar way – their intrinsic maliciousness as people (or a class or community of people, for that matter), but the instability and magnetic psychological force of crowd belief and behaviour.

So, importantly, Girard argues that the significance of the Bible's narrative accounts of these events is not directed to the end of rendering a guilty verdict on any particular individual or collective – whether Caiaphas, Pilate, or Peter, the Jews or the Romans. It is structured, that is, not by some vaguely specified juridical imperative to pass judgement on a particular ethnic, religious, or subcultural group, but to illustrate the chaotic movement and immense force of mob dynamics. In this sense, the New Testament presents Jesus, and only Jesus, as occupying the true 'moral high ground'.

Importantly, Jesus's acceptance of his persecution and death was accompanied by an equal refusal – unlike Oedipus – to accept his alleged 'guilt' by participating in the fantasies of his persecutors; he goes to his death, that is, without becoming mimetically drawn into the sacrificial mechanism which claims him as its victim. It is in light of this that Robert Hamerton-Kelly claims that the Passion is a 'deconstruction' rather than a 'destruction' of surrogate victimage: 'it leaves the sacrificial structures in place while exposing them for what they are and thereby enabling us to withdraw credibility and allegiance from them.' It is, in other words, a 'dialectical' overcoming of sacrifice, because it 'supersedes it while leaving it intact.'[33] The source of Jesus's often – pointed-to 'pacifism' is therefore not merely some radical existential 'choice' or 'ethical stance', but a *structural* necessity for the possibility of the 'Kingdom of God' replacing the violent sacred. Indeed, any straightforward 'destruction' of the old system through force – supernatural or otherwise – would have been simply its *continuation*. It would have been, in the words of Jesus, Satan attempting to cast out Satan (Mark 3: 23).

The understanding of the Passion outlined above has engendered some very interesting articulations of the notions of 'salvation' and 'atonement' in Christian theology. More radically, Girard's reading of the Gospels challenges some of the most deeply entrenched and institutionally legitimated dogmas of Christian eschatology and soteriology. One challenge emanating from Girard's thought has been directed at the traditional understanding of atonement, a Christian doctrine which was given its most refined articulation by the medieval philosopher and theologian Anselm of Canterbury in his *Cur Deus homo* [*Why God Became Man*], written in 1098. Anselm ventured the idea that the sinful behaviour of humanity had so offended God's 'infinite honour' that adequate compensation could only be achieved by the infliction of an infinite penalty on one who was able to bear infinite suffering. As no human could possibly bear this, God became man in order that this penalty be exacted. Jesus's death was thought necessary for human salvation, in other words, because it spared us the considerable wrath of God.[34]

There are, however, serious problems with this (Anselmian) doctrine, even in its own terms. In accordance with a certain economic logic inherent in the original formulation, one might ask what constitutes God's 'mercy' if He must be repaid in *full*. And how can a debt be paid by the one to whom it is *owed*? Further, how does the somehow 'necessary' slaying of an innocent person represent 'justice' – ostensibly 'biblical' or otherwise? Beyond these admittedly standard objections, Girard notes his dissatisfaction with the Anselmian atonement in the light of its irreducible incommensurability with the Gospels themselves (*TH* 183–4/206–8).[35] Perhaps most perversely, the Anselmian doctrine places God the Father in the moral company of those infamous Machiavellian utilitarians: Herod and Pilate. God is here somehow perversely included in the company of those who believe that it is better for an innocent man to die than a nation (or world) to be destroyed.

For Girard, therefore, the Anselmian doctrine of the atonement tends to perpetuate a key element of surrogate victimage: the projection of human violence onto the divine, a construal of a God who derives satisfaction only through sacrificial offerings (*TH* 215/238–9). To the contrary, for Girard, the 'salvation' which Christ offers is best understood anthropologically, not metaphysically: we are 'saved' through Christ (Acts 4: 12), that is, because it is through him that the complicity between violence and the sacred was fully broken. So where classical theologies were correct in tying the Cross to salvation, Girard argues that they invariably misconstrued this relationship in deference to the old sacred which the Bible overcame. Pursuing the Girardian line of thought here (in reference to

Paul; 2 Cor. 5: 20), the Catholic theologian Raymund Schwager argues that the atonement should be construed as a reconciliation not of humanity to God, but of *God to humanity*.[36] Jesus' life and teachings reveal, in fact, that humanity can be reconciled to God without any sacrificial intermediary – indeed, that humanity can *only* be reconciled to God in this way (*TH* 183/197). Therefore, the 'grace' resultant upon Jesus' death is not the product of the Father somehow being avenged, but by the fact that if we all lived like Jesus we would not have to *die* like him – we would be free from scandals and the violence that follows in their wake. Girard's critique of the doctrine of sacrificial atonement can be clarified in terms of the manifest incompatibility between God-the-Son and the Anselmian God-the-Father. Where Anselm's God needs to exact revenge on his own creation, Jesus invites all to refrain from taking revenge, to 'devote themselves to the project of getting rid of violence, a project conceived with reference to the true nature of violence, taking into account the illusions it fosters, the methods by which it gains ground' (*TH* 197/221).

It has become commonplace, if not even somewhat banal, to note Jesus' lack of complicity with any form of violence (see, for instance, Matt. 5: 9; 5: 38–48; Mark 12: 28–34): his non-vengeance and good will extended even towards those who were torturing and killing him (Luke 23: 34); his post-resurrection return to the community that sacrificed him to proclaim the message of peace (John 20: 19); and his instruction to those who are attacked to 'turn the other cheek' (Matt. 5: 39) (cf. *TH* 197/221). Girard suggests that, by taking the prophets' denunciation of bloodshed and sacrifice and carrying it to its (theo)logical conclusion, Jesus institutes a social space in which *all* violence is abandoned (we might note here, for instance, that Paul's 'conversion' and subsequent discipleship are deeply imbricated in his abandonment of persecution (Acts 26: 12–18)). But it needs to be stressed that the representations of violence in the Gospels make far more of it than a mere object of the moral gaze; violence is not simply an ethical phenomenon, that is, but an *anthropological* one. It is therefore subject not merely to possible moral approbation, but to sociopsychological exploration. These themes of non-violence and the prioritization of love have been emphasized by authors before. Girard stresses, however, that Jesus' programme is not just prescriptive – it is the culmination of the rigorous deconstruction of violence that the prophets began to unravel.

Girard discusses, for instance, the story of the woman whom the scribes and Pharisees bring before Jesus, informing him that she had been caught in the act of adultery, quoting to him Moses' command that such women be stoned (John 8: 3–11) (*IS* 54–61/80–7). This was, needless to say, potentially a very difficult episode for Jesus: his assent to or condoning of the killing would have been at the price of betraying his own teachings; on the other hand, if Jesus *opposed* the stoning, this opposition could not help but seem to be an outright expression of contempt for Judaic Law. (Parenthetically, it is also worth noting that the legal proscription that rendered adultery a capital crime – for women only – had become contentious enough by the time of Jesus such that it was no longer universally observed.) Resisting delivering a verbal juridical-religious pronouncement on or explicit evaluation of the case, Jesus bent down and began writing in the sand with his finger. When those gathered persisted in their questioning, Jesus drew near to the crowd and said, 'Let whoever is without sin among you cast the first stone at her!' After this, he recommenced writing in the sand and slowly, one by one, each withdrew, 'convicted by their own conscience' (John 8: 9). Eventually only Jesus and the woman were left; standing up, Jesus said to her, ' "Woman, where are they? Has no one condemned you?" "No one, Lord," she answered. "Neither do I condemn you," Jesus said. "Go and sin no more".'

Here, Jesus might be construed as 'transcending' the (Judaic) Law – and not 'breaking' it in any straightforward sense – insofar as his behaviour *exceeds* the Law in the *direction of the Law itself*. Again, he is presenting (or even embodying) not simply some 'ethical stance', but a *cognitive insight* pertaining to the Law itself and the often ignoble uses to which it is put. Jesus' fulfilling of the spirit of the Law, therefore, is effected by showing that the Law itself can augment or encourage what it attempts to retard – its complicity with violence and injustice (*IS* 58–9/84–5). Violence used – and, undoubtedly, still uses – the Law and its proclaimed righteousness as a cover and alibi. (We should recall, for instance, that Paul's persecution of Christians before his conversion was *underwritten* by Law.)

So here we can see in what way Girard's claims concerning the cognitivity of biblical texts hold while maintaining that such cognitive veracity is not somehow equivalent to asserting that the Bible itself is somehow 'incomplete theory' (or perhaps *complete* theory, incompletely formalized). And nor are these claims equivalent to asserting that the New Testament displays wisdom that is completely recoupable in straightforwardly 'humanistic', 'scientific', or secular terms. For Girard, to the contrary, a real God lies behind these texts (*S* 163/231; *TH* 219/242), and, as such, we need to pay close attention to those aspects of these that are most susceptible to being ignored or passed over in embarrassed silence – of becoming, in other words, casualties of modern prejudices and resentments. As such, Girard refuses to back away from even the most currently unfashionable of biblical terms. We will consider Girard's treatment of some of those terms in a moment, but we first need to say just a little more about his somewhat atypical willingness to entertain them in the first instance.

The *skandalon*

As insistent as Girard is in claiming the anthropological veracity of biblical texts, his is a position that nonetheless needs to be distinguished from those strains of conservative religious interpretation that operate under the names 'evangelical' and, sometimes, 'fundamentalist'.[37] We have already seen that Girard's biblical hermeneutics stresses the intrinsically temporal, narrative basis of biblical auto-critique – his claim that the unveiling of violence in the Bible is a progressive process, replete with a host of fits, starts, and even reversals. This feature necessarily pits him against those religious scholars who are given to making incautiously large claims concerning the putative 'inerrancy' of sacred texts: a doctrinal position that affirms that all passages of the Bible are not only divinely inspired, but *literally true*.

Conservative strains of religious thought have inevitably been characterized by strident affirmations of a belief in the inviolable singularity of Christianity but, equally, have been stymied by a correlative inability adequately to *specify* this singularity. Invariably, such scholars seem to have wanted to ignore – or perhaps have conspired to overlook – the omnipresence of anthropological and mythological reiterations of death and resurrection motifs pervading cultural and religious history. And where such comparisons *are* entertained, however, statements specifically addressing the differences between the Christian story and (other putative) myths are typified by blanket assertions that, where the myths mentioned are little more than simple nonsense, the Christian story somehow possesses complete historical veridicality. That is, they assert that Christianity differs from myths largely in that Christian narratives just so happen to be *true*. Where, traditionally, Christian thinkers have been able assert – and perhaps, to some extent, perceive – the difference between Christianity and other religions, they were not able adequately to specify this; anti-Christian thinkers, on the other hand, could note its continuity with other traditions but were unable to see the true nature of those continuities (*TH* 445/467).

Girard contends that he is able to specify the difference sought by conservative religious scholars, but does not underwrite this specification with notions of biblical inerrancy. He, too, emphasizes the 'historical' nature of biblical narrative but insists, to the contrary, that 'history' does not adequately encapsulate the genre of most biblical texts – especially the Gospels – as history *per se* isn't able to document the unconscious mechanisms at work in mimetic desire and the scapegoat mechanism. His thesis draws attention to the idea of a narrative progression in biblical texts, and so one might conclude that any ideological commitment fundamentally incompatible with the idea that the Bible represents a relationship between God and His people – as is the case with the fundamentalist refiguring of this relationship by construing the Bible as little more than a series of detemporalized, propositional assertions – is going to represent, for Girard, a falsification of the text.[38]

In addition, the somewhat perverse reading of supernatural 'divine violence' furnished by conservative scholars in the twentieth century prompted a (commensurate) liberal *evacuation* of eschatology, an evacuation about which Girard is equally dissatisfied: 'Sacrificial Christianity still believes in divine thunderbolts, while its progressive *double* completely stifles the apocalyptic dimension and so deprives itself of the most valuable card that it has in its hands, under the flimsy pretext that the first priority [of biblical religion] is to *reassure* people' (*TH* 442–3/464). So his unflattering depiction of fundamentalist doctrine is matched equally with a critique of 'liberal' religious scholarship, such as that represented by figures like Albert Schweitzer and (Martin Heidegger's pupil) Rudolf Bultmann. Where Schweitzer reads Jesus as an apocalyptic cult figure whose chief benefit was to engender some non-apocalyptic religious movements, Bultmann regards the appearance of apocalyptic themes or motifs anywhere in biblical texts as unfortunate relics of a 'prescientific' mentality. Girard distances himself from liberalism of this sort primarily because he doesn't wish to avoid engaging the traditional language and the apocalyptic texts, an avoidance which he sees as a lamentable but predictable offshoot of the more general inability adequately to handle those texts that cannot be accommodated within the sacrificial theological paradigm (*TH* 259–60/283). We will now briefly turn our attention to the presence in Girard's work of some of those terms that liberal critics have typically avoided, having seen them as unfit for useful redeployment, or that conservative scholars have utilized only within a sacrificial idiom.

One of the most surprising elements of Girard's religious hermeneutics has been his exposition of the role of 'Satan' in the Gospel narratives, a personage he claims to be utterly central to any satisfactory comprehension of Judeo-Christian anthropology: 'Far from being absurd or fantastic, [the evangelists] use another language to reformulate a theory of scandals and the working of a mimetic violence that initially decomposes communities and subsequently recomposes them, thanks to the unanimous scapegoating triggered by the decomposition' (*IS* 182/237; see also *S* 198–212/277–95; *J* 154–68/174–89). Here Girard introduces the term and affirms its centrality with respect to what he sees as the demythologizing force of the New Testament:

> By revealing that mechanism and the surrounding mimeticism, the Gospels set in motion the only textual mechanism that can put an end to humanity's system of mythological representation based on the false transcendence of a victim who is made sacred because of the unanimous verdict of guilt. This transcendence is mentioned directly in the Gospels and the New Testament. It is even given many names, but the main one is Satan. (*S* 166/234–5)

His inventory of the appearances of 'Satan' and the family of descriptors applied to him allows Girard easily to map onto it the symptoms and violent pathologies of desire. 'Satan' is, for Girard, the chief biblical personification of the power of conflictual desire, the divisiveness which engenders violence and accusation. (Indeed, the term itself is actually a Hebrew word that means 'the accuser'.)[39] Satan symbolizes those paths of false transcendence (idolatry) which lead to surrogate victimage – he is, in other words, the lie concealing the innocence of the victim, 'hidden since the foundation of the world' (Matt. 13: 35). He is, as John puts it in a somewhat condensed fashion, the 'father of lies' and a 'murderer from the beginning' (John 8: 44). It is in a related sense that Satan is also referred to as the 'prince of darkness' or the 'prince of this world' – Satan, that is, is both the *archon*, the ruler or prince of human culture, and the *arche*, the 'beginning', the spirit of murder that founds the earthly *polis* (*S* 187–8/262–5). He is, Girard contends, the 'concealed producer-director of the Passion' (*IS* 182/237).

The depiction of Satan that Girard has developed most fully is that of the 'model-rival'. He points out that Satan is often associated with – indeed sometimes almost synonymous with – the noun *skandalon* (verb form: *skandalizein*), which used to be translated into English as 'stumbling block' (or, in French, as *'pierre d'achoppement'*), and now is more commonly – and regrettably – rendered 'scandal' or 'obstacle'. What the most recent renderings of the term lose, Girard maintains, is the psychopathological character of the designation captured by the original term. Representing more than a kind of (invariably physical) obstacle that can be disposed with, the biblical label designates a more diffuse *force* of attraction/repulsion, a temptation 'causing attraction to the extent that it is an obstacle and forming an obstacle to the extent that it can attract' (*TH* 416/439; cf. *TH* 132/154; *GR* 198; *IS* 16–18/34–6). The *skandalon*, in other words, depicts the model-obstacle dynamic associated with the 'double-bind'; it is a kind of desire that, John informs us, is the antithesis of Christian love (1 John 2: 10–11).[40]

The first time that Jesus foretells of his violent death (Matt. 16: 21–3), Peter seems appalled by his resignation. The disciple therefore attempts to instil in Jesus some worldly ambition: 'Instead of imitating Jesus, Peter wants Jesus to imitate him'; and yet, 'had Jesus imitated Peter's ambition, the two thereby would have begun competing for the leadership of some politicized "Jesus movement". Sensing the danger, Jesus vehemently interrupts Peter: "Get behind me, Satan, you are a scandal [*skandalon*] to me, because the way you think is not God's way but man's"' (Mark 8: 33; Matt. 16: 23).[41] His rebuke consists in alerting Peter that he (Jesus) will die by being crucified, not in being 'triumphant' in the way expected – Jesus will not resist his captors or defend himself through recourse to physical force.

To 'renounce Satan' is to renounce, therefore, the evil attendant upon the rivalry and violence of cultural formation – not to engage in a 'war' against it; as Jesus once asked a gathered crowd: 'How can Satan cast out Satan?' (Mark 3: 23). The answer is, of course, 'he can't' – but he can always *try*, through surrogate victimage. In his rebuke to Peter, Jesus is expressing both a temptation to be, and his refusal *of* being, the kind of messiah desired by his disciples (*S* 194/272), most probably a Davidic messiah who would violently reinstate a worldly kingdom for his people.[42] His disciples, in other words, turned Jesus into an 'idol' and in so doing lost sight of his actual teachings (*TH* 418–19/441–2). And here we can discern the meaning of the common designation of Satan as a 'tempter'; indeed, the same kinds of worldly temptations offered by Peter are presented to Jesus in his ordeal with Satan (Matt. 4: 1–10; Luke 4: 3–12).

Satan, we are told, offers to Jesus 'all the kingdoms of the world and the glory of them' if Jesus bows down and worships him. This offer of false transcendence, of idolatry, renders Satan the chief model-obstacle. And just as Satan proves to be a *skandalon* to Jesus, Jesus proves to be a *skandalon* to his disciples – just as God Himself, as Isaiah points out, could be a *skandalon* to the Israelites (Isa. 8: 14–15).

As the consummate tempter, however, Satan is also portrayed as interminably envious, a disposition that we are told is engendered by his formidable pride (Job 1: 8, 9; 1 Tim. 3: 6; Isa. 14: 13). Envy, in fact, is the vice most often ascribed to Satan; indeed, his 'fall' was caused by his rivalry with and envy of God, wrought by his (futile) attempts to attain and maintain an independence from God. As Jean-Michel Oughourlian has pointed out, the construal of Satan as constitutionally envious runs right through the commentaries of the Church Fathers, from Saints Cyprian and Tertullian to Gregory the Great and Thomas Aquinas.[43]

Employing Girardian terminology, Satan could be said to be the pseudo-masochist's divinity of choice, an insuperable *skandalon* valued precisely for his omnipotent insuperability. Of all figures present and alluded to in the Bible, only Jesus can be said to be totally free of idolatry, of the *skandalon*. What has profoundly disturbed Satan's rule – the very workings of this world, in other words – is the Cross. Where Satan means 'the accuser', the term used to describe the Spirit of God in the Gospels – especially the Gospel of John – is the *'paraclete'*, a Greek term which means, quite literally, 'defender of the accused' (*GR* 201).[44]

It bears noting here that what might be called Girard's 'anthropological rehabilitation' of the Judeo-Christian texts should be seen not as somehow making – or endeavouring to make – all other approaches to biblical texts redundant, but rather as augmenting these from another perspective. His unusual willingness to discuss the 'demonic', 'Satanic', and 'apocalyptic' dimensions of the Judeo-Christian texts seemingly bypasses both the liberal reticence to engage these texts as well as the equally undesirable conservative endorsement of them from the sacrificial perspective of divine violence (which is, of course, the same reason as to why the former ignore them). Girard is strongly of the view that the contemporary relevance of texts such as the book of Revelation cannot be ignored: 'As for the terrors of the Apocalypse, no one could do better in that respect nowadays than the daily newspaper' (*TH* 260/283). Indeed, the 'judgement' of God and his 'punishment' for humanity often consist precisely in God leaving humanity to its own idols, its sacrifices – its own devices (Acts 7: 42–3; Rom. 1: 18–32).

Girard's point, of course, is not that the 'end of the world is nigh'; but, equally, he argues that a serious consideration of the apocalyptic texts disallows one from participating in the kinds of technocratic or managerialist optimisms typified by convictions such as that, for instance, which would seek to propose 'anger management' as a possible solution to intense cultural fragmentation or breakdown. The eclipse of the sacred, the constantly eroded salvific power of ritual, the generalized crisis of authority ('legitimation crisis'), and the loosening of legal constraints characteristic of modernity and late modernity cannot be seen – as certain conservatives might like to see them – as irrevocable evidence of decline, decadence, and decomposition. But nor should these features be viewed as the slightly disfigured harbingers of a new dawn of the 'liberation' of desire and capital – as admittedly unlikely, but unambiguous, signs of endless progress. Of the latter, Girard has the following to say:

> Those who claimed to be governed by the pleasure principle, as a rule, are enslaved to models and rivals which makes their lives a constant frustration. But they are too vain to acknowledge their own enslavement. Mimetic desire makes us believe we are always on the verge of becoming self-sufficient through our own transformation into someone else.[45]

Undoubtedly, Girard possesses a typically amodern willingness to express doubts about desire, a term which not only names a central theoretical preoccupation of contemporary theory, but subsists as a normative declaration that the substantive basis of morality and psychological well-being can be somehow based on 'what people want'.[46] It is here that one can best see, and repudiate, the claim that biblical religion itself is somehow intrinsically 'conservative', a claim that has sometimes been broached of Girard himself.[47] Girard's recognition that cultural order depends on certain patterns of hierarchization has often meant that a certain conservative design is read into his project; here, an interviewer from *Diacritics* expresses the concern well:

Diacritics: Politically you seem inevitably to come down on the side of order and law against all forms of violent excess. Where would you situate your work and its political/ethical implications in relation to Marx or to Bataille?

RG: The expression 'order and law' is reminiscent of 'law and order.' To American readers, at least, it suggests some recent alignments in American domestic politics. These alignments mean little more than the distribution of good and bad political grades to those who come down 'for' or 'against' law and order. Since everybody resorts to the same simplistic dichotomies, the thinking is the same on both sides. This is as it should be. 'Violent excess' on the one hand, 'law and order' on the other have always fed on each other. What else could they feed upon? If they did not, we would be rid, by now, of both of them.

   If our readers recall the questions you asked me, and the answers I gave, they might be a little surprised, wouldn't you think, to find that I am the one who inevitably comes down on the side of order and law. All you have to do, apparently, to make that verdict inevitable is to maintain that the victims are real behind the texts that seem to allude to them. Does it inevitably follow that the impeccable revolutionary credentials go to those for whom the victims are not real? That would be a great paradox indeed! There are signs, I am afraid, that this paradox is not merely intertextual. It may well be the major fact of twentieth-century life. (*DB* 228; cf. *S* 115/167)

As should be clear, there is no part of Girard's work that articulates the desire for a return to some kind of Hobbesian absolutist state: 'From the moment cultural forms begin to dissolve', he affirms, 'any attempt to reconstitute them artificially can only result in the most appalling tyranny' (*TH* 286/310–11; cf. *TE* 282). And it is precisely this kind of appalling tyranny that Girard sees as the focus of the book of Revelation, a book essentially about the potentially catastrophic consequences of human violence in a time and culture which veers unstably between the Gospel and myth: 'We are in a place between the full revelation of the scapegoat and the totally mythical. In history, we are always between the gospel and myth.'[48]

   Therefore, the book of Revelation should not be ignored in futile efforts to 'improve' on Christianity by excising those elements of biblical texts which do not immediately pander to agendas set by our own resentments. Girard argues that the book of Revelation warns us that a damaged Satan is potentially far more destructive than one let loose in a world in which he has free rein (*TH* 253/277). The peace offered in the Gospels is not the one of the old *anthropos* (of Satan casting out Satan) – but passing to this peace from the 'peace' maintained by the victimage mechanism is by no means an easy transition. However, such claims, as they stand, are too schematic or cursory. Their importance should not be passed over quickly; it is fitting, then, that we conclude this chapter with a consideration of historical Christianity, elements of its 'world-historical' impact, and Girard's complex relationship to it.

Historical Christianity

Girard argues that the impact of the biblical tradition on history has been a generalized movement in the direction of the desacralization of culture. One of the ways in which this desacralization has operated was considered in the final section of the previous chapter – the textual supersession whereby myths gradually give way to 'texts of persecution'. As Richard Golsan puts it, myth is the 'casualty of Judeo-Christian revelation, and so, too, are the sacrificial practices which originally founded social and cultural order.'[49] (Myths, in the sense in which Girard describes them, are no longer being generated.) We will recall that texts of persecution provide accounts of communities in the throes of sacrificial crises which the deaths of scapegoats do not avert. This relative failure of surrogate victimage means that a complete mythic crystallization of events does not take place – even when that violence is seen by persecutors to be 'divinely' decreed.

It would be a grave mistake, however, to see in the claim about the progressive historical desacralization of culture some prefabricated apologetic for *historical* Christianity – a tradition which has, obviously enough, been all too ready to assimilate the radicalness of biblical teachings into the sacrificial structures which these teachings uncovered. It is widely accepted, for instance, that with the conversion of Constantine in 324 AD the success of Christianity became increasingly tied to the success of the Roman empire, just as the striving for this success became a key determinant of (ostensibly) 'Christian' ethical behaviour. The image of 'Christus Victor' and the social praxis of anti-violence which had emerged in the early Church were rapidly made victims of the far more worldly task of empire building.[50]

It is important, therefore, to recognize that Girard's theses which affirm the Judeo-Christian demythologization of sacred violence are not upheld such as to minimize the less than universally edifying history of Christian 'mission', of the vast amounts of blood shed in the name of so-called Christian 'defences of the faith'. Historically, the Bible's – and, more specifically, the Gospels' – message has too easily been recuperated by the sacrificial structures that it had unveiled. To put the same point slightly more provocatively, one might say that historical Christianity became *one of the principal mechanisms for hiding its own revelation* – an 'elaboration of a per-version', an 'imaginary construction which resists the Gospels' revelation itself.'[51] (As Søren Kierkegaard was prompted to say: 'My position is that the whole prevailing official proclamation of Christianity is a conspiracy against the Bible.')[52]

Historical Christianity, tragi-ironically, pitted itself against the Gospels in a seeming attempt to revivify the violent sacred that Jesus – and the prophetic tradition that had preceded him – laid bare. Where the first attempt to crush revelation was evidenced by the violence exerted in Jesus's execution itself, the second – in some ways far more effective – attempt at the same went under the name 'Christendom'. Christianity, to frame this in a less extreme way, absorbed Christ's teachings in perhaps the only manner that it could: through the doctrine of the sacrificial atonement. Even Friedrich Nietzsche, certainly no friend or ally of monotheism, was able to see the recrudescence of the primitive sacred in the Chris-tianity of the nineteenth century: 'I am ashamed to recall what the Church has made of this symbolism: has it not placed an Amphitron story at the threshold of the Christian "faith"?'[53] (The Amphitron myth fits the Dionysian model far better than most; Nietzsche thought that Christianity, in other words, had betrayed itself and become a degraded kind of paganism (*TH* 222).)

One should be wary, therefore, of claiming to detect in Girard's thesis of the biblical erosion of surrogate victimage an attempt to mitigate atrocities of Christian history (perhaps by subsuming these within some idealized picture of a terminally peaceful Christian 'ideology'); rather, he attempts to point to the textual sources which ostensibly *engendered* Christianity, resources that effectively provide a critique of such practices from *within*. Indeed, to grant Girard's claim concerning the radicalness of the unveiling of violence in the Judeo-Christian scriptures also draws attention to the very real possibility that sacrificial culture's fiercest critics could very easily become its most faithful perpetrators. That Christians would mistake terribly Jesus's message, in fact, tends not to undermine this message but to corroborate it in important respects by attesting historically to the insidiousness, pervasiveness, contagiousness, and seeming intractability of violence in culture. Indeed, perhaps the character and intensity of Christian violence itself is related to the fact that it was first in 'Christian' cultures that the initial, intense conflicts between a growing awareness of scapegoating and the biblical demand for giving it up were felt most acutely.

But here, another important clarification is in order. As our previous discussion of Guillaume de Machaut's *Judgement of the King of Navarre* should disclose, the desacralization of culture does not somehow put scapegoating to an *end*. By claiming that myth is a 'casualty' of biblical monotheism, what is being asserted is merely that the *effectiveness* of surrogate victimage – its underwriting of social unanimity and its ability to obscure its real origin – has been permanently undermined. The progressive failure of the scapegoat mechanism is itself symptomatic of a correlative inability adequately to *sacralize* violence, a failure prompted by the 'indirect and unperceived but formidably constraining influence of the Judaeo-Christian scriptures' (*TH* 138/161). But this failure is not equivalent to a decrease either in the incidence or in the severity of violence – quite the opposite. Girard argues that as the surrogate victimage mechanism fails it needs to operate with greater levels of intensity to achieve the same ends (*TH* 127–8/149–51).

A key predicate in Girard's hypothesis is that the effectiveness of surrogate victimage exists in direct proportion to the extent that its operation remains concealed behind the effects it generates; and, correlatively, it loses this functionality in direct proportion to the extent that these operations are revealed. It would, however, be grossly inaccurate to assume that the revelation of surrogate victimage is somehow equivalent to some kind of Edenic 'end of violence' or a state of 'heaven on earth'. In the short and medium terms at least, the uncovering of the mechanism simply means that the polarization typical of the victimage mechanism no longer produces the unanimity required of it, and, therefore, that the *esprit de corps* produced by collective violence is slowly undermined. That is, rather than uniting the community, the biblical revelation in fact *multiplies* social fracturing and fractiousness. Thus, to affirm that successful victimage is – almost by definition – invisible is by no means equivalent to maintaining that unsuccessful victimage, therefore, is one that doesn't produce victims – it is, rather, victimage whose *victims have become visible* (*as* victims). Indeed, this 'unsuccessful' victimage can produce far more violence than the former, as it allows for an environment where vengeance is easily perpetuated. As Girard argues, biblical demystification is not necessarily constituted or accompanied by any *political panaceas*: 'Religious truth and social usefulness do not necessarily go hand in hand.'[54]

In a related way, Girard argues that the failure of the sacred during modernity can be readily detected in some varieties of contemporary totalitarianism and extreme forms of nationalism, political forms which represent *reversions* to the primitive sacred – but reversions whose brutality is all the more evident to us insofar as they *cannot be successfully completed*. Girard argues that these contemporary 'tribalisms', undermined, historically, by the Judeo-Christian texts, lack the 'authenticity' of their anthropological precursors:

> Our contemporary world revives primitive violence without rediscovering the absence of knowledge that endowed former societies with a relative innocence and prevented them from being unlivable. When modern societies which have increasingly distanced themselves from primitive religion over the centuries without ever making a complete break yield to totalitarian temptations, they again come close not to primitive religion but to its disintegration. (*J* 120/139)

The first thing to note here is that Girard ties the typical violence of modernity to the *breakdown* of 'tribalism', not tribalism *itself*. In this way, he avoids turning ritual or myth *themselves* into scapegoats; for him, the naïve condemnation of myth is one of the worst forms of ignorance. Therefore, his work should not be situated within the Enlightenment tendency of theorists such as J. G. Frazer and E. B. Tylor, who saw in myth and ritual poor attempts at science (just as 'legend' supposedly incarnated a failed attempt at history) – inventions of the 'superstitious' mind invoked to explain the physical world. To the contrary, to deny that myths are premeditated, 'rational', or intellectual constructs – as Girard does – is not equivalent to asserting that they are 'irrational' or that they are not *well founded* (*TH* 42–3/50–1; *TE* 214). Girard holds that we have to take very seriously the dangers from which they have provided protection and view myth and ritual as functional forms of knowledge (*VS* 82/125–6). He argues that both the dismissal of myth (as we see with Frazer) and the fetishization of their internal logics (as we see with Lévi-Strauss) are inherently dangerous modes of thought. The spectres of industrial pollution and nuclear war are just two threats that should cause Western societies to take heed of a law that so-called primitive people understand very well: whoever uses violence will, in turn, be used by it (*VS* 261/389; cf. *DB* 205).

One of Girard's criticisms of J. G. Frazer's *The Golden Bough* was that its overt ethnocentrism precluded Frazer from seeing *Western*, industrialized 'tribalism' – tribalism of the present. Although Frazer's notion of the scapegoat captured a pervasive social and cultural dynamic, he so restricted its application that the considerable scapegoating present in so-called civilized societies utterly escaped him.[55] In *Violence and the Sacred*, for instance, Girard does not hesitate to point – albeit in a somewhat qualified way – to the 'primitivism' and 'tribalism' of certain forms of nationalism and the general imperative for 'developed' nations to partake in the progressive acquisition of armaments. 'Post-religious' societies are no less inclined to revert to the use of the sacred in order to restore social harmony.

> The ideology of ritual cannibalism brings to mind the nationalistic myths of our own modern world. . . . A sacrificial cult based on war and the reciprocal murder of prisoners is not substantially different from nineteenth century nationalistic myths with their concept of an 'hereditary enemy'. To insist on the differences between two myths of this type is in effect to succumb to the mystique of the myths themselves, to turn away from the identical reality residing at the center of each. (*VS* 279–80/418)

It is in light of Girard's assertion concerning the breakdown/resurgence of tribalism that the violence of modernity can be understood. This, of course, supplies the much-needed context in which to interpret Girard's somewhat opaque references in *Violence and the Sacred* to the 'sacrificial system' being 'virtually worn out', without entailing that violence is 'no longer a threat; quite the contrary' (*VS* 295/441). Girard suggests that this profound and pronounced exacerbation of violence is, in fact, predicted by Jesus in the Gospel of Matthew when he says 'I have not come to bring peace, but a sword' (Matt. 10: 34). Jesus, that is, well understands that the traditional means for securing peace will be irrevocably undermined through his death.

This is something that Nietzsche also well understood; in fact, Girard argues that the philosopher formulates this in a far more powerful and decisive manner than any religious thinker had been able to do up to him: 'He put his finger on that "sword" that Jesus said he brought, the sword destructive of human culture' (*GR* 254). Where Hobbes saw this 'deadly' 'equality of man' as a state of nature, Nietzsche could not accept the English philosopher's bio-logical essentialism; he knew where this social dynamic came from: ' "Equality of souls before God", this falsehood, this *pretext* for the *rancune* of all the base-minded, this explosive concept which finally became revolution, modern idea and principle of the decline of the entire social order – is *Christian* dynamite.'[56]

One might hazard a guess that a good proportion of contempo-rary secularists would probably prefer not to see 'the equality of all souls' as 'Christian dynamite', as a 'pretext for the rancune' of the 'base-minded' – indeed, many would no doubt be likely to want to see this doctrine as representing, in fact, a *liberation* from the 'Christian'. Regardless, it is difficult not to concede that the biblical tradition has made some very deep and lasting impacts on contemporary ideals of justice and on legal practice itself, impacts which themselves have since become part of standard secular approaches in these areas, and are difficult to dispense with regard-less of an individual person's state of irreligion. Notions such as 'equality before the law', the rights of the accused to legal repre-sentation or advocacy, the necessity of witnesses in prosecution, and an 'absolute' measure of justice are just some of the juridical and judicial legacies of biblical anthropology.[57] And while wanting to consign, in fact, *all* religion to the dustbins of history, the Oxford political theorist Larry Siedentop is forced begrudgingly to admit that political liberalism itself – with its assertion of the equality of all before the law, and its construal of social institutions open to criticism – must acknowledge its uniquely Christian roots;[58] it was biblical principles, in fact, that undermined and deposed slavery and then serfdom, and the principle of 'charity' (*caritas*) that pro-duced institutions like the hospital.[59] Additionally, a lot of work has gone into examining the ways, for instance, in which notions such as the 'rights-bearing' individual[60] and certain 'revolutionary' imperatives for social justice[61] are also biblical legacies. (Of partic-ular note here is the work of the Italian philosopher Gianni Vattimo – a theorist who has pursued this theme and who uses Girard as an explicit resource to this end. For Vattimo, it is too 'naïve and schematic' to conceive of modernity as a sort of general emancipa-tion from the Christian tradition.)[62] What such analyses tend towards is an acknowledgement that many of the purported 'secular' values and the demystifying energies (*Entzauberungen*) of

European modernity – *and* postmodernity – were not so much anti-thetical to the Judeo-Christian moral tradition as *effects* of it.[63]

So while he is more than prepared to acknowledge its horrors, Girard doesn't want to turn historical Christianity itself into a scapegoat. He takes issue with what he sees as a highly pervasive, indeed, seemingly 'universal', wager that – given historical Christianity – regards it as 'intrinsically perverse rather than as perverted by the enormous human ingenuity in the service of this perversion' (*GR* 254). Neither does he believe this perversion of the biblical ethos to be something located exclusively in the 'past' – nor exclusively Christian. Indeed, the shape of contemporary 'secular' political discourse could be said to be held under the sway of a certain kind of desacralization attendant upon the biblical texts. We live in a time where scapegoating itself now must go through an additional filter or phase of sacralization, whereby – to make the scapegoating convincing to themselves – it is both displaced and augmented by victimizers accusing the victims of, in fact, being the chief victim-izers. It is here that Girard detects a somewhat opportunistic and morally corrupt injection of the 'Christian problematic' into contemporary discourses of victimization: 'Never before in history have people spent so much time throwing victims at one another's heads as a substitute for weapons . . . We go on persecuting, but in our world everybody persecutes in the name of being against persecution; that's what we call propaganda.'[64] What we witness here is a world that remains a very long way from one that might properly be designated 'Christian', but one that is nonetheless thoroughly permeated by the values of the Bible.

Conclusion: sacred allergies

In 1987, Thomas F. Bertonneau posed Girard the following question: 'How far is your interest in religion, or indeed the religious element, responsible for the defensive attitude many people seem to take toward your theory?' Girard's response: 'I would say ninety-eight-and-a-half per cent; maybe ninety-nine-and-a-half.'[65] While Girard's answer neglected to mention that it is also this element that could well constitute a large factor of *attraction* to others, his response would – one is prone to conclude – represent only a slight exaggeration. Throughout the twentieth century, at least, religious reflection has undoubtedly existed on the margins of the academy.

Girard's work flaunts a seeming disregard for this status of religious reflection insofar as it has not simply entertained such reflections at the hermeneutic level – as scholars such as Paul Ricoeur and Rudolph Otto have done – but has instead attempted to carry out a wholesale epistemological inversion which asserts that the traditions that most 'educated' minds regard as supernatural fantasy – Judaism and Christianity – tell us much more about the 'natural' paroxysms of violence found in the modern world than the social sciences to which we claim undying allegiance.

And it is here, no doubt, that Girard and even some of his most sympathetic commentators part ways. Thinkers such as Eric Gans, Tobin Siebers, Jean-Pierre Dupuy, and Paul Dumouchel have offered largely secular renderings of his work. But this kind of reading is something that Girard has strenuously resisted; he has balked at the idea that the biblical tradition, once it has deployed its anthropology or ethics, can be left – somewhat like the tonsils or the appendix – as a salutary reminder of a certain developmental necessity, a *historical* necessity, devoid of any essential contemporary function. Along with philosophers such as Emmanuel Levinas, Jean-Luc Marion, Charles Taylor, and Gianni Vattimo, Girard rejects the idea that philosophy and the humanities have no need for religious, and particularly biblical, reflection.

Although Girard's work offers a hypothesis of the ways in which human culture is epistemologically, axiologically, and fictively entangled in the structures of the violent reflexes of terminally religious polities, he suggests provocatively that, in 'comparison with the astonishing work of demystification effected by the Gospels, our own exercises in demystification are only slight sketches' (*TH* 179/202). Here one is reminded of the idea of the French philosopher and theologian Henri de Lubac that contemporary secularism and atheism are simply new and attractively packaged religions which keep cultural violence very much alive: 'It is generally conceded that Christianity "inaugurated the struggle against false gods." But some people would like to take over from it, as though it could not complete the task itself. They would like to make philosophy the heir to Christianity. . . . In that case the false gods still have a promising future!'[66]

It is, no doubt, not the task of this author to evaluate the extensive range of competing claims broached above. The issues raised in the last section of this chapter are far too broad and complex to admit of any schematic or brief treatment – and so here our task must remain primarily one of exposition. It is for the reader, then, to consider the issues raised so far. But, in order for the reader to do this, he or she needs to have perhaps a clearer idea of what kind of theory Girard has offered us, the ways in which it has been developed, and the kinds of possibilities that exist for critiquing it. It is to these issues that we will now, finally, turn.

5

Conclusion

My claims are scandalously out of proportion with the general
temper of the times and . . . my literary background . . . must be
regarded by almost everybody as the worst possible recommenda-
tion for the type of research that interests me.

René Girard, *DB*

'Any coincidence', said Miss Marple to herself, 'is always worth
noticing. You can throw it away later if it is only a coincidence.'

Agatha Christie

Girard's above assessment of his own thinking in relation to 'the
general temper of the times', while inflected perhaps with a certain
defensiveness – and, no doubt, some humour – would seem to be
at least roughly accurate. For those familiar with the (interdisciplinary) terrain, it seems clear that Girard cuts an unusual figure in
the contemporary humanities academy. His penchant for broad
interdisciplinary systematization, his preference for parsimonious
explanations of socio-cultural phenomena, and his unabashed
declarations on religion are all features that cause him to stand
out somewhat in an academy which has, for a large part of the
twentieth century at least, predominantly privileged the local, the
partial, the particular, and the secular.

These features of his work have, however, neither prevented
Girard from attaining and sustaining a high scholarly profile in
continental Europe, nor stopped his work from being redeployed
in a startlingly diverse array of disciplinary contexts. The Canadian
philosopher Paul Dumouchel has argued that Girard has offered the

scholarly community an 'objective thought content', a 'theoretical ensemble relatively independent of its author and thus open to the inquiry and criticism of all. Girard is certainly a privileged interpreter of this theory', he goes on, 'but he is none the less only one among others, often the one most surprised by the trails or deadlocks it contains.'[1] Dumouchel's assessment is cogent. As unique as it may be, Girard's transdisciplinary hermeneutics is not so idiosyncratically articulated or hidebound to each and every intellectual commitment of its author that it stands or falls solely in its context of enunciation; Girard has proffered not simply *research*, that is, but a research *programme*.[2] His is an *oeuvre* that has exerted considerable and ongoing influence on a wide variety of work in the humanities and social sciences.

Indeed, if the value of Girard's output were to be assessed solely in terms of its capacity to generate or provoke *additional* theoretical work, then it would prove highly valuable in this respect at least. Here we should note not simply the *fact* of this uptake, but its range and calibre; Girard's work has often been extended by those who are formidable scholars in their own right – his writing has provoked a series of engagements that have not been restricted to a single domain or discipline, but have run the gamut from chemistry and psychology to politics and biophysics. It would be extremely difficult to name another twentieth-century thinker in the humanities who has so drawn thinkers both in the humanities and in the sciences. (Indeed, it is very nearly as difficult a task to bring to mind any thinker about which this could be said to be *true at all*.)

One of the most interesting examples of a body of work that has developed out of certain Girardian problematics is that of Eric Gans (*b.* 1941), currently professor of Romance languages at the University of California, Los Angeles. Beginning with the publication of *The Origin of Language* in 1981, Gans has set about devising and revising a genetic theorization of language and culture – of the 'human' as such – which takes proto-human mimesis as its departure point.[3] In a body of work that is both remarkably fresh and critically acute – a project in some ways even more ambitious than Girard's 'fundamental anthropology' – Gans's 'generative anthropology' draws on central elements of Girard's work and then reshapes them in the context of a general theory of language, signification, and the emergence of human self-consciousness.

For Gans, standard accounts of biological evolution, although necessary for complete accounts of human development, are not sufficient to account for hominization; what he designates 'positive' (empirical, physical) anthropology requires supplementation with a 'generative' anthropology of the kind that he specifies. He argues that what (necessarily gradualist) empirical accounts fail to account for in any evolutionary reconstruction of the origin of humanity is the necessarily *punctual* status of this origin. Gans argues, that is, that self-consciousness and language cannot somehow 'creep up' on the nascent human unannounced, without this creature's awareness of their presence.

He argues that language, rather than simply being a necessary, non-physical effect of physical evolution, should be seen as a development arising because of the insufficiency of pre-human modes of interaction (primarily non-symbolic imitation) to prevent the inchoate species from self-destruction. His genetic hypothesis attempts to reconstruct the punctual emergence of representation and self-consciousness from the animal's immanent relation to the world, which he construes as being precipitated by an intensification of mimetic rivalry sufficient to pose a greater danger to the species' survival than any possible external threat.[4] Non-symbolic or gestural imitation is transcended by the nascent human, Gans argues, at the moment that such imitation is blocked as a result of the mimetic contagion and convergence of attention on a single object.

Gans's scene of hominization remains in many respects close to Girard's, but the former reads the designation of the scapegoat in terms of the birth of language. This hypothetical origin of language – what Gans calls the 'originary scene' – is characterized by the first sign, which rescinds what it designates and is therefore termed by him the 'aborted gesture of appropriation'. This is, as Gans argues, 'the emergence of the vertical sign-relation from the horizontal one of animal interaction':[5] the birth of the human, and the necessary precursor to the subsequent diachronic development of syntactical forms. Although Gans's body of work is substantial, coherent, and potentially far-reaching, the questions that he has raised have yet to be properly considered by the scholarly community at large.

Another line of development stemming from explicitly Girardian problematics – or, rather, several lines of development – can be seen in much of the significant intellectual output of the French CREA (*Centre de Recherche Epistémologie Appliquée*), an institute whose members have included such esteemed thinkers as Francisco Varela, Jean-Pierre Dupuy, and Henri Atlan,[6] and whose explicit mission it is to investigate the relationships between models of self-organization in the biological and physical sciences, and cultural theory. For instance, Varela (a neurobiologist) and Dupuy (a political philosopher) have together looked at theories of cognition in relation to Girard's work;[7] Ilya Prigogine, the Nobel prize-winning chemist, has drawn explicit parallels between his notion of 'dissipative structures' and Girard's hypothesis of surrogate victimage;[8] and the biophysicist Henri Atlan has discussed the notion of self-organization in physical systems and Girard's model of social upheaval and consolidation.[9]

One of the founding members of the CREA was Jean-Pierre Dupuy, currently professor of social and political philosophy at the Ecole Polytechnique, Paris, and visiting professor in the departments of French and Italian studies and political science at Stanford University. Dupuy has done a lot of very interesting work at the intersections of political philosophy, systems theory, economics, and cognitive science. He has brought Girardian thinking to bear on a startlingly wide range of fields, although, at present, relatively little of his work has appeared in English translation. He has, for instance, discussed the extent to which major theorists of the market economy and utilitarian ethics are haunted by the ghost of sacrifice and continue, in fact, to legitimate it in one form or another.[10] He has also engaged with the phenomenon of self-reference in philosophy, anthropology, economics, and critical theory, bringing the work of Girard to bear on what the cognitive scientist Douglas Hofstadter has called 'tangled hierarchies'.[11] Pointing to structural and logical isomorphisms between what he sees as tangled hierarchies in a variety of disciplines, Dupuy has brought an anthropological sensibility to the logical structures of formal systems; he argues, for instance, that self-referential paradoxes and self-fulfilling prophecies exhibit the 'logic of the sacred'.

But perhaps what Dupuy is best known for is his highly original work in economics; along with fellow economists and political philosophers Paul Dumouchel, Mark Anspach, André Orléan, and Michel Aglietta, Dupuy argues that Girard's work offers invaluable resources for economic theory, and supplies substantial evidence for their sustained contestation of what they see as the 'objectivistic', even 'fetishistic', tendencies of orthodox economics – both *laissez faire* and Marxist. Common to the Girardian economists is the idea that exchange serves far more than simple instrumental functions: it is neither limited, nor owes its genesis, to the facilitation of the satisfaction of material needs; and nor does money serve merely to increase the efficiency of this exchange – both are, instead, heavily implicated in social life and relations.[12] To this end, Dupuy,

Dumouchel, and Anspach especially have examined the anthropological character of modern market economies and both the positive and deleterious social implications of their amelioration of
those forms of reciprocal obligation common to 'gift economies'.[13]
They have also examined the ways in which such market economies, although 'secular', maintain certain features common to
religiously framed exchange. For instance, the presence of incorpo-
real mediators, spirits, in the gift exchange persist in displaced form
in theories of liberal political economy, perhaps predominantly in
Adam Smith's idea of the 'invisible hand', which – like the victimage mechanism – diverts individual violence into common peace
and so absolves people of the responsibility for their actions.[14]

Another notable explorer and developer of Girard's work is the
French philosopher and historian of science Michel Serres. William
Johnsen has described the relationship that has developed between
Serres's and Girard's work as a 'theoretical *renga*', the noun referring to the Japanese form of linked poetry in which units of the
poem are written by two or more poets.[15] Serres's work is utterly
infused with Girardian ideas and problematics, although the
deployment of Girard's thought in his theoretical corpus more often
than not works through tacit deployment and endorsement rather
than explicit citation (Girard's presence, in other words, *permeates*
rather than *punctuates* Serres's work).

Serres asserts that his work is broadly 'structuralist' in orientation and operation,[16] but he has qualified this with the further claim
that the structuralism to which he aligns himself is not the linguistic variety but the mathematical one as practised by the poly-
cephalic 'mathematician' Nicolas Bourbaki.[17] His main mode of
operation, then, is the construction of theoretical models based on
perceived structural analogies between objects; he points to isomorphisms that exist between seemingly disparate phenomena by
tracing their common contours.[18] An ongoing concern of Serres is
the place of violence in science, which, he argues, does not simply
emerge with 'technology' or other applications of scientific reason,
but instead takes refuge in its language, finds an unassuming home
in its concepts: 'It is not politics or sociology that is projected onto
nature, but the sacred. Beneath the sacred, violence.'[19]

Serres has, for instance, looked at the notions of 'turbulence' and
'noise' from a Girardian perspective by remapping the problematic
of the sacred onto ancient atomism; he paints a suggestive picture
in which natural and human history are possessed by a homologous process of emergence: an ongoing fracas where equilibrium is

followed by a displacement. He claims that (socio-psychological) mimesis and violent polarization/differentiation find some rigorous correlates respectively in the Epicurean description of the laminal circulation of atoms and the *clinamen* – chaos, followed by a slight, random, atomic declination.[20] He has also looked at the role of exclusion in the Platonic dialogues, exclusions which inaugurate Platonism just as the scapegoat is the disavowed cornerstone of the polity.[21] He has repeatedly discussed the origin of geometry from a range of perspectives, including one that presents homologies between the geometric solution of rendering commensurate incommensurate values (through the formulation of the first apagogic proof), and mimesis and resolutions through victimage.[22] More recently, in *Genesis*, Serres proposed a new object for philosophy: the 'multiple';[23] in this book he again takes up the notion of 'noise', positing it as a kind of generative condition/chaotic state – an 'Ur-Noise' – prior to discrimination of the discrete elements of which both social and natural experience are comprised.[24]

Of course, there are many other notable instances of such work, with the selection of the above examples determined by no more than a desire for a small sample to point towards both the quality and the genuine diversity of the work being undertaken. In addition to these, however, we have a Girardian psychology, as pursued by the Sorbonne's Jean-Michel Oughourlian and others; the philosophy of Andrew McKenna, Stephen L. Gardner, and Gianni Vattimo; the literary criticism of Sandor Goodhart and Cesáreo Bandera; and the theological work of Raymund Schwager, James Alison, Robert Hamerton-Kelly, and James G. Williams. (Given that these are all significantly indebted to Girard's oeuvre, the disciplinary designations given above should serve as no more than rough guides – as should be no surprise, this secondary literature is an inherently interdisciplinary body of work.)

To draw attention to the extent of the uptake of Girard's work, as well as its quality, is of course by no means equivalent to insinuating that it possesses some kind of universal scholarly appeal. Far from it. In an article which appeared in *Comparative Criticism* in the late 1970s, Richard Gordon compared Girard's theory of surrogate victimage to British Leyland: 'it is hard to produce the goods with antiquated machinery', he asserted; Girard's work, Gordon went on, 'has the utterly predictable demerits of its pedigree; its tone of brilliant self-confidence is the fruit merely of wide reading with a closed mind. Like so much contemporary meta-writing, it has little, either of interest or profit, to offer us.'[25]

Putting aside for a moment the kind of performative inconsistency in Gordon's avowed declaration that Girard's work has little of interest to offer 'us' in the context of an article devoted to a protracted discussion of that very work, what is of interest here is the author's notion of Girard as somehow undeniably *passé*. Gordon's charge of 'antiquated machinery' in the quote above, and his insistent tying of Girard to the failed anthropological projects of the nineteenth century in the article proper, evinces a mode of temporalization that would appear, in the very least, highly contentious. The author seems given to expressing repeatedly his perplexity as to how, through Girard, the past somehow came to inhabit the present and even disguise itself as such; it is sufficient in Gordon's eyes to quash any rumours concerning the perspicacity of Girard's work simply by noting that the very scale and tenor of Girard's project belongs to some bygone era of sweeping theoretical ambition.

There is certainly an element of descriptive perspicacity in Gordon's tacit intellectual history. His 'argument from antiquated machinery' has numerous allies in twentieth-century anthropology. from E. E. Evans-Pritchard to Claude Lévi-Strauss, Georges Dumézil, Renato Rosaldo, and James Clifford, the vast majority of twentieth-century anthropologists have long considered that general theories of the sort that Girard proposes are, in principle, impossible. Despite their manifest incompatibilities, late-functionalist, structuralist, and poststructuralist theories have together laboured tirelessly to indicate the kinds of *aporiae* attendant upon any bid to produce the level and type of systematization that Girard attempts. And here what one observes to be true of anthropology could be seen equally as symptomatic of a far more pervasive cultural and intellectual consensus which expresses itself as hostile, either explicitly or implicitly, to broad analytic systematization – indeed, the only widespread forms of systematization being undertaken currently seem to be by other disciplines *on behalf* of the human sciences.[26]

But it seems to be a mistake to think that simply *reminding* Girard of his synthesizing ambitions is somehow adequate to the task of throwing into question his whole enterprise; as a scholar, he is not so easily embarrassed. Girard is, rather, acutely aware of his theoretical operation – he confesses to suffering from an *idée fixe*, even calling his 'insistence on the religious significance of the collective murder' 'somewhat tiresome' (*GR* 256).[27] And he is equally acutely aware of how his work must appear to many, perhaps most, fellow scholars – that it 'must unwittingly recommence an adventure that has already run its full course and failed somewhere in the accumulated writing of western philosophy' (*DB* 203).

It is not the place here to entertain even a partial consideration of the hugely complex issues that would arise in any consideration of the relationship between Girard's work and some of the most pervasive explicit and tacit assumptions of the contemporary humanities academy; and nor is here the place directly to assess or respond to those specific critiques of Girard that have been broached over the last twenty-five years.[28] What I propose to do, rather, is briefly to *contemplate* Girard's work such that we can know what it actually is, what is at stake in criticizing it, and how this might best be done.

One way into this issue is to acknowledge straight up that Girard *may well* be unwittingly recommencing an already intellectually exhausted adventure. But it also needs stressing that it is very hard to *know* this if we do not attend to the actual specifics of his project, to the actual evidence he brings to bear upon it, and to the modes of reasoning he employs to present and develop it. Despite such a seemingly modest demand in the assessment of his work, Girard notes how rarely, however, this actually ever happens; he confesses that he finds distressing the extent to which 'many people condemn it or even sometimes applaud it with no reference to the data, as if its merit or lack of merit depended on some intrinsic virtue.'[29]

Girard's observation here deserves some attention; if we choose to assess his work simply by reference to some putative 'intrinsic property', theoretical or otherwise, then we will tend to erode the specificity of our assessment by conflating the possible failure of Girard's attempt at systematic anthropology with the failure of *any attempt whatsoever*. The danger here, of course, is not simply that critique, if undertaken in this manner, loses its specificity – it's that we thereby leave ourselves open to being charged with the same crime of which we accuse him. This critique can only but assume the form of a particularly debilitating Batesonian double-bind: asserting that the only valid sweeping theory which can be maintained is one which proscribes sweeping theories. The very attempt to oppose broad systematization through the same kind of systematization reveals a brazen epistemological surety of the limits of our own knowledge, a scepticism held with little less than apodeictic certainty.

And it is here that we might find that certain (ostensibly) 'modernist' assumptions concerning 'progress' and the universality of *a priori* knowledge that were thought to have been shown out through some proverbial intellectual front door will have been shown to be capable of re-entering through the back window. What are we to make of the assertion that history is neither linear nor progressive when we are simultaneously informed that such a view is itself a fixed point from which the present can, indeed must, be understood? What are we to do when told in flatly reductive and sweeping terms that reductionism and sweeping theories must no longer hold our allegiances as scholars?

This is to simplify, of course, an enormously complicated state of affairs. There are often highly persuasive intellectual and ethical justifications for our general wariness towards broad theoretical systematization; we are, for instance, aware of the probability of being duped by representation itself and perhaps equally mindful about the kinds of violence that such duping (and such representation) may both accompany and engender (*TE* 222; 335–42). But are such concerns, in themselves, sufficiently persuasive reasons permanently to close the issue at hand? What is worth noting here is that, at the very least, the theoretical challenges to unified projects have been *no more conclusive than the projects that these attempted to displace* (*DB* 209).[30] Girard notes the paradox here and its application to the realm of religion:

> The kind of anthropological research undertaken before World War II – in which theorists struggled to account for resemblances among myths – is regarded as a hopeless 'metaphysical' failure by most anthropologists nowadays. Its failure seems, however, not to have weakened anthropology's skeptical scientific spirit, but only to have weakened further, in some mysterious way, the plausibility of the dogmatic claims of religion that the earlier theorists had hoped to supersede: if science itself cannot formulate universal truths of human nature, then religion – as manifestly inferior to science – must be even more devalued than we had supposed.[31]

To the contrary, Girard wants to suggest that we are in no position to know whether the syntheses of the kind which he attempts to produce are possible until we have actually done them. It might be the case that an indeterminate number of these cannot be done; and Girard's project should certainly be open to critique if it fails to do what it sets out to do. The question is whether it should stand condemned for setting out to do it in the first instance.

It is easy, however, to give a distorted account of both what is at stake in Girard's intellectual project and what is at stake in possible resistances to it. The way in which I have pursued the discussion so far should not necessarily create the impression that Girard's project is somehow inherently and implacably hostile to those contemporary philosophical trends sometimes (perhaps problematically) called 'poststructuralist' or 'postmodern'.[32] Indeed, Girard's work has a complex, and perhaps irresolvably ambiguous, relationship to poststructuralism – he has, for instance, repeatedly protested against systems of 'static classification' and 'essentialist' modes of thought; and his thought has some surprising affinities with the work of Jacques Derrida.

Girard does not, in addition, hold to any classical philosophical conception of 'reason'. He argues, for instance, that, in its archetypal form, the sacrificial crisis is not amenable to a 'rational' or 'philosophical' solution that would ostensibly pit itself against the 'unreason' of violence (*VS* 2/11). Reason itself is easily enlisted in the perpetuation of violence and in so doing renders violence more insidious by disguising it behind the ostensibly neutral demands of (so-called) 'detached' rationality.[33] 'Reason', that is, possesses a remarkable capacity to endow barbarism with an aura of 'nobility' by supplying it with intellectual alibis and by dissimulating behind signs like 'progress' or 'historical necessity'; barbarism, that is, rarely *desires to appear as such* – it invariably has 'good reasons' with which to bolster itself (*TE* 208; *TH* 399). And just as reason can be employed to cover for violence, violence can easily dispense with this valuable alibi at will (which is also, in some important respects, *exactly the same thing*): 'Men always find it distasteful to admit that the "reasons" on both sides of a dispute are equally valid – which is to say that *violence operates without reason*' (*VS* 46/73). Reason itself, Girard argues, is tainted with violence, itself a 'child of the foundational murder' (*TE* 208).

Equally, Girard has not claimed to have discovered any 'absolute truth' (*TH* 435/457). But, by the same token, he refuses to turn the inherent limitations of human cognitive capacities into an idol somehow worthy of worship; he is careful not to absolutize these limitations such that pointing them out itself becomes the *sole object of any legitimate theoretical operation* – he contests the notion that 'critical insight develops in proportion to increasing skepticism' (*S* 1/8). Rather, he argues that the abandonment of the philosophical notion of 'truth' does not mean the *end of knowledge*:

> The present cognitive nihilism is rooted in a purely philosophical idea of truth and of the means to reach that truth. All established methodologies, such as structuralism, are dogmatically bound to the

> idea of truth. The sciences of man in their past and present state still
> share in an ideal of direct mastery and immediate evidence . . . This
> avaricious ideal dominates both empiricism and phenomenology,
> which are never abandoned without a fight because their practition-
> ers cannot see any possibility of knowledge. . . . The only intellectual
> activity they conceive is the interminable and solemn burial of
> 'Western philosophy'. (*DB* 213)

Girard is using the word 'dogmatic' here not simply pejoratively,
but descriptively – the adjective means, in fact, a philosophical (*a
priori*) tenet.[34] For Girard, then, the (self-diagnosed) failure of dogmatic knowledge is the perfect opening for hypothesis; it presents
itself as 'the threshold of hypothetical knowledge' (*DB* 213). Knowledge is hypothetical to the extent that it is not the result of phe-
nomenological 'intuition' or empirical observation alone (nor does
it claim that it is); as such, Girard's central concepts do not, indeed
cannot, operate independently from the ethnological, ethological,
and literary evidence he brings to bear on them, ideas which he
expresses in an inherently tentative idiom. He is not interested in
deductive certainties, that is, but in inferences drawn that seem to
fit best the available evidence.

To put this another way, in somewhat more concrete terms,
Girard believes that phenomena that he and other anthropologists
examine seem highly improbable, unlikely, or unexpected without
the hypothesis that he puts forward to explain these. What interests
him primarily is the often-noted, but rarely theorized, repetition of
structurally isomorphic mythemes, ritemes and prohibitions found
in a wide range of texts and practices across an equally wide range
of traditions and cultures. (He takes clear examples and then
generalizes where the narrative presented is more ambiguous.) For
instance, one of the ways in which Girard attempts to validate his
reading of myth is by providing detailed comparisons with texts
not generally considered mythical in terms of *genre*. He points out
that those texts traditionally thought of as myths possess some
striking structural affinities with the figures and events portrayed
in scapegoat texts or 'texts of persecution'. The above claims can be
rephrased as a series of questions: What is the likelihood that the
convergence of mythical patterns across a broad range of cultures
would share the same patterns to a very high degree of consistency
without there being a common mechanism that would bring these
into effect? And, secondly, what is the chance – allowing for a
moment the reality of genuine violence behind texts of persecution
– that the analogies to mythical texts do not suggest a similar vio-

lence? For Girard, the common patterns in myth and ritual are too striking not to attempt to put them into a wider interpretative frame; the motifs and practices do not allow us to pretend that every variation is a uniquely independent cultural form.

In light of this, to critique Girard effectively would perhaps involve (1) explaining all that Girard explains more economically; (2) showing that the phenomena under examination are not as improbable as Girard seems to think, given the postulate of the irreducible difference of cultures; (3) showing that Girard does not resolve the problems he seems to; (4) pointing to internal, logical (or logico-semantic) inconsistencies in his account; or (5) showing that the putative isomorphisms (the 'constants') between myths and rituals are not truly isomorphic, or that a significant proportion of them are sufficiently disanalogous to a degree which effectively undermines Girard's hypothesis.

Surprisingly, very rarely have *any* of these tasks been undertaken; much of what is offered instead are theses about what 'good cultural theory' should do. One of the senses that one gets when examining these is that Girard's highly specific construal of cultural phenomena is felt to be overly restrictive or 'reductive'. At first glance, it is hard to see exactly why this is the case – contemporary cultural theory is no stranger to a host of reductions (especially of the ontological kind); even violence itself is commonly seen to be central to – perhaps even the ultimate determinant of – culture and representation. (For instance, Peter Berger asserts, as if it were self-evident, that 'violence is the ultimate foundation of any political order.')[35] Indeed, outside the context of social and cultural theory, one might suggest that theory *per se* is reductive, as the very move from the particular to the abstract involves conceptual and taxonomic 'typing' of some sort or another. But here, and despite their own reductions, Girard argues that some theorists in the humanities and social sciences have ostensible problems even with *this* dimension of their profession:

> the most unavoidable process of abstraction, the very type of generalization that makes you able to walk into the street without being run over by a car, is already tainted with the impurity of reductionism. You are a 'reductionist' above all if you pursue the type of goal that any researcher outside the Humanities takes for granted that he should pursue.[36]

No doubt, any effective approach to hypothesis will need to respect the complexity of the phenomena it investigates, and hold this in some kind of tension with the will-to-abstract.[37] Indeed, in light of this, it is important then that one does not expect *too much* from Girard's explanatory scheme, to believe that he somehow offers (quite literally) a 'theory of everything' – that, for instance, his use of the term 'myth' exhausts all of its possible uses, or that his theory of the same provides an account of everything that passes under that name: 'I do not claim', he says, 'to be a complete critic' (*DB* 224).

Even on its own terms, it may well be the case that the theory of surrogate victimage will prove to be a far more partial account of cultural genesis and order than Girard claims it to be. I leave it to others to assess just how much Girard's hypothesis explains and the veracity of what he attempts – it has not, needless to say, been the task of this book to try to address such issues directly. Nonetheless these are, I feel, questions that must be addressed, as the stunning scope, range, and importance of Girard's thinking demand that we examine it in a world increasingly perplexed by the dangerous and frightening admixture of violence and the sacred.

In what he hoped would be the beginning of an extended discussion with Girard in *Diacritics*, the renowned French philosopher Philippe Lacoue-Labarthe was led to assert that 'there is every reason to believe, at least as far as I am concerned, that . . . we are still a long way from the point when anyone will have measured the scope of the question Girard has raised.'[38] My own feeling is that these words are as true today as they were in 1978, twenty-five years after they appeared.

Notes

Introduction

1 Translations of French texts are mine, unless otherwise noted.
2 Much of the biographical information here is derived from James G. Williams's overview provided in *GR* 1–6.
3 These books were translated respectively as *Deceit, Desire, and the Novel: Self and Other in Literary Structure* (1966) and *Resurrection from the Underground: Feodor Dostoevsky* (1997).
4 For instance, the queer theorist Eve Kosofsky Sedgwick has made highly innovative use of Girard's notion of mimetic desire to analyse homosociality in *Between Men: English Literature and Male Homosocial Desire*. And Eric Gans of UCLA has drawn on (and reformulated) Girard's notion of mimetic desire to develop an account of the origin of language. For a brief account of the latter, see the discussion in the final chapter.
5 In terms of the order of the chapters, I have chosen to mirror the chronological development of Girard's thought itself.
6 During this time, Girard also released *Critique dans un souterrain* (1976), which contains an earlier, short monograph on Dostoevsky – *Dostoïevski: du double à l'unité* (1963) – as well as other pieces which were published in journals between 1963 and 1972, some of which appeared (minus the piece on Dostoevsky) in English in *'To Double Business Bound': Essays on Literature, Mimesis, and Anthropology* (1978).
7 For an alternative contextualization of Girard's place in recent intellectual history, see Eugene Webb, *The Self Between: From Freud to the New Social Psychology of France*, pp. 3–25, 152–53; and, by the same author, 'The New Social Psychology of France: The Girardian School'. See also William A. Johnsen, 'Myth, Ritual, and Literature after Girard', and Girard's own essay 'Theory and its Terrors'.

Chapter 1   Mimetic Desire

1   Aristotle noted in *Poetics* (§4) that the human being 'is the most imi-
    tative [*mimetic*] creature in the world, and learns at first by imitation.'
    Much more recent work could, of course, be enlisted to support this
    contention. See, for instance, items by the developmental psychologist
    Andrew N. Meltzoff cited in the bibliography.
2   Quotation taken from a postscript written for the English translation
    of *Dostoïevski: du double à l'unité* not contained in the original text. It is
    also worth noting here that, after the publication of *DD* and *RU*, Girard
    moved away from the term 'mediator' to describe the imitated
    Other/s, and towards 'model/rival'. In this study, the terms are used
    interchangeably.
3   The very term 'ape' itself alludes to the increased imitative propensity
    of primates. For more on the imitative capacity of human and non-
    human animals, see William B. Hurlbut, 'Mimesis and Empathy in
    Human Biology'.
4   There are parallels here between Girard's distinction between appetite
    and desire and G. W. F. Hegel's contention that desire (*Begierde*) is the
    permanent principle of (human) self-consciousness, that 'self-
    consciousness in general is Desire.' Hegel, *Phenomenology of Spirit*,
    §167, pp. 104–5.
5   Girard, 'Generative Scapegoating', p. 122.
6   Sandor Goodhart, *Sacrificing Commentary*, p. 100.
7   In Girard's *DD*, and for much of *RU*, mimetic desire goes mostly under
    the name of 'triangular desire'. In this chapter, the term 'mimetic
    desire' will be used exclusively. Schematically speaking, Freudian
    theory could also be said to be 'triangular', although its coordinates
    and their relations bear only superficial resemblance to Girard's ideas,
    as we will soon see.
8   The other possibility here might be one derived from Hegel, which
    could be characterized as *un désir du désir de l'Autre* [a desire for the
    Other's desire]. See Hegel, *Phenomenology*, §§166–96, pp. 104–19. See
    note 35 below.
9   See Roberto Calasso, *The Ruin of Kasch*, pp. 135–70. Milan Kundera
    makes the following effusive declaration: 'At last, an occasion to cite
    René Girard; his *Mensonge romantique et vérité romanesque* is the best
    book I have ever read on the art of the novel.' Kundera, *Testaments
    Betrayed: An Essay in Nine Parts*, p. 184.
10 Girard, *Critique dans un souterrain*, p. 16.
11 Girard, 'Literature and Christianity: A Personal View', p. 36. On inter-
    textual approaches to literary interpretation, see Paisley Livingston,
    'From Work to Work'. (It is important to note, however, that Girard
    does use some extratextual material in his analysis of literary works:
    biographies.)

12 Here one should be sensitive to the epistemological method of procedure. The Canadian philosopher Paul Dumouchel points out that Girard's practice of intertextual comparison – and, one might add, the movement of the novelist's *oeuvre* itself – is inherently epistemological. See Dumouchel, 'Introduction', *Violence and Truth: On the Work of René Girard*, p. 247. Cf. Adolf Grunbaum, 'Can a Theory Answer More Questions than One of its Rivals?'; and Alasdair MacIntyre, 'Epistemological Crises, Dramatic Narrative, and the Philosophy of Science', esp. p. 69.

13 Cf. Charles Taylor's argument that the modern obsession with the self has, in fact, eroded any real, ontologically thick, kind of subjectivity. See Taylor, *Sources of the Self: The Making of the Modern Identity*, pp. 506–13.

14 This essay appears in *Critique dans un souterrain*, pp. 137–75. As Carl Rubino notes, the relationship between Camus, Meursault, and Clamence is a kind of Moebius strip. Carl Rubino, review of *'To Double Business Bound': Essays on Literature, Mimesis, and Anthropology*, p. 1020.

15 Anthony Wilden, *System and Structure: Essays in Communication and Exchange*, p. 470.

16 Lat. *æmulus*: rival.

17 Girard has all but dropped the distinction between 'internal' versus 'external' mediation in recent work. Because the vast majority of his output has concentrated on internal mediation (which is usually denoted by the term 'conflictual mimesis', or even sometimes simply 'mimetic desire') this has resulted in some degree of confusion about his writing, with some objecting that he argues implausibly that *all* desire is conflictual. Although Girard has, to some extent, contributed to this confusion, he has also argued against this reading of his work (see GR 62–5). One of the sources of this confusion is that internally mediated desire (unlike externally mediated desire) is a far more common object of Girard's concerns, central as it is to his theorization of myth, violence, and hominization.

18 Gregory Bateson, *Steps to an Ecology of Mind*. The title of Girard's collection of essays *'To Double Business Bound'* contains a double allusion – in one direction to a line from Shakespeare's *Hamlet*, and in another to Bateson's formulation. Compare also with the notion of the 'pragmatic paradox' in P. Watzlawick et al., *The Pragmatics of Human Communication*.

19 This is taken from an afterword written for the English edition.

20 Jean-Pierre Dupuy, 'Le Signe et l'envie', *L'Enfer des choses*, p. 70.

21 Bruno Latour has accused Girard of a disdain for objects, for implausibly claiming that objects 'do not count'. See Latour, *We Have Never Been Modern*, p. 45. While it is true enough that Girard's theory of desire is not object-oriented, he actually sees the 'disappearance' of the object as a pathological psychological state which originates in the progressive intensification of conflictual mimesis. More specifically, the

disappearance of the object is one of the symptoms of *paranoia*, 'the disappearance of the object and the persistence of rivalry in its pure state' (*TH* 348/371). Approached slightly differently, Girard does not claim that objects are somehow intrinsically valueless, but that the properties of any said object are not sufficient to explain the intensities of rivalry it (ostensibly) provokes; indeed, the removal of objects in the area of human affairs will *often have no impact on the intensity of a particular rivalry* (*TH* 90/99). This says nothing, of course, about the capacity for objects to 'act' or physically impact upon the world; Girard's concerns, for instance, about weapons proliferation make no secret of this.

22   Girard, 'Literature and Christianity: A Personal View', p. 36.
23   Girard has reservations about the terms 'masochism' and 'sadism' – and particularly their conceptual ties to the thought of Freud and Krafft-Ebing – and so designates these (somewhat *sous rature*) respectively as 'pseudo-masochism' and 'pseudo-sadism'. For the sake of economy, I will refer simply to Girard's ideas without 'pseudo'.
24   In light of the awkwardness of writing 'she or he', I will simply alternate between male and female pronouns.
25   See, for instance, Albert Ellis, *Humanistic Psychotherapy: The Rational-Emotive Approach*.
26   This claim, concerning violence and modernity, may seem perverse given the horrendous violence of the modern era; suffice to say, that violence is less easily legitimately channelled during modernity – or that its efficacy as an agent of producing social solidarity has been degraded – is not in the slightest incompatible with ever more brutal deployments of it. This is an idea that will be examined in chapter 4.
27   The question of whether the contemporary world can be equated with a continuation or repudiation of modernity – or, indeed, both of these simultaneously – is a question far too complex to be entertained here. Nonetheless, those elements of modernity already mentioned – the erosion of traditional sources of authority, as well as the ethico-political imperative of 'equality' – are still very much in effect (irrespective of one's preferred label for describing the contemporary world).
28   Interestingly, Stephen Gardner observes that a common tendency of philosophical modernity is a reversion to paganism which replaces the Socratic imperative – that philosophy is a question for self-knowledge (wisdom) – with a conception of philosophy as a quest for *Being*. Gardner, *Myths of Freedom*, p. 42.
29   Alexis de Tocqueville, *Democracy in America*, vol. 2, pp. 137–40. Cf. *DD* 117–22/122–7. See also Wolfgang Palaver, 'Hobbes and the Katéchon: The Secularization of Sacrificial Christianity', pp. 57–9.
30   Cf. Jean-Pierre Dupuy's observations on Weber's analysis of capitalism in 'Le Signe et l'envie', pp. 17–97.
31   See esp. note 19 of chapter 2.

32 It is worth noting that Girard has also engaged with the work of Jacques Lacan, and that of Gilles Deleuze and Felix Guattari. On Lacan, see *TH* 402–9/425–32. On Deleuze and Guattari, see *DB* 84–120/*Critique dans un souterrain*, pp. 199–250.

33 Cited in *VS* 170/250. Originally from Sigmund Freud, 'Group Psychology and the Analysis of the Ego', p. 105.

34 Freud, 'The Ego and the Id', pp. 31–3.

35 Girard's insistence on the 'objectlessness' of desire has allowed certain commentators such as Philippe Lacoue-Labarthe to conflate mimetic desire with a certain kind of (Kojèvian) Hegelianism. Alexandre Kojève, in his famous lectures on Hegel, formulated a notion of desire as directed towards some possible future state, rather than any object. That is, desire is constituted *as* desire insofar as it is mediated by an Other: something is desirable because it is the object of the Other's desire. Despite Girard's claims to have found the notion of mimesis in certain literary works, there is little doubt that Kojève's reading of Hegel impacted upon his work (as it did on most French intellectuals of Girard's generation); Girard even goes so far as to say that his early work was somewhat 'contaminated' by the Hegelian climate of the 1950s! (*DB* 201). But there are dangers in overstressing this connection. Mimetic desire, as desire directed towards the being of the other through an *object*, is not equivalent to an objectless desire centred in a quest for *recognition* by the other: 'the dynamics of mimetic rivalry are rooted in the disputed object and not in that "Hegelian desire for recognition" which I have always viewed as derivative – insofar as it resembles Hegel's – of more elementary mimetic interferences over an object' (*DB* 201; cf. *TH* 16/24; 320/344). The Hegelian notion is a form of speculative idealism in that, for Hegel, desire is always essentially desire for another's desire, a desire for recognition. Kojève, *Introduction to the Reading of Hegel: Lectures on the Phenomenology of Spirit*, pp. 13–15. See Jean-Pierre Dupuy's distinction between Girard's notion – un désir *selon l'Autre* – and Hegel's – un désir *du désir de l'Autre* – in *Ordres et desordres: enquête sur un nouveau paradigme*, p. 133. Cf. Robert Hamerton-Kelly, *Sacred Violence*, pp. 199–207.

36 This essay first appeared in Girard, *Critique dans un souterrain*, pp. 5–40. Cf. Girard's essay 'Narcissism: The Freudian Myth Demythified by Proust', pp. 293–311.

37 For a critique of the psychoanalytic idea of 'ambivalence' and a very interesting reflection on this phenomenon in terms of the relations between Friedrich Nietzsche and Richard Wagner, see *DB* 61–83.

38 Here we see an important divergence between Girard's thinking and those, usually philosophical, notions of mimesis as inhering purely in the realm of representation. For Girard mimesis is able to generate representations but it also, at certain stages, precludes them; that is, it precludes those self-representations concerning the fact that we are imitating. There is no need to have propositional knowledge of how

to imitate or that one is imitating in order that one does so; to put it in terms with which analytic philosophers are familiar: knowledge *how* does not necessarily imply knowledge *that*. The standard reference here is Gilbert Ryle, *The Concept of Mind*, pp. 25–61. See also Nathan Brett, 'Knowing How, What and That'; and Willard Van Orman Quine, *Quiddities*, pp. 18–21, 108–10.

39 I have used the term 'subject' up until now somewhat in deference to the standard theoretical lexicon of the contemporary humanities academy.

40 In some ways, Girard's notion of the 'self' as a 'field' or function of interdividual relations both draws on and radicalizes an older tradition of French thinking about psychology which operated relatively independently of the Freudian tradition. See Eugene Webb, 'The New Social Psychology of France: The Girardian School', pp. 259–60.

41 Jacques Lacan, *Écrits*, p. 835.

42 Eugene Webb argues that this feature is one of the things that distinguishes the 'Girardian school' from other psychological approaches; see Webb, *The Self Between*, p. 88.

43 See note 38 above. See also Eric Gans, *Signs of Paradox*, pp. 1–9.

44 Sigmund Freud, 'On Narcissism', pp. 67–102.

45 Henri Atlan and Jean-Pierre Dupuy, 'Mimesis and Social Morphogenesis: Violence and the Sacred from a Systems Analysis Viewpoint', p. 1264.

46 Webb, *The Self Between*, p. 101.

47 Perhaps the best-known proponent of this has been Jean-Michel Oughourlian, currently professor of psychiatry and psychopathology at the Sorbonne; see the bibliography for references (as well as those such as François Roustang's *Un destin si funeste* and Mikkel Borch-Jacobsen's *Le Lien affectif*).

Chapter 2   Sacrificial Crisis and Surrogate Victimage

1 This principle can be illustrated in a number of domains. For competition to be possible in sport, for instance, individuals or teams are required to operate in highly analogous ways – in terms not simply of explicit rules, but of the host of those tacitly learnt bodily habits strictly 'unnecessary' to the game. It is also evident in those highly stylized stagings of combat often found in primitive rituals (*VS* 166–8/246–8; 278–80/416–18).

2 For an example of this approach in the anthropological arena, for instance, see Victor Turner, *The Ritual Process*, pp. 179–80.

3 Although his theoretical trajectory is markedly different from Girard's, Elias Canetti is another theorist who has perceived very acutely the crowd's role in abolishing differences. See *Crowds and Power*.

4   The blood feud, therefore, is a particularly vivid anthropological example of what communications theorists call a 'positive feedback loop' – an escalating (non-linear) process of self-reinforcement, susceptible to 'runaway.'

5   Paul Dumouchel, 'Introduction', *Violence and Truth*, p. 12. Conflict, therefore, does not necessarily destroy the reciprocity of human relations – indeed, it makes it more complete, albeit in the direction of reprisal rather than peaceful coexistence (*IS* 22/42).

6   If the depiction of the 'sacrificial' crisis offered so far appears a little overblown it bears noting that, firstly, what Girard is here describing *formally* has a range of intermediate instantiations that don't always exhibit the degree of dissolution depicted. Secondly, the ethnological evidence that Girard enlists to support his contentions regarding the sacrificial crisis cannot be considered in any depth here; more will be said about this in the next chapter.

7   That there is no natural 'end point' to human violence is partly attributable to the lack of dominance hierarchies present in non-human animals. This is the subject of the first section of the next chapter.

8   The seeming implication of this point is that sacrificial crises – or even blood feuds more specifically – are phenomena that occur only in 'primitive' societies. Although the original anthropological context in which the blood feud was discussed relies on the absence of a judicial institution that transcends antagonists, the sacrificial crisis, when present in 'modern' industrial nations, is able to erode those institutions such as the judiciary that would otherwise intervene at times of social crisis.

9   The sacrificial crisis might be seen to have an epistemological and axiological analogue in what the critical theorist Jürgen Habermas dubbed a 'legitimation crisis'. See Habermas, *Legitimation Crisis*.

10 The origin of our use of the term 'scapegoat' is derived from the book of Leviticus in the Hebrew Bible, and describes the act of ritual purification which involves the selection and sacrifice of an animal, a goat, which is slaughtered for the atonement of sins (Lev. 16: 5–10). But the term 'scapegoat' [*bouc émissaire*] in Girard's writings, as in its more widespread usage, describes not simply the more formal ceremonial practices of sacrificial atonement (of which the Leviticus ritual is but one – and, in some senses, an atypical – example), but the seemingly spontaneous psychological mechanism which names that polarization of violence effected though the substitutionary selection of a victim. See Girard, 'Generative Scapegoating', pp. 73–8.

11 Gregory Bateson, *Steps to an Ecology of Mind*, p. 315. The operation of surrogate victimage, as the hypothetical solution to the sacrificial crisis, has some strong analogues in interdisciplinary observations concerning self-organizing systems. The emergence of order from disorder (in Girard's case, through surrogate victimage) is the result of a random fluctuation in a chaotic system that inaugurates the process

of (re)structuration. A number of scientists and philosophers, such as the (Nobel Prize-winning) chemist Ilya Prigogine, the biophysicist Henri Atlan, and the political philosopher Jean-Pierre Dupuy, have drawn interesting parallels between the morphogenetic scope of Girard's theory and theories of self-organization in the physical sciences. See, for instance, Ilya Prigogine, 'Order out of Chaos', p. 60; see also Henri Atlan and Jean-Pierre Dupuy, 'Mimesis and Social Morphogenesis', p. 1265.

12   For an excellent collection of the kind of images being discussed here, see Sam Keen, *Faces of the Enemy*.

13   As Guy Lefort remarks in *Things Hidden*: 'the only true scapegoats are those we cannot recognize as such'(*TH* 129/152). (And again, here we could make use of the insights proffered by the philosophy of mind of Gilbert Ryle, already mentioned.) Henri Atlan, while endorsing the tenor of Girard's theses in this area, argues that scapegoating need not be unwitting for it to have the kinds of social effects that Girard describes. See Atlan, 'Founding Violence and Divine Referent', pp. 192–208.

14   This is, of course, to simplify a very complicated state of affairs. The long history of anti-Semitism in Europe is a factor that complicates this already multifaceted era in German history; but a consideration of this is, needless to say, beyond the scope of the current chapter.

15   In acknowledging the pervasiveness of this transference of hostility from 'within' to 'without', we are surely able to recognize a constitutive element of the morphogenesis of certain kinds of 'foreign' war, the militarized result of the process in which internal fracturing and social unrest are directed outwards towards an external enemy, who is often construed – and actually seen – as responsible for the domestic crisis. Perhaps, even more radically, Girard suggests, we should regard the persistent reference to 'foreign war' in mythical narratives as the displaced representation of civil disorder (*VS* 249/370–1).

16   See James George Frazer, *The Golden Bough*. See also Albert Henrichs, 'Loss of Self, Suffering, Violence'.

17   It is interesting to note that Girard's use of the term '*émissaire*' renders more explicit the relationship between kingship and victimage. Although usually translated as 'surrogate', in French it also carries the meaning of what, in English, is called an 'emissary': one who, especially in a governmental capacity, 'stands in for' or 'represents' others.

18   Morphogenetic: derived from Gk *morphos* (shape) + *gignesthai* (to be born).

19   Girard is not the first thinker to link the phenomenon of prohibitions to sacrifice and, in turn, to relate both to an originary collective murder, Freud also undertook to demonstrate the connections between these in his last – and almost universally disparaged – works. (For Girard's overview and assessment of other theorizations of sacrifice, see *VS* 1–67/9–104.) Initially inspired by the work of

W. Robertson Smith, Freud proposed – in *Totem and Taboo* and *Moses and Monotheism* – that the origin of religion and human society lay in a founding murder of a father by his sons, a 'primal horde', carried out by them in order to get sexual access to the mother; in this scheme, sacrifice then emerged as a ritual repetition of this originary event. Freud's Lamarckianism allowed him to posit that the memory of this event was (biologically) passed down through subsequent generations and had climactic and pathological expressions, usually ritual sacrifice – a veritable 'return of the repressed', driven by the guilt incurred through a memory of the original event. Although Girard appreciates Freud's positing of an actual collective murder as his model for sacrifice (*VS* 178/262), he doesn't accept either Freud's sexual essentialism or the invocation of 'guilt' as the re-energizing factor; that is, Girard takes exception both to the mechanism Freud describes and to how he thought that it operated (*VS* 193–222/283–325). Moreover, Girard argues that Freud's *single* murder does not account for the cultural diversity that such an act should account for. (That is, Girard's mechanism is not simply a 'one-off' affair; it is not, as he says, 'a kind of accident that cannot be repeated'.) See Girard, 'Generative Scapegoating', p. 121.

20 No doubt, the contentiousness of the very designations 'primitive' and 'modern' invites whole series of qualifications and clarifications that cannot be taken up here; to do so would necessitate entering a domain in which we would have to engage in a substantial consideration of complex issues concerning anthropology as a discipline, its relations to colonial power, and its deep imbrication in certain implicit ideas about linear temporalization and 'progress'. Here it must simply suffice to note that the term 'primitive' as it is used by Girard does *not* denote those meanings of the term predicated on a Darwinian construal of 'savages' and their place in the evolutionary history of the species. In the context of Girard's work, the term 'primitive' equates to what otherwise would be denoted by the term 'pre-state': an adjectival designation of those cultural structures where prohibitions and the assigning of objects to individuals are underwritten by kinship and totemic obligations; where the division of labour is ritually prescribed; and where the society as a whole functions without the presence of an (ostensibly) neutral judiciary, but operates instead by virtue of a social structure provided by immanentist religious beliefs and practices. Given these initial qualifications – and not without considerable trepidation – I will from now on invariably use the term without scare quotes.

21 It is important to note that the phrase 'surrogate victimage mechanism' refers only to the spontaneous socio-psychological phenomenon by which violence converges on a victim, not the *ritual repetition of this act*, for which Girard usually deploys the term 'sacrifice' (*TH* 33/41).

22 For an excellent discussion of the relationships between kingship and sacrifice, see Simon Simonse, *Kings of Disaster*. Elias Canetti is another thinker who has brought out some of these connections. See *Crowds and Power*, pp. 410–20.

23 Jacques Derrida, 'Plato's Pharmacy', pp. 63–171. Cf. *VS* 95/143–4; 296–7/442–4.

24 It is worth noting that he does not often speak of 'religion' [*la religion*] *per se*, but more often of 'the religious', or 'the religious sense' [*le religieux*], which for him is a synonym of 'the sacred' [*le sacré*].

25 Andrew McKenna, 'Aristotle's Theater of Envy: Paradox, Logic, and Literature', p. 646.

26 As befits the topic, Girard situates most of his discussion of 'the sacred' in relation to anthropology, rather than, say, sociology or political science, and so much of his discussion of the sacred is located in the domain of primitive religion. This by no means precludes the extension of this thesis concerning the sacred to contemporary, industrial, societies. Although Girard's notion of 'the sacred' is neither, strictly speaking, exclusively 'non-Western' nor 'non-modern', it requires certain qualifications contingent on the presentation of material in subsequent chapters. This says nothing, of course, of the value of such extensions – extensions which Girard himself continually undertakes. (For instance, he argues that in political forms of totalitarianism we can see a fierce recrudescence of the 'primitive sacred' (*J* 119/138–9).)

27 Although it is perhaps a perennial temptation in humanities scholarship to overinvest the theoretical import of etymology, cursory reflections in this area tend to reiterate, perhaps even corroborate, some key Girardian theses. The Latin term '*sacer*' [holy], from which we derive the English terms 'sacred' and 'sacrifice', can be rendered as both 'sacred'/'holy' and 'accursed'. (From this Latin origin are derived a series of such related terms as *sacrare* [Lat. 'to set apart']. The English terms 'sacrifice' and 'sacred' come to us from the Latin via the Old French term *sacrificium*, a combination of *sacer* [holy] and *facere* [to make].)

28 Mark R. Anspach, 'Violence Against Violence: Islam in Comparative Context', p. 9. Therefore, contrary to the romantic constructions peculiar to modern anthropology and comparative religion, typified by the work of theorists such as Mircea Eliade, primitive religion doesn't 'celebrate' the sacred or attempt to put us 'in touch' with it – rather, it attempts to keep it at a safe distance (*VS* 267/398). (Cf. E. E. Evans-Pritchard, *Nuer Religion*.) Asserting this is not equivalent, however, to succumbing to the Enlightenment temptation to construe the function of primitive religion as somehow to 'promote' violence; at least in a utilitarian sense, it prevents and curtails it – it is actually one of the

primary functions of religion to stop reciprocal violence through judi-
cious doses of non-reciprocal violence (*VS* 55/86).

29 Lat. 'The voice of the people/popular opinion – the voice of God'.

30 The main distinction between 'ancient' and 'primitive' societies is the
presence of (broadly) socio-political 'institutions' in the former, and
their absence in the latter (*IS* 89/122–3).

31 Having said this, however, the propensity – equally in evidence
during Western modernity – to endow 'sacred victims' with almost
supernatural capacities for causing harm, as well as their typical characterization as somehow 'utterly Other', nonetheless moves in this
direction.

32 Much the same could be said of Girard's view of violence itself. We
should, however, be very careful to distinguish Girard's insistence
on the socio-historical pervasiveness of violence, and its (again, socio-
historical) centrality to cultural and social stucturation, from the idea
that violence is an inescapable metaphysical absolute, somehow
inscribed in the very 'nature of things'. This distinction is, unfortunately, lost on John Milbank, who complains that Girard's socio-
scientific explanations are predicated on an almost Hobbesian
metaphysics of violence. See John Milbank, *Theology & Social Theory:
Beyond Secular Reason*, pp. 392–8. But there is a genuine and significant
difference between Girard and the theoretical systems evinced by
Hobbesian anthropology, Hegelian historicism, Nietzschean 'genealogy', and Heraclitian metaphysics, the latter of which all agree that
violence is not simply historically pervasive, but somehow *ontologically fundamental*. To the contrary, Girard's account of violent humanity more closely resembles the Augustinian 'fallen state' than the
Hobbesian 'state of nature'. (A good account of the differences
between Hobbes and Augustine can be found in Eric Vogelin, *The New
Science of Politics*, 59–72. Cf. *DB* 199–201 and Jean-Pierre Dupuy, *Ordres
et desordres*, p. 125.)

33 Interestingly enough, Girard points to the presence of the same fear
in Platonism, and so gives philosophy itself a particularly interesting
anthropological reading (*TH* 15–17/23–6). Cf. Cesáreo Bandera, *The
Sacred Game*, pp. 43–87.

34 Mikhail Bakhtin, *Rabelais and his World*, p. 40. There are very real differences, however, between Bakhtin's analysis of carnival and Girard's
analysis of ritual which I am not able to go into here.

35 Serres, 'The Origin of Language: Biology, Information Theory, &
Thermodynamics', in *Hermes: Literature, Science, Philosophy*, pp.
71–83.

36 See Émile Durkheim, *The Elementary Forms of the Religious Life*. See also
Eric Gans, 'The Sacred and the Social'.

37 These views are, in fact, hardly mutually exclusive. See, for instance,
Voltaire, *Philosophical Dictionary*.

Chapter 3   Myth, Tragedy, History

1   Jacob Bronowski, *The Ascent of Man*, p. 412.
2   Jacques Lacan, *The Seminar, Book II*, p. 5. For a riposte to the Lacanian-style objections similar to the one offered here, see Eric Gans, *Signs of Paradox*, pp. 13–50.
3   See note 3 of chapter 1.
4   Cf. Gans, *Originary Thinking*, pp. 8–9. Although in *TH* Girard draws on the work of Monod, more recent work in this area could now be cited. Recently, for instance, a very interesting series of theses on 'mirror neurons' – neurons located in the ventral premotor area of the frontal lobes of monkeys – have been ventured that have some interesting potential to corroborate the increasing functional role of imitation in the evolution of primates and humans. See G. Rizzolatti et al., 'Neurones Related to Reaching-Grasping Arm Movements in the Rostral Part of Area 6 (Area 6a)'; Vittorio Gallese and Alvin Goldman, 'Mirror Neurons and the Simulation Theory of Mind-Reading'; Giacomo Rizzolatti and Michael Arbib, 'Language within our Grasp'; and V. S. Ramachandran, 'Mirror Neurons and Imitation Learning as the Driving Force behind the "Great Leap Forward" in Human Evolution'.
5   Cf. Girard, 'Generative Scapegoating', p. 129. Here the reader may detect similarities between Girard's hypothesis of hominization through surrogate victimage and the thesis of Freud's *Totem and Taboo*. See note 19 of chapter 2.
6   Donald Davidson was one of the few contemporary philosophers working in the analytic tradition who has argued for the idea that language itself is a requirement for the emergence of (properly human) desire. See Davidson, *Inquiries into Truth and Interpretation*, pp. 279–81.
7   It is interesting to note, in this respect, that the etymological origin of the term 'category' [Fr. *catégorie*] is the Latin *categoria*, which means 'accusation'.
8   The structuralist A. J. Greimas offers a typically structuralist assessment when he says, 'We perceive differences, and thanks to that perception, the world "takes shape" in front of us, and for our purposes.' Greimas, *Sémantique structurale: recherche de méthode*, p. 19.
9   For an interesting discussion of sign systems as 'proxies', see Steven Maras, 'A Semiotics of the Proxy'.
10   Girard, 'Generative Scapegoating', p. 129.
11   Philippe Sollers, 'Is God Dead? "The Purloined Letter" of the Gospel', pp. 191–2. The parallels between Girard and certain psychoanalytic ideas of others could prove very suggestive here. See, for instance, Jacques Lacan, *Écrits: A Selection*, p. 104; and Julia Kristeva, *Revolution in Poetic Language*, p. 75.
12   The 'justification' referred to here is not 'conspiratorial' in any sense; none of the institutions of the sacred are primarily 'strategic' or 'apolo-

getic' forms that attempt to embody an already formed theological or metaphysical framework; they are, rather, responses to the experience of the sacred (*VS* 89–92/135–40).

13 The bulk of Girard's engagement with Lévi-Strauss can be found in *VS* 223–49; *DB* 155–77, 178–98; & *TH* 105–25. Also of note is Girard's essay 'Disorder and Order in Mythology'.

14 Jean-Pierre Vernant, *Myth and Society in Ancient Greece*, pp. 186–7. The distinction here is that the irrational may be seen as (capturing) the Real – and fiction itself may possess internally coherent logics. Vernant's point is that the predominant view of myth is that neither of these is the case.

15 See Kenneth Burke, 'Doing and Saying', and Carl Jung, *The Gnostic Jung*. For a brief (although now somewhat dated) history of the conceptualizations of myth in European intellectual history, see Alasdair MacIntyre, 'Myth'.

16 The etymological root of the Greek word for myth – from the Greek *muthos* [fable] – is *mu*, which means to 'keep secret' or 'to close'. *Mu* is the common root not only of 'myth', but of the terms 'mute' and 'mutate'.

17 Philippe Sollers, 'Is God Dead?', p. 192. A qualification is in order; the lynching which Sollers says is 'unconscious' is not, according to Girard, repressed 'into' a (Freudian) unconscious; rather 'it is detached from man and made divine' (*VS* 136/204). It becomes the quasi-transcendent source of culture. Lacan's phrase was 'the unconscious is structured like a language.' See Jacques Lacan, *The Seminar, Book III*, p. 167.

18 Laurence Coupe, *Myth*, p. 116.

19 'The plague is universally presented as a process of undifferentiation, a destruction of specificities. This destruction is often preceded by a reversal. The plague will turn the honest man into a thief, the virtuous man into a lecher, the prostitute into a saint. Friends murder and enemies embrace. Wealthy men are made poor by the ruin of their business. Riches are showered upon paupers who inherit in a few days the fortunes of many distant relatives. Social hierarchies are first transgressed, then abolished. Political and religious authorities collapse. The plague makes all accumulated knowledge and all categories of judgement invalid' (*DB* 136–7).

20 Mircea Eliade, *Histoire des croyances et des idées religieuses*, p. 84. See *IS* 83/115.

21 On the Ojibwa myth, compare these references with René Girard, 'Generative Scapegoating', pp. 95–105.

22 See also Clarence Maloney, ed., *The Evil Eye*.

23 A good summary reference here is Robert Hamerton-Kelly, *Sacred Violence*, pp. 37–8.

24 Cf. James G. Williams, *The Bible, Violence, and the Sacred*, pp. 14–20.

25 Jean-Pierre Dupuy, 'Totalization and Misrecognition', p. 75.

26 Ibid.
27 Northrop Frye, *Anatomy of Criticism: Four Essays*, pp. 364–6.
28 The exception for Girard here is Shakespeare, whose work doesn't remythologize violence at all. We will consider Shakespeare following our discussion of Greek tragedy.
29 Gil Bailie, *Violence Unveiled*, pp. 32–3.
30 Sandor Goodhart has offered a subtle and sophisticated reading of the *Theban Plays* oriented by a Girardian hermeneutic. See his *Sacrificing Commentary: Reading the End of Literature*, pp. 13–41.
31 'If the art of tragedy is to be defined in a single phrase, we might do worse than call attention to one of its most characteristic traits: the opposition of symmetrical elements' (*VS* 44/71).
32 But, Girard argues, it would be a mistake to see the rivalries in which Oedipus is implicated as (Freudian) *Oedipal rivalries*. The mechanism which draws in antagonists has no basis in psychoanalytic 'complexes', but is best seen as 'fratricidal' battles, not because 'brotherly' rivalry has a more secure basis in 'human nature', but because this designation indicates – far better than its biologized alternative – both the incidentality of sexuality to the conflict and the kind of de-hierarchization and antagonistic mirroring characteristic of violent reciprocity (*VS* 65/100–1).
33 See, for instance, Roberto da Matta, *Carnavals, bandits et héros* and 'Carnival in Multiple Planes'.
34 For a very interesting discussion and application of mimetic desire to psychopathological phenomena (by a practising psychiatrist and professor of psychiatry at the Sorbonne), see Jean-Michel Oughourlian, *The Puppet of Desire*.
35 It is perhaps this feature that provides the Aristotelian tradition with its *raison d'être*. But although the theory 'tragic flaw' is inadequate to the extent that it perpetuates the mythic vision itself, it is also irrelevant to much Greek tragedy, even on its own terms – for instance, the extant plays of Aeschylus or the majority of Euripides' *oeuvre*.
36 Paradoxically, for a purported 'political' play, commentators remain terminally undecided regarding Shakespeare's *political allegiances* – Mark Antony, Octavius Caesar and the Empire, or Brutus and the Republic?
37 Golsan, *René Girard and Myth*, p. 47.
38 Claiming that Girard asserts that traces of victimage can be found in historical texts should not be confused with the (incorrect) notion that Girard's hypothesis of surrogate victimage is some 'historical narrative' of the kind undertaken by Freud in his account of the primal murder in *Totem and Taboo*. That is, surrogate victimage is not, strictly speaking, a 'history' that Girard postulates, but a *méchanisme* that both produces and distorts history.
39 Although Girard took up the subject of texts of persecution first in *Things Hidden Since the Foundation of the World* (*TH* 126–38/136–62),

this discussion should now be viewed as a preparatory study, as something of a preface to the far more nuanced and comprehensive consideration of the same phenomenon in *The Scapegoat* (*S* 1–44/ 7–67).

40 Roberto Calasso, *The Ruin of Kasch*, p. 160.
41 Bruno Latour, *We Have Never Been Modern*, p. 45.

Chapter 4 Non-Sacrificial Violence: The Judeo-Christian Scriptures

1 *Le Monde*, 27 October 1972.
2 The formal features of this degradation were discussed in the final section of the previous chapter.
3 See, for instance, Alfred North Whitehead, *Science and the Modern World*; M. B. Foster, 'The Christian Doctrine of Creation and the Rise of Modern Natural Science'; Richard Hooykaas, *Religion and the Rise of Modern Science*; and Peter E. Hodgson, 'The Christian Origin of Science'.
4 Philippe Sollers, 'Is God Dead? "The Purloined Letter" of the Gospel', p. 191.
5 This is, of course, an abbreviated list. A good early representative of this kind of critique of Christianity is presented by the late second-century philosopher Celsus in his *On the True Doctrine: A Discourse Against the Christians*, esp. pp. 55–68. For an incisive commentary on the Celsian critique, see Thomas F. Bertonneau, 'Celsus, the First Nietzsche: Resentment and the Case Against Christianity'.
6 'Non-anagogical' here means, roughly, 'literal-minded'. Campbell, cited in Bailie, *Violence Unveiled*, p. 128.
7 I *presume* that this would be the case; Girard has not actually, to my knowledge, ever discussed Campbell's work. Gil Bailie *has*, however, and I see no reason to doubt his conclusions. See Bailie, *Violence Unveiled*, pp. 128–32.
8 Girard, 'Violence in Biblical Narrative', p. 387.
9 Raymund Schwager, *Must There be Scapegoats? Violence and Redemption in the Bible*, pp. 47–67.
10 Cf. Walter Wink, *Engaging the Powers*, p. 147.
11 McKenna, *Violence and Difference*, pp. 201–21. This does not, of course, imply that theology is proscribed, merely that the theoretical and anthropological import of these texts functions, in the first instance, to clarify their theological import.
12 Girard is, of course, not the first thinker to undertake a genre analysis of biblical 'myths' only to find that they don't quite fit the genre. See, for instance, C. S. Lewis's essay 'Modern Theology and Biblical Criticism'. Much the same point has been made by the theologian Hans Frei, albeit in a decidedly more sustained, intellectually rigorous

fashion than that provided by Lewis. See Frei, *The Eclipse of Biblical Narrative.*

13 Gil Bailie, *Violence Unveiled*, pp. 128–30.

14 As it stands, there is a substantial and continually growing amount of Girardian theological literature that derives its initial orientation from Girard's work. See works in the Bibliography by Anthony W. Bartlett, Sandor Goodhart, Raymund Schwager, James Alison, Robert G. Hamerton-Kelly, and James G. Williams.

15 The title of the French edition of Girard's book-length examination of the book of Job is *La Route antique des hommes pervers* (1985), a phrase taken from Job 22: 15, where Eliphaz asks Job 'Will you keep to the ancient way that the wicked have travelled?' In the French edition of the book, Girard uses a capital 'D' when referring to '*le Dieu des victimes*', and a small d ('dieu') in other cases. The text of the English translation, unfortunately, fails to render this distinction.

16 While offering a fundamentally sympathetic treatment of Girard's reading of Job – a treatment that is ingenious in its own right – the Jewish literary and cultural theorist Sandor Goodhart contests Girard's claim that the narrator is himself given to the proclivities of the mob perspective. See Goodhart, *Sacrificing Commentary*, pp. 168–211, esp. pp. 185–8.

17 And even the 'God' who *does* exert revenge and demand sacrifice – with few exceptions – gets humans to exact his revenge for him. See Schwager, *Must There be Scapegoats?*, p. 67.

18 Girard, 'Generative Scapegoating', p. 141. Sandor Goodhart contests this claim. See Goodhart, *Sacrificing Commentary*, pp. 99–212, esp. pp. 99–121.

19 Max Weber, *Ancient Judaism*, esp. pp. 19–22; 86; 475–7; 492–5.

20 Eric Gans, 'The Victim as Subject: The Esthetico-Ethical System of Rousseau's *Rêveries*', p. 4.

21 The second of these consists of fragments taken from Nietzsche's notebooks and published posthumously.

22 Nietzsche, 'The Anti-Christ', §62, p. 198.

23 Nietzsche, *The Will to Power*, §1052, pp. 542–3; cf. 'The Anti-Christ', §§2–7, pp. 127–31.

24 Nietzsche, *The Will to Power*, §246, p. 142.

25 Nietzsche, *On the Genealogy of Morals*, and *Ecce Homo*, §7, p. 332.

26 It may strike the reader as unusual that Oedipus is here included in the 'Dionysian'. But Nietzsche's supplanting of the (early) antithesis of the 'Apollonian versus the Dionysian' with 'Dionysus versus the Crucified' (in his later works) effectively transposed much that had fallen under the heading of the 'Apollonian' into the category of the 'Dionysian'. The 'Dionysian', for Nietzsche, extends far beyond what would be considered strictly 'Dionysian', taking in Greek tragedy and primitive religion almost *in toto*.

27 An analogous point has been elaborated at length by Stephen L. Gardner. See his *Myths of Freedom*.

28 Michel Foucault might be seen to follow a similar trajectory to Nietzsche in his *Discipline and Punish*; in this analysis Foucault is given to lamenting what he sees as the 'interiorization' of prisoner reform, an operation which takes place in the prisoner's 'soul' rather than being inflicted on his body – an interiorization achieved through Christian 'technologies' structurally homologous to confession.

29 For more on Girard's engagement with Nietzsche, see 'The Founding Murder in the Philosophy of Nietzsche'; 'Strategies of Madness: Nietzsche, Wagner, and Dostoevski' (*DB* 61–83); and 'Nietzsche and Contradiction'.

30 Sollers, 'Is God Dead?', p. 191. Sollers is here alluding to Jesus, who quotes Psalm 118: 22: 'The stone that the builders rejected has become the chief cornerstone.' This Christian 'return of the repressed' is, no doubt, equivalent to a decisively *non*-Nietzschean 'transvaluation of all values', a transvaluation which carries out a replacement of *pharmakos* by *Christos* through a series of semiotic reinscriptions, the replacement, for instance, of the usual term 'scapegoat' in the New Testament with the phrase 'lamb of God'. So while the New Testament preserves the functional equivalence of these terms, the latter one replaces the 'distasteful and loathsome connotations' of the goat with the lamb, and in so doing makes the innocence and goodness of the victim and the barbarity of the killing manifest (*S* 117/169). Needless to say, this semiotic transvaluation – of the reinscription of linguistic markers which uphold the innocence and goodness of the victim – is not something that *can* be upheld if the cultural and social benefits of the surrogate victimage mechanism are to be sustained.

31 Girard, 'Foreword', James G. Williams, *The Bible, Violence, and the Sacred*, pp. v–vi.

32 Golsan, *René Girard and Myth*, p. 100.

33 Hamerton-Kelly, *Sacred Violence*, p. 60. The central Hegelian concept here is surely '*Aufhebung*', which designates, simultaneously, negation, preservation, and progress.

34 Eugene Webb notes that, as widespread as Anselm's doctrine of sacrificial atonement has been throughout (Latinate) Christendom, it remains anathema to the Eastern Christian tradition. Eugene Webb, *The Self Between: From Freud to the New Social Psychology of France*, pp. 180–1.

35 Cf. Anthony W. Bartlett, *Cross Purposes*.

36 Raymund Schwager, *Must There be Scapegoats?*, p. 209; cf. *TH* 215/239.

37 These positions can, of course, be distinguished, with the 'evangelical' scholar somewhat closer to 'liberalism' than his or her fundamentalist colleague; nonetheless, they share a common philosophical genealogy. The origins of the division can be seen in the differing strands of post-Humean thought; where 'liberal' theology developed out of a line

beginning with Kant and continuing through to Schleiermacher, conservative theology comes from Thomas Reid through to the 'Princeton school' of theology. See Nancey Murphy, *Beyond Liberalism and Fundamentalism*, pp. 4–6.

38 Perhaps, more centrally, Girard repudiates the idea of a 'sacrificial atonement' and the correlative notions of 'divine punishment' that invariably go along with fundamentalism and certain kinds of evangelical Christianity. That is, the mood of conservative claim of the singularity of the Christian tradition is invariably accompanied by a threat and an emphasis on the apocalyptic texts. See Williams, *The Bible, Violence, and the Sacred*, pp. 1–3.

39 To describe Satan as a 'personification' is not to 'liberalize' orthodoxy by rendering innocuous a previously ontological agent by turning it somehow into a 'figure of speech'. Girard points out that the New Testament repeatedly indicates that evil has power only insofar as it is embodied in a particular person or group; Satan is, therefore, both the true subject of every worldly kingdom (instantiated through surrogate victimage) and not a subject at all (*TH* 210). As Dante would have us believe, Satan's first deception is to trick us into believing he doesn't exist; undoubtedly, Girard would agree – but may add that Satan's (equally pernicious) second deception is to trick us into believing that he *does*. The Gospels point out that Satan is not an autonomous subject, gaining whatever power he can by manifesting in people; but he *is* a (perhaps *the*) real subject insofar as he is the reality of cultural formation and scandal.

40 Here we can see another deployment of the Christian comprehension of Law – from the (vaguely) 'sociological' use (discussed above) to the more 'psychological'. In a (decidedly pre-Lacanian) observation, Paul notes in his Letter to the Romans that that which is forbidden to us by Law can, *for that reason alone*, cause us to obsess over its acquisition! (Lacan posited that desire is, in effect, a by-product of the Law: Lacan, *The Seminar, Book VII*, pp. 83–4; 177. Judith Butler also – mistakenly, I believe – ascribes this view to Michel Foucault: Butler, *Subjects of Desire*, p. 218.) Law, in other words, may 'stir up' desire solely by virtue of presenting us with model-obstacles. 'Shall we say, then', Paul says, 'that the Law itself is sinful? Of course not! But it was the Law that made me know what sin is. If the Law had not said, "Do not desire what belongs to someone else", I would not have known such a desire' (Rom. 7: 7). The point here, of course, is that the Law itself can be a *skandalon*.

41 Girard, 'Are the Gospels Mythical?'

42 Webb, *The Self Between*, p. 190.

43 Jean-Michel Oughourlian, *The Puppet of Desire*, pp. 70–1.

44 The theory of the (Anselmian) sacrificial atonement represented the Paraclete as the one who begged for mercy on behalf of sinners before a violent God, rather than the advocate who testifies for the oppressed and accused before persecutors. The former interpretation figures the

situation of God's relationship to humanity as one of a trial before God; this accusatory mould makes God a somewhat Satanic figure: an 'adversary' or 'accuser' (*TH* 209).

45 Girard, 'Literature and Christianity: A Personal View', p. 36.

46 For an exposition and interesting (secular) critique of this moral doctrine, see Bob Brecher, *Getting What You Want?*

47 For instance, in one of the best-known and most often-cited critiques of Girard, Hayden White draws parallels between Girard and the conservative Catholic ideologue Joseph de Maistre; Girard, like de Maistre, is an 'apologist of reaction', someone who desperately wants to turn the clock back to pre-modernity. White goes so far as to suggest that Nazi Germany may embody the Girardian notion of a healthy culture. White, 'Ethnological "Lie" and Mythical "Truth"', p. 8. It would be exceedingly difficult to see how White's misprision of Girard's work could have been more complete. See Cesáreo Bandera, 'The Doubles Reconciled', p. 1011. As should be obvious to the reader at this point, it has never been part of Girard's project to valorize violence in any respect, *especially* as a means for securing social or cultural unanimity or harmony. As seen in the previous chapter, Girard's interest in and epistemological valuation of biblical texts is predicated upon the way in which they *condemn* violence. White has misconstrued normativity with descriptivity; that violence structures a culture does not somehow earn it Girard's ethical endorsement. Perversely, White somehow manages to read *La Violence et le sacré* as a *defence* of the sacred.

48 Girard, 'Generative Scapegoating', p. 145.

49 Richard Golsan, *René Girard and Myth*, p. 88.

50 J. Denny Weaver, 'Atonement for the Non-Constantinian Church'. Also see Walter Wink, *Engaging the Powers*, p. 150. For another account of the links between Christian violence, post-Constantinian Christianity, and the 'sacrificial atonement', see Charles K. Bellinger, *The Genealogy of Violence*, pp. 98–112.

51 Philippe Sollers, 'Is God Dead?', pp. 195, 192.

52 Cited in Bellinger, *The Genealogy of Violence*, p. 98.

53 Nietzsche, 'The Anti-Christ', §55.

54 Girard, 'Generative Scapegoating', p. 141.

55 Girard's work follows Durkheim's in that it rejects the construal of a fundamental opposition between 'primitive' and contemporary modes of thought (unlike, say, Lévi-Bruhl or Frazer).

56 Friedrich Nietzsche, 'The Anti-Christ', §62, p. 198. As for the doctrine of the 'equality of all souls', Alasdair MacIntyre points to the biblical sources of this now widespread (secular) doctrine. See Alasdair MacIntyre, *A Short History of Ethics*, pp. 110–11.

57 Harold J. Berman, *The Formation of the Western Legal Tradition*; Richard O'Sullivan, *The Spirit of the Common Law*, pp. 65–109; Rudolph Brasch, *Thank God I'm an Atheist*, pp. 117–26; Alvin J. Schmidt, *Under the Influence*, pp. 248–71.

58 Larry Siedentop, *Democracy in Europe*, esp. pp. 162–5; 212–14.
59 Siedentop, *Democracy in Europe*, p. 203. As contentious as Siedentop's argument concerning the Christian undermining of slavery and serfdom may seem, it is a thesis that finds ample corroboration. See, in this respect, Paul Johnson, *A History of Christianity*, pp. 147–9; James Walvin, *Black Ivory*, esp. pp. 194–8; David Brion Davis, *Slavery and Human Progress*, pp. 109–31; and Robert William Fogel, *Without Consent and Without Contract*, esp. pp. 204–21. On the hospital, see *IS* 167/217–18 and Schmidt, *Under the Influence*, pp. 151–69.
60 Adam Seligman, *Modernity's Wager: Authority, the Self, and Transcendence*, p. 12. See also Marcel Mauss, 'A Category of the Human Mind: The Notion of Person; the Notion of Self'; Louis Dumont, 'A Modified View of Our Origins: The Christian Beginnings of Modern Individualism'; and Seligman, *The Problem of Trust*, pp. 124–46.
61 Although there are many ways of pursuing this idea, one of the most common is that Marxism, say, took up Judeo-Christian eschatology and reinscribed it within a secular frame. On this, see Michael Walzer's very interesting *Exodus and Revolution*, which discusses the impact of biblical texts – particularly Exodus, Numbers, and Deuteronomy – in shaping radical political thought and action as well as providing a critique for some of its most violent and unrealistic forms.
62 Vattimo's main target here is Hans Blumenberg's *The Legitimacy of the Modern Age*. See especially Vattimo, *Beyond Interpretation*, pp. 49–52; and *Belief*, pp. 39–42.
63 This thesis has its sociological origins in the work of Max Weber.
64 Girard, 'Generative Scapegoating', pp. 140, 142. Of course, this is not the only 'internationalization' of which we can speak. Jacques Derrida has recently pointed to what he sees as a certain globalization of biblical ethics, an internationalization of the idea of 'forgiveness' through the language of international human rights, of 'crimes against humanity'; the notion of forgiveness, he claims, finds its grounding and ultimate point of origin in doctrines of the 'sacredness' of the human – a notion ultimately derived from the 'Abrahamic memory of the religions of the Book, and in a Jewish but above all Christian interpretation of the "neighbour" or the "fellow man".' Jacques Derrida, *On Cosmopolitanism and Forgiveness*, p. 30. Cf. *TE* 342.
65 'The Logic of the Undecidable: An Interview with René Girard', p. 9.
66 Henri de Lubac, *The Discovery of God*, p. 179.

Chapter 5   Conclusion

1 Paul Dumouchel, '*Ouverture*', *Violence and Truth*, ed. Dumouchel, p. 24.
2 The notion of a 'research programme' referred to here is deployed in the sense used by Imre Lakatos, in 'Falsification and the Methodology of Scientific Research Programmes'.

3 By 'genetic', Gans is referring to the notion of origin in its non-biological sense. See the bibliography for a listing of his major publications. Gans has also established the excellent online journal *Anthropoetics: The Journal of Generative Anthropology*, which is located at ⟨http://www.anthropoetics.ucla.edu⟩.

4 Gans thus holds that a hypothesis of the sort that he suggests provides a highly plausible solution to the seemingly intractable problem of how language, as a system of conventional signs, could be established without presupposing an already existing language that would serve as the medium through which this convention could be established. That is, language must emerge in a collective event, because a single originator would be faced with the problem of representational solipsism – of having, in short, no one to communicate with.

5 Gans, *Signs of Paradox*, p. 15.

6 In English, the CREA is best rendered 'Centre for Applied Epistemology'. The relationships between Girard's work and physical systems were considered in a number of conferences throughout the 1980s at Cerisy and Stanford, California. See work in the bibliography by the authors mentioned.

7 Jean-Pierre Dupuy and Francisco J. Varela, 'Understanding Origins: An Introduction'.

8 Ilya Prigogine, 'Order out of Chaos'.

9 Henri Atlan and Jean-Pierre Dupuy, 'Mimesis and Social Morphogenesis'.

10 Jean-Pierre Dupuy, 'Deconstruction and the Liberal Order'. Dupuy points out how John Rawls's critique of utilitarianism, articulated in his *A Theory of Justice* (1971), is predicated on a wariness of sacrificial logics. Dupuy's reflection continues, in effect, earlier discussions of utilitarianism in the mid-twentieth century initiated by H. J. McCloskey, but brings to these a much-needed anthropological perspective. See McCloskey, 'The Complexity of the Concepts of Punishment'; 'A Note on Utilitarian Punishment'; and 'Utilitarian and Retributive Punishment'.

11 Douglas R. Hofstadter, *Gödel, Escher, Bach*, p. 10.

12 This perspective is not, of course, unique to Girard. The defining moment in such an approach to exchange is inaugurated by the French anthropologist Marcel Mauss in his book *The Gift*. Mauss remains, for these economists, another central influence.

13 Anspach, 'Global Markets, Anonymous Victims'; Dumouchel and Dupuy, *L'Enfer des choses*, esp. pp. 137–65; 197–210; Dupuy, 'Shaking the Invisible Hand'.

14 Dupuy, 'Shaking the Invisible Hand'; Anspach, 'Global Markets, Anonymous Victims'.

15 William Johnsen, '*Frères amis*, not Enemies: Serres Between Prigogine and Girard'.

16 Serres, *Hermés I: La communication*, pp. 32–3.

17   Bourbaki is not, in fact, a mathematician at all, but a French *société anonyme* which, since 1939, has written thirty-one volumes of the monumental *Éléments de mathématique*. See Paul R. Halmos, 'Nicolas Bourbaki'.

18   Serres makes this methodology explicit; it 'examines one or two particular models reduced to a form (or to several): a preestablished, transitive order. Then, analogically, it finds this form or structure in other domains, *et similia tam facilia*. Whence its power of comprehension, of classification and of explication: geometry, arithmetic, mechanics, method, philosophy.' Serres, *Hermés I: La communication*, p. 121.

19   Serres, *La Naissance de la physique dans le texte de Lucréce*, pp. 165–6.

20   This is treated at length in his *La Naissance*. An excerpt of this appears in English in *Hermes: Literature, Science, Philosophy*, pp. 98–124.

21   Serres, *Hermes: Literature, Science, Philosophy*, pp. 65–70.

22   Ibid., pp. 125–33.

23   Serres, *Genesis*, p. 4.

24   Ibid., p. 7.

25   Richard Gordon, 'Reason and Ritual in Greek Tragedy', p. 289.

26   See, for instance, Edward O. Wilson, *Consilience*, esp. pp. 137–297.

27   Cf. Girard, 'The Founding Murder in the Philosophy of Nietzsche', pp. 227–9.

28   One of the reasons for this is that, firstly, such a task has been taken up with considerable subtlety and rigour elsewhere. A very thoughtful consideration and discussion of some of the major criticisms of Girard are taken up by Richard J. Golsan in his *René Girard and Myth*, pp. 111–28. See also Golsan's interview with Girard on pp. 129–49 of the same volume. The second reason for my reticence to engage with the critiques is that some of the best known and most often cited actually misconstrue his work in quite fundamental ways. Both Hayden White and Nancy Jay, for instance, believe that Girard argues that sacred violence is actually a *good way* to establish social order, even a way to be preferred over others! See Hayden White, 'Ethnological "Lie" and Mythical "Truth"'; and Nancy Jay, *Throughout your Generations Forever*, p. 131. Philippe Lacoue-Labarthe misattributes to Girard Hegel's view of desire: *un désir du désir de l'Autre* [a desire for the Other's desire], rather than Girard's actual theorization, which is *un désir selon l'Autre* [the desire following the desire of the Other]. Secondly, Lacoue-Labarthe attributes to Girard the peculiar belief that mimetic desire is fundamentally competitive, 'from its inception infused with hatred and rivalry'. Philippe Lacoue-Labarthe, *Typography: Mimesis, Philosophy, and Politics*, pp. 102, 112. This is simply not the case; see *GR* 62–5 and Girard's *Quand ces choses commenceront*, pp. 70–6. Toril Moi and Sarah Kofman both argue that Girard's notion of mimesis privileges 'masculine desire' over 'feminine desire' and that Girard cannot stand the idea of 'feminine' 'self-sufficiency'. See Moi, 'The Missing Mother: The Oedipal Rivalries of René Girard'; and

Kofman, 'The Narcissistic Woman: Freud and Girard'. Girard, of course, would not support 'feminine self-sufficiency', but neither would he support 'masculine self-sufficiency'; he subscribes to the idea of the 'supremacy' (let alone the existence) of neither 'masculine desire' nor 'feminine desire'. (One might here hazard a guess that this is perhaps the reason why the queer theorist Eve Kosofsky Sedgwick found Girard's mimetic desire an ideal theoretical model for her reading of English literature. See Sedgwick, *Between Men*.)

29   Girard, 'Origins: A View from the Literature', p. 39.
30   For instance, Paul Dumouchel challenges Rodney Needham's contention that general theories require monothetic schemes of classification. See his introduction to *Violence and Truth*, pp. 8–10. And John O'Carroll and I have taken up a discussion of Girard's and Gans's work in relation to contemporary intellectual trends, especially postcolonialism, phenomenology, and deconstruction, in our essay 'Notes on Generative Anthropology: Towards an Ethics of the Hypothesis'.
31   Girard, 'Are the Gospels Mythical?'
32   See, for instance, Andrew McKenna's book *Violence and Difference*.
33   Although it succumbs to some excesses typical of its genre, see Karlis Racevskis's *Modernity's Pretences* for some vivid illustrations of this.
34   Lat. *dogma*: 'philosophical tenet'.
35   Peter Berger, *Invitation to Sociology*, p. 69. Max Weber shows his fundamental agreement with this assertion of the necessary relation between violence and political formation: 'The state is a relation of men dominating men, a relation by means of legitimate . . . violence.' Weber, *Politics as a Vocation*, p. 1. With regard to violence and representation, we could, of course, mention the work of Jacques Derrida and Michel Foucault.
36   Girard, 'Origins: A View from the Literature', p. 31.
37   Perhaps an additional problem here is that Girard is highly *explicit* about his reductions, where others may not be so: 'The mimetic scheme should be highly conspicuous, in a position where it is most vulnerable to criticism' (*TE* 209); 'The value of a critical thought depends not on how cleverly it manages to disguise its own systematic nature' (*DD* 3). Secondly, the reduction Girard employs is explanatory, not metaphysical or ontological – the latter is far more common in philosophy and social theory.
38   Lacoue-Labarthe, 'Mimesis and Truth', p. 10.

References and Bibliography

Major works by Girard (in French)

Mensonge romantique et vérité romanesque. Paris: Grasset, 1961.
Dostoïevski: du double à l'unité. Paris: Plon, 1963.
La Violence et le sacré. Paris: Grasset, 1972.
Critique dans un souterrain. Includes *Dostoïevski: du double à l'unité* (1963). Paris: Grasset, 1976.
Des choses cachées depuis la fondation du monde, with Jean-Michel Oughourlian and Guy Lefort. Paris: Grasset, 1978.
Le Bouc émissaire. Paris: Grasset, 1982.
La Route antique des hommes pervers. Paris: Grasset, 1985.
*Shakespeare: les feux de l'envie, trans. Bernard Vincent. Paris: Grasset, 1990.
Quand ces choses commenceront . . . entretiens avec Michel Treguer. Paris: Arléa, 1994.
Je vois Satan tomber comme l'éclair. Paris: Grasset, 1999.
Celui par qui le scandale arrive. Paris: Desclée de Brouwer, 2001.

*This book was written in English, but published first in French translation.

Major translations and works in English by Girard

Proust: A Collection of Critical Essays, ed. Girard. New York: Prentice-Hall, 1962.

Deceit, Desire, and the Novel: Self and Other in Literary Structure, trans. Yvonne Freccero. Baltimore and London: Johns Hopkins UP, 1966.

Violence and the Sacred (1972), trans. Patrick Gregory. Baltimore: Johns Hopkins UP, 1977.

'To Double Business Bound': Essays on Literature, Mimesis, and Anthropology. Baltimore: Johns Hopkins UP, 1978.

The Scapegoat (1982), trans. Yvonne Freccero. Baltimore: Johns Hopkins UP, 1986.

Things Hidden Since the Foundation of the World (1978), with Jean-Michel Oughourlian and Guy Lefort, trans. Stephen Bann and Michael Metteer. Stanford: Stanford UP, 1987.

Job, the Victim of his People (1985), trans. Yvonne Freccero. Stanford: Stanford UP, 1987.

A Theater of Envy: William Shakespeare. New York: Oxford UP, 1991.

The Girard Reader, ed. James G. Williams. New York: Crossroad, 1996.

Resurrection from the Underground: Feodor Dostoevsky (1963), trans. James G. Williams. New York: Crossroad, 1997.

I See Satan Fall Like Lightning (1999), trans. James G. Williams. Maryknoll, NY: Orbis, 2001.

Selected articles/shorter publications by Girard

'Literature and Christianity: A Personal View'. *Philosophy and Literature* 23, 1999: 32–43.

'Violence in Biblical Narrative'. *Philosophy and Literature* 23, 1999: 387–92.

'Are the Gospels Mythical?' *First Things: The Journal of Religion and Public Life* 62, April 1996 ⟨http://www.firstthings.com/ftissues/ft9604/girard.html⟩.

'Origins: A View from the Literature'. In Dupuy and Varela, *Understanding Origins*, 27–42.

'Theory and its Terrors'. In *The Limits of Theory*, ed. Thomas M. Kavanagh. Stanford: Stanford UP, 1989, 225–54.

'The Founding Murder in the Philosophy of Nietzsche'. In Dumouchel, *Violence and Truth*, 227–46.

'Generative Scapegoating'. In *Violent Origins: Walter Burkert, René Girard, and Jonathan Z. Smith on Ritual Killing and Cultural Formation*, ed. Robert G. Hamerton-Kelly. Stanford: Stanford UP, 1987, 73–145.

'The Logic of the Undecidable: An Interview with René Girard' (conducted by Thomas Bertonneau). *Paroles Gelées – UCLA French Studies* 5, 1987: 1–24.

'Nietzsche and Contradiction'. *Stanford Italian Review* 1, 1–2, 1986: 53–65.

'Disorder and Order in Mythology'. In Livingston, *Disorder and Order*, 80–97.

'Narcissism: The Freudian Myth Demythified by Proust'. In *Psychoanalysis, Creativity, and Literature: A French-American Inquiry*, ed. Alan Roland. New York: Columbia UP, 1978, 293–311.

Further reading

Aglietta, Michel and André Orléan, *La Violence de la monnaie*. Paris: Presses Universitaires de France, 1982.

Alison, James, *Raising Abel: The Recovery of the Eschatological Imagination*. New York: Crossroad Herder, 1996.

——, *The Joy of Being Wrong: Original Sin through Easter Eyes*. New York: Crossroad Herder, 1998.

——, *Faith Beyond Resentment: Fragments Catholic and Gay*. London: Dartman, Longman & Todd, 2001.

Attali, Jacques, *Noise: The Political Economy of Music*, trans. Brian Massumi. Minneapolis and London: University of Minnesota Press, 1985.

Bailie, Gil, *Violence Unveiled: Humanity at the Crossroads*. New York: Crossroad, 1995.

Bandera, Cesáreo, *Mímesis conflictiva: ficción literaria y violencia en Cervantes y Calderón*. Madrid: Gredos, 1975.

——, *The Sacred Game: The Role of the Sacred in the Genesis of Modern Literary Fiction*. University Park: Pennsylvania State UP, 1994.

Bartlett, Anthony W., *Cross Purposes: The Violent Grammar of Christian Atonement*. Harrisburg, PA: Trinity Press, 2001.

Baudler, Georg, *Töten oder Lieben: Gewalt und Gewaltlosigkeit in Religion und Christentum*. Munich: Kösel, 1991.

Borch-Jacobsen, Mikkel, *Le Lien affectif*. Paris: Aubier Montaigne, 1991.

Chilton, Bruce, *The Temple of Jesus*. University Park: Pennsylvania State UP, 1992.

Deguy, Michel, ed., *René Girard et le problème du mal*. Paris: Grasset, 1982.

Dieckmann, Bernhard, *Judas als Südenbock: eine verhängnisvolle Geschichte von Angst und Vergeltung*. Munich: Kösel, 1991.

Dumouchel, Paul, ed., *Violence and Truth: On the Work of René Girard*. Stanford: Stanford UP, 1988.

Dumouchel, Paul and Jean-Pierre Dupuy, eds, *L'Enfer des choses: René Girard et la logique de l'économie*. Paris: Seuil, 1979.

——, *Colloque de Cerisy: L'Auto-organisation de la physique au politique*. Paris: Seuil, 1983.

Dupuy, Jean-Pierre, *Ordres et desordres: enquête sur un nouveau paradigme*. Paris: Grasset, 1982.

——, *Le Sacrifice et l'envie: le libéralisme aux prises avec la justice sociale*. Paris: Calmann-Lévy, 1992.

Dupuy, Jean-Pierre and Francisco J. Varela, eds, *Understanding Origins: Contemporary Views on the Origin of Life, Mind, and Society*. Dordrecht: Kluwer, 1992.

Gans, Eric, *The Origin of Language: A Formal Theory of Representation*. Berkeley: University of California Press, 1981.

——, *The End of Culture: Toward a Generative Anthropology*. Berkeley and Los Angeles: University of California Press, 1985.

——, *Science and Faith: The Anthropology of Revelation*. Savage, MD: Rowman & Littlefield, 1991.

——, *Originary Thinking: Elements of Generative Anthropology*. Stanford: Stanford UP, 1993.

——, *Signs of Paradox: Irony, Resentment, and Other Mimetic Structures*. Stanford: Stanford UP, 1997.

Gardner, Stephen L., *Myths of Freedom: Equality, Modern Thought, and Philosophical Radicalism*. Westport, CT, and London: Greenwood Press, 1998.

Goodhart, Sandor, *Sacrificing Commentary: Reading the End of Literature*. Baltimore and London: Johns Hopkins UP, 1996.

Hamerton-Kelly, Robert G., *Sacred Violence: Paul's Hermeneutic of the Cross*. Minneapolis: Fortress, 1992.

——, *The Gospel and the Sacred: Poetics of Violence in Mark*. Minneapolis: Fortress, 1994.

Juilland, Alphonse, ed., *To Honor René Girard*. Special issue of *Stanford French and Italian Studies* 34 (1986).

Lagrange, François, *Rene Girard ou la christianisation des sciences humaines*. New York: Peter Lang, 1994.

Livingston, Paisley, ed., *Disorder and Order: Proceedings of the Stanford International Symposium (Sept. 14–16, 1981)*. Special issue of *Stanford Literature Studies* 1, 1984.

——, *Models of Desire: René Girard and the Psychology of Mimesis*. Baltimore: Johns Hopkins UP, 1992.

McCracken, David, *The Scandal of the Gospels: Jesus, Story, and Offense*. New York and Oxford: Oxford UP, 1994.

McKenna, Andrew, *Violence and Difference: Girard, Derrida, and Deconstruction*. Urbana and Chicago: University of Illinois Press, 1992.

Oughourlian, Jean-Michel, *The Puppet of Desire: The Psychology of Hysteria, Possession, and Hypnosis*, trans. Eugene Webb. Stanford: Stanford UP, 1991.

Palaver, Wolfgang, *Politik und Religion bei Thomas Hobbes: eine Kritik aus der Sicht der Theorie Girards*. Innsbruck: Tyrolia, 1991.

Roustang, François, *Un destin si funeste*. Paris: Editions de Minuit, 1976.

Schwager, Raymund, *Must There be Scapegoats? Violence and Redemption in the Bible*, trans. Maria L. Assad. San Fransisco: Harper & Row, 1987.

——, *Jesus in the Drama of Salvation: Toward a Biblical Doctrine of Redemption*, trans. James G. Williams. New York: Herder & Herder, 1999.

Serres, Michel, *Hermés III: La traduction*. Paris: Minuit, 1974.

——, *La Naissance de la physique dans le texte de Lucréce: fleuves et turbulences*. Paris: Minuit, 1977, esp. 127–66.

——, *The Parasite*, trans. Lawrence R. Schehr. Baltimore: Johns Hopkins UP, 1982.

——, *Rome: The Book of Foundations*, trans. Felicia McCarren. Stanford: Stanford UP, 1991, esp. 89–136.

——, *Genesis*, trans. Geneviève James and James Nielson. Ann Arbor: University of Michigan Press, 1995.

Simonse, Simon, *Kings of Disaster: Dualism, Centralism and the Scapegoat King in the Southeastern Sudan*. Leiden and New York: E. J. Brill, 1992.

Smith, Theophus and Mark Wallace, eds, *Curing Violence*. Sonoma, CA: Polebridge, 1994.

Swartley, Willard M., ed., *Violence Renounced: René Girard, Biblical Studies, and Peacemaking*. Telford, PA: Pandora Press, 2000.

Vattimo, Gianni, *Belief*, trans. David Webb and Luca D'Isanto. Cambridge: Polity, 1999.

Webb, Eugene, *The Self Between: From Freud to the New Social Psychology of France*. Seattle and London: University of Washington Press, 1993.

Williams, James G., *The Bible, Violence, and the Sacred: Liberation from the Myth of Sanctioned Violence*. Valley Forge, PA: Trinity Press, 1991.

Other works

Anspach, Mark R., *From the Double Bind to Autonomy: Epistemological Challenges in Contemporary French Theory*. Diss., Stanford University, 1991.

——, 'Violence Against Violence: Islam in Comparative Context'. *Terrorism and Political Violence* 3, 3, 1991: 9–29.

——, *A charge de revanche, les formes élémentaires de la réciprocité*. Paris: Seuil, 2001.

——, 'Global Markets, Anonymous Victims'. *UNESCO Courier*, May 2001: 47–51.

Aristotle, *On the Art of Poetry* [*Poetics*], trans. Ingram Bywater. Oxford: Oxford UP, 1920.

Atlan, Henri, 'Founding Violence and Divine Referent'. In Dumouchel, *Violence and Truth*, 192–208.

Atlan, Henri, and Jean-Pierre Dupuy, 'Mimesis and Social Morphogenesis: Violence and the Sacred from a Systems Analysis Viewpoint'. *Applied Systems and Cybernetics (Proceedings of the International Congress on Applied Systems Research and Cybernetics, III)*, ed. G. E. Lasker. New York, Pergamon Press, 1981, 1263–8.

Bakhtin, Mikhail, *Rabelais and his World*, trans. Hélène Iswolski. Bloomington: Indiana UP, 1984.

Bandera, Cesáreo, 'Literature and Desire: Poetic Frenzy and the Love Potion'. *Mosaic* 8, 2, 1975: 33–52.

——, 'The Doubles Reconciled'. Review of *Mensonge romantique et vérité romanesque, La Violence et le sacré*, and *Des choses cachées depuis la fondation du monde*, by René Girard. *Modern Literary Notes* 93, 1978: 1007–136.

Bateson, Gregory, *Steps to an Ecology of Mind*. New York: Ballantine, 1972.

Bellinger, Charles K., *The Genealogy of Violence: Reflections on Creation, Freedom, and Evil*. Oxford: Oxford UP, 2001.

Berger, Peter, *Invitation to Sociology: A Humanistic Perspective*. New York: Doubleday, 1963.

Berman, Harold J., *The Formation of the Western Legal Tradition*. Cambridge, MA: Harvard UP, 1983.

Bertonneau, Thomas F., 'Celsus, the First Nietzsche: Resentment and the Case Against Christianity'. *Anthropoetics: The Journal of Generative Anthropology* 3, 1, 1997 ⟨http://humnet.ucla.edu/humnet/anthropoetics/Ap0301/CELSUS.htm⟩.

Blumenberg, Hans, *The Legitimacy of the Modern Age*, trans. Robert M. Wallace. Cambridge, MA: MIT Press, 1983.

Brasch, Rudolph, *Thank God I'm an Atheist: The Religious Origins of Expressions, Customs and Institutions*. Sydney: Collins, 1987.

Brecher, Bob, *Getting What You Want? A Critique of Liberal Morality*. London: Routledge, 1998.

Brett, Nathan, 'Knowing How, What and That'. *Canadian Journal of Philosophy* 4, 1974: 293–400.

Bronowski, Jacob, *The Ascent of Man*. London: BBC Publications, 1973.

Burke, Kenneth, 'Doing and Saying: Thoughts on Myth, Cult and Archetype'. *Salmagundi* 7, 1971: 100–19.

Butler, Judith, *Subjects of Desire: Hegelian Reflections on Twentieth-Century France*. New York: Columbia UP, 1999.

Calasso, Roberto, *The Ruin of Kasch*, trans. William Weaver and Stephen Sartarelli. London: Vintage, 1994.

Canetti, Elias, *Crowds and Power*, trans. Carol Stewart. New York: Farrar, Straus & Giroux, 1984.

Carrithers, Michael, Steven Collins, and Steven Lukes, eds, *The Category of the Person*. Cambridge: Cambridge UP, 1985.

Celsus, *On the True Doctrine: A Discourse Against the Christians*, trans. R. Joseph Hoffman. New York: Oxford UP, 1987.

Coupe, Laurence, *Myth*. London and New York: Routledge, 1997.

Davidson, Donald, *Inquiries into Truth and Interpretation*. Oxford: Clarendon Press, 1984.

Davis, David Brion, *Slavery and Human Progress*. New York: Oxford UP, 1984.

Derrida, Jacques, 'Plato's Pharmacy'. *Dissemination*, trans. Barbara Johnson. London: Athlone Press, 1981, 63–171.

——, *On Cosmopolitanism and Forgiveness*, trans. Mark Dooley and Michael Hughes. London and New York: Routledge, 2001.

Dumont, Louis, 'A Modified View of our Origins: The Christian Beginnings of Modern Individualism'. In Carrithers et al., *The Category of the Person*, 93–122.

Dumouchel, Paul, 'Introduction'. In Dumouchel, *Violence and Truth*, 1–21.

Dupuy, Jean-Pierre, *L'Erreur*. Lyon: Presses Universitaires de Lyon, 1982.

——, 'Mimésis et morphogénèse'. In Deguy, *René Girard et le problème du mal*, 225–78.

——, 'De l'économie considerée comme théorie de la foule'. *Stanford French Review*, summer 1983: 245–64.

——, 'Shaking the Invisible Hand'. In Livingston, *Disorder and Order*, 129–45.

——, 'Totalization and Misrecognition'. In Dumouchel, *Violence and Truth*, 75–100.

——, 'Common Knowledge, Common Sense'. *Theory and Decision* 27, 1989: 37–62.

——, 'Deconstruction and the Liberal Order'. *SubStance* 62/63, 1990: 110–24.

——, 'Tangled Hierarchies: Self-Reference in Philosophy, Anthropology, and Critical Theory'. *Comparative Criticism* 12, 1990: 105–23.

——, 'The Self-Deconstruction of Convention'. *SubStance* 74, 1994: 86–98.

——, 'Mimesis and Social Autopoiesis: A Girardian Reading of Hayek'. *Paragrana* 4, 2, 1995: 192–214.

——, 'The Autonomy of Social Reality: On the Contribution of Systems Theory to the Theory of Society'. *Evolution, Order and Complexity*, ed. Elias L. Khalil and Kenneth E. Boulding. London and New York: Routledge, 1996, 61–88.

Dupuy, Jean-Pierre and Francisco J. Varela, 'Understanding Origins: An Introduction'. In Dupuy and Varela, *Understanding Origins*, 1–25.

Durkheim, Émile, *The Elementary Forms of the Religious Life*, trans. Joseph Swain. New York: Free Press, 1965.

Eliade, Mircea, *Histoire des croyances et des idées religieuses*. Paris: Payot, 1978.

Ellis, Albert, *Humanistic Psychotherapy: The Rational-Emotive Approach*. New York: McGraw-Hill, 1973.

Evans-Pritchard, E. E., *Nuer Religion*. Oxford: Clarendon Press, 1956.

Fleming, Chris and John O'Carroll, 'Notes on Generative Anthropology: Towards an Ethics of the Hypothesis'. *Anthropoetics* 8, 2, 2002/2003 ⟨http://www.anthropoetics.ucla.edu/~ap0802/fleming.htm⟩.

Fogel, Robert William, *Without Consent and Without Contract: The Rise and Fall of American Slavery*. New York: Norton, 1991.

Foster, M. B., 'The Christian Doctrine of Creation and the Rise of Modern Natural Science'. *Mind* 43, 1934: 446–68.

Foucault, Michel, *Discipline and Punish: The Birth of the Prison*, trans. Alan Sheridan. Harmondsworth: Penguin, 1977.

Frazer, James George, *The Golden Bough: A Study in Magic and Religion* (1890), ed. Robert Fraser. Oxford and New York: Oxford UP, 1994.

Frei, Hans, *The Eclipse of Biblical Narrative*. New Haven: Yale UP, 1974.

Freud, Sigmund, 'The Ego and the Id'. *The Standard Edition of the Complete Psychological Works*, ed. and trans. James Strachey. London: Hogarth Press, 1953–66, vol. 19, 12–59.

——, 'Group Psychology and the Analysis of the Ego'. *The Standard Edition of the Complete Psychological Works*, ed. and trans. James Strachey. London: Hogarth Press, 1953–66, vol. 18, 69–143.

——, 'On Narcissism'. *The Standard Edition of the Complete Psychological Works*, ed. and trans. James Strachey. London: Hogarth Press, 1953–66, vol. 14, 67–102.

Frye, Northrop, *Anatomy of Criticism: Four Essays*. Princeton: Princeton UP, 1957.

Gallese, Vittorio and Alvin Goldman, 'Mirror Neurons and the Simulation Theory of Mind-Reading'. *Trends in Cognitive Sciences* 2, 1998: 493–501.

Gans, Eric, 'Pour une esthétique triangulaire'. *Esprit* 429, 1973: 564–81.

——, 'Differences'. *Modern Language Notes* 96, 4, 1981: 792–808.

——, 'Le Logos de René Girard'. In *René Girard et le problème du mal*, ed. Michel Deguy and Jean-Pierre Dupuy. Paris: Grasset, 1982, 179–214.

——, 'The Victim as Subject: The Esthetico-Ethical System of Rousseau's *Rêveries*'. *Studies in Romanticism* 21, 1, 1982: 3–31.

——, 'The Sacred and the Social: Defining Durkheim's Anthropological Legacy'. *Anthropoetics* 6, 1, 2000 ⟨http://www.anthropoetics.ucla.edu/ap0601/durkheim.htm⟩.

Golsan, Richard, *René Girard and Myth*. New York and London: Garland, 1993.

Gordon, Richard, 'Reason and Ritual in Greek Tragedy. On René Girard, *Violence and the Sacred* and Marcel Detienne, *The Garden of Adonis*'. *Comparative Criticism* 1, 1979: 279–310.

Greimas, A[lgirdas] J[ulien], *Sémantique structurale: recherche de méthode*. Paris: Larousse, 1966.

Grivois, Henri, 'Adolescence, Indifferentiation, and the Onset of Psychosis'. *Contagion: Journal of Violence, Mimesis, and Culture* 6, 1999: 104–21.

Grunbaum, Adolf, 'Can a Theory Answer More Questions than One of its Rivals?' *British Journal for the Philosophy of Science* 27, 1976: 1–23.

Habermas, Jürgen, *Legitimation Crisis*, trans. Thomas MacCarthy. Cambridge: Polity, 1975.

Halmos, Paul R., 'Nicolas Bourbaki'. *Scientific American* 196, May 1957: 88–99.

Hegel, G. W. F., *Phenomenology of Spirit*, trans. A. V. Miller. Oxford and New York: Oxford UP, 1977.

Henrichs, Albert, 'Loss of Self, Suffering, Violence: The Modern View of Dionysus from Nietzsche to Girard'. *Harvard Studies in Classical Philology* 88, 1984: 205–40.

Hodgson, Peter E., 'The Christian Origin of Science'. *Logos* 4, 2, 2001: 138–59.

Hofstadter, Douglas R., *Gödel, Escher, Bach: An Eternal Golden Braid*. Harmondsworth, Penguin, 1979.

Hooykaas, Richard, *Religion and the Rise of Modern Science*. Edinburgh and London: Scottish Academic Press, 1972.

Hubert, Henri and Marcel Mauss, *Sacrifice: Its Nature and Function*, trans. W. D. Halls. Chicago: University of Chicago Press, 1964.

Hurlbut, William B., 'Mimesis and Empathy in Human Biology'. *Contagion: Journal of Violence, Mimesis, and Culture* 4, 1997: 14–25.

Jameson, Frederic, *The Political Unconscious: Narrative as a Socially Symbolic Act*. Ithaca, NY: Cornell UP, 1982.

Jay, Nancy, *Throughout your Generations Forever: Sacrifice, Religion, and Paternity*. Chicago and London: University of Chicago Press, 1992.

Johnsen, William A., 'Myth, Ritual, and Literature after Girard'. *Literary Theory's Future(s)*, ed. Joseph Natoli. Urbana and Chicago: University of Illinois Press, 1989, 116–48.

——, '*Frères amis*, not Enemies: Serres Between Prigogine and Girard'. Forthcoming.

Johnson, Paul, *A History of Christianity*. New York: Atheneum, 1987.

Jung, Carl, *The Gnostic Jung*, ed. R. A. Segal. London: Routledge, 1992.

Keen, Sam, *Faces of the Enemy: Reflections of the Hostile Imagination*. San Francisco: Harper, 1986.

Kofman, Sarah, 'The Narcissistic Woman: Freud and Girard'. *Diacritics* 10, 3, 1980: 36–45; repr. in *French Feminist Thought: A Reader*, ed. Toril Moi. Oxford: Blackwell, 1987, 210–26.

Kojève, Alexandre, *Introduction to the Reading of Hegel: Lectures on the Phenomenology of Spirit*, trans. James H. Nichols. Ithaca and London: Cornell UP, 1969.

Kristeva, Julia, *Revolution in Poetic Language*, trans. Margaret Waller. New York: Columbia UP, 1984.

Kundera, Milan, *Testaments Betrayed: An Essay in Nine Parts*, trans. Linda Asher. New York: Harper, 1984.

Lacan, Jacques, *Écrits*. Paris: Seuil, 1966.

——, *Écrits: A Selection*, trans. Alan Sheridan. London: Tavistock, 1977.

——, *The Seminar, Book II: The Ego in Freud's Theory and in the Technique of Psychoanalysis, 1954–55*, trans. Sylvana Tomaselli. Cambridge: Cambridge UP, 1988.

——, *The Seminar, Book VII: The Ethics of Psychoanalysis, 1959–60*, trans. Dennis Porter. London: Routledge, 1992.

——, *The Seminar, Book III: The Psychoses, 1955–56*, trans. Russell Grigg. London: Routledge, 1993.

Lacoue-Labarthe, Philippe, 'Mimesis and Truth'. *Diacritics* 8, 1, 1978: 10–23.

——, *Typography: Mimesis, Philosophy, and Politics*, ed. and trans. Christopher Fynsk. Cambridge, MA: Harvard UP, 1989.

Lakatos, Imre, 'Falsification and the Methodology of Scientific Research Programmes'. In *Criticism and the Growth of Knowledge*, ed. Imre Lakatos and Alan Musgrave. Cambridge: Cambridge UP, 1970, 91–196.

Latour, Bruno, *We Have Never Been Modern*, trans. Catherine Porter. Cambridge, MA: Harvard UP, 1993.

Lewis, C. S., 'Modern Theology and Biblical Criticism'. In *Christian Reflections*, ed. Walter Hooper. Grand Rapids, MI: Eerdmans, 1967, 152–66.

Lienhardt, Godfrey, *Divinity and Experience: The Religion of the Dinka*. Oxford: Oxford UP, 1961.

Livingston, Paisley, 'From Work to Work'. *Philosophy and Literature* 20, 2, 1996: 436–54.

Lubac, Henri de, *The Discovery of God*, trans. Alexander Dru. Grand Rapids, MI: Eerdmans, 1996.

McCloskey, H. J., 'The Complexity of the Concepts of Punishment'. *Philosophy* 37, 1962: 307–25.

——, 'A Note on Utilitarian Punishment'. *Mind* 72, 1963: 599.

——, 'Utilitarian and Retributive Punishment'. *Journal of Philosophy* 64, 1967: 91–110.

MacIntyre, Alasdair, 'Myth'. In *The Encyclopedia of Philosophy*, vol. 5, ed. Paul Edwards. New York and London: Macmillian, 1967, 434–7.

——, 'Epistemological Crises, Dramatic Narrative, and the Philosophy of Science'. In *Paradigms and Revolutions*, ed. Gary Gutting. Notre Dame, IN: University of Notre Dame Press, 1980, 55–74.

——, *A Short History of Ethics: A History of Moral Philosophy from the Homeric Age to the Twentieth Century*. London and New York: Routledge, 1998.

McKenna, Andrew, 'Aristotle's Theater of Envy: Paradox, Logic, and Literature'. In *Philosophical Designs for a Socio-Cultural Transformation: Beyond Violence and the Modern Era*, ed. Tetsuji Yamamoto. Tokyo: Ecole des Hautes Etudes en Sciences Culturelles, 1998, 632–54.

Maloney, Clarence, ed., *The Evil Eye*. New York: Columbia UP, 1976.

Maras, Steven, 'A Semiotics of the Proxy'. *Social Semiotics* 12, 1, 2002: 115–29.

Matta, Roberto da, *Carnavals, bandits et héros*, trans. Danielle Birck. Paris: Seuil, 1983.

——, 'Carnival in Multiple Planes'. In *Rite, Drama, Festival, Spectacle: Rehearsals Toward a Theory of Cultural Performance*, ed. J. MacAloon. Philadelphia: ISHI, 1984, 208–40.

Mauss, Marcel, 'A Category of the Human Mind: The Notion of Person; the Notion of Self'. In Carrithers et al., *The Category of the Person*, 1–25.

——, *The Gift: The Form and Reason for Exchange in Archaic Societies* [1923–4], trans. W. D. Halls. London: Routledge, 1990.

Meltzoff, Andrew N., 'The Human Infant as homo imitans'. In *Social Learning: Psychological and Biological Perspectives*, ed. T. R. Zentall and B. G. Galef. Hillsdale, NJ: Erlbaum, 1988, 319–41.

——, 'Infants' Understanding of People and Things: From Body Imitation to Folk Psychology'. In *The Body and the Self*, ed. José Luis Bermúdez, Anthony Marcel, and Naomi Eilan. Cambridge, MA: MIT Press, 1995, 43–69.

Milbank, John, *Theology & Social Theory: Beyond Secular Reason*. Oxford: Blackwell, 1990.

Moi, Toril, 'The Missing Mother: The Oedipal Rivalries of René Girard'. *Diacritics* 12, 1982: 21–31.

Murphy, Nancey, *Beyond Liberalism and Fundamentalism: How Modern and Postmodern Philosophy set the Theological Agenda*. Valley Forge, PA: Trinity Press International, 1996.

Nietzsche, Friedrich, *On the Genealogy of Morals and Ecce Homo*, trans. Walter Kaufmann. New York: Vintage, 1967.

——, *The Will to Power*, trans. Walter Kaufmann and R. J. Hollingdale. New York: Vintage, 1967.

——, 'The Anti-Christ'. *Twilight of the Idols/The Anti-Christ*, trans. R. J. Hollingdale. Harmondsworth: Penguin, 1968, 123–99.

Orléan, André, 'Mimétism et anticipations rationelles: une perspective Keynesienne', *Recherches Economiques de Louvain* 52, 1, 1986: 45–66.

——, 'La Théorie mimétique face aux phénomènes'. In Juilland, *To Honor René Girard*, 121–33.

——, 'Money and Mimetic Speculation'. In Dumouchel, *Violence and Truth*, 101–12.

——, 'Mimetic Contagion and Speculative Bubbles'. *Theory and Decision* 27, 1989: 63–92.

——, 'The Origin of Money'. In Dupuy and Varela, *Understanding Origins*, 113–43.

O'Sullivan, Richard, *The Spirit of the Common Law*. Worcester: Fowler Wright, 1965.

Palaver, Wolfgang, 'Hobbes and the Katéchon: The Secularization of Sacrificial Christianity'. *Contagion: Journal of Violence, Mimesis, and Culture* 2, 1995: 57–74.

Prigogine, Ilya, 'Order out of Chaos'. In Livingston, *Disorder and Order*, 41–60.

Quine, Willard Van Orman, *Quiddities: An Intermittently Philosophical Dictionary*. Cambridge, MA: Harvard UP, 1987.

Racevskis, Karlis, *Modernity's Pretences: Making Reality Fit Reason from Candide to the Gulag*. Albany: State University of New York Press, 1998.

Ramachandran, V. S., 'Mirror Neurons and Imitation Learning as the Driving Force behind the "Great Leap Forward" in Human Evolution'. ⟨http://www.edge.org/documents/archive/edge69. html⟩.

Rizzolatti, Giacomo and Michael Arbib, 'Language within our Grasp'. *Trends in Neurosciences* 21, 1998: 188–94.

Rizzolatti, Giacomo, M. Gartilucci, R. M. Camaerda, V. Gallex, G. Luppino, M. Matteli, and L. Fogassi, 'Neurones Related to Reaching-Grasping Arm Movements in the Rostral Part of Area 6 (Area 6a)'. *Experimental Brain Research* 82, 1990: 337–50.

Rubino, Carl, Review of *'To Double Business Bound': Essays on Literature, Mimesis, and Anthropology*. *Modern Literary Notes* 93, 1978: 1018–21.

Ryle, Gilbert, *The Concept of Mind*. London: Hutchinson, 1949.

Schmidt, Alvin J., *Under the Influence: How Christianity Transformed Civilization*. Grand Rapids, MI: Zondervan, 2001.

Sedgwick, Eve Kosofsky, *Between Men: English Literature and Male Homosocial Desire*. New York: Columbia UP, 1985.

Seligman, Adam, *The Problem of Trust*. Princeton: Princeton UP, 1997.

——, *Modernity's Wager: Authority, the Self, and Transcendence*. Princeton and Oxford: Princeton UP, 2000.

Serres, Michel, *Hermés I: La communication*. Paris: Minuit, 1968.

——, *Hermes: Literature, Science, Philosophy*, ed. Josué V. Harari and David F. Bell. Baltimore and London: Johns Hopkins UP, 1982.

——, 'Dream'. In Livingston, *Disorder and Order*, 248–54.

——, *Conversations on Science, Culture, and Time* (with Bruno Latour), trans. Roxanne Lapidus. Ann Arbor: University of Michigan Press, 1995.

Siebers, Tobin, 'Language, Violence, and the Sacred: A Polemical Survey of Critical Theories'. In Juilland, *To Honor René Girard*, 203–19.

Siedentop, Larry, *Democracy in Europe*. Harmondsworth: Penguin, 2000.

Sollers, Philippe, 'Is God Dead? "The Purloined Letter" of the Gospel'. In Juilland, *To Honor René Girard*, 191–6.

Taylor, Charles, *Sources of the Self: The Making of the Modern Identity*. Cambridge, MA: Harvard UP, 1992.

Tocqueville, Alexis de, *Democracy in America*, vol. 2, ed. P. Bradley. New York: Vintage, 1990.

Turner, Victor, *The Ritual Process*. Chicago: Aldine, 1969.

Vattimo, Gianni, *The Transparent Society*, trans. David Webb. Cambridge: Polity, 1992.

——, *Beyond Interpretation: The Meaning of Hermeneutics for Philosophy*, trans. David Webb. Cambridge: Polity, 1997.

——, *After Christianity*, trans. Luca D'Isanto. New York: Columbia UP, 2002.

Vernant, Jean-Pierre, *Myth and Society in Ancient Greece*. London: Methuen, 1982.

Vogelin, Eric, *The New Science of Politics: An Introduction*. Chicago: Chicago UP, 1990.

Voltaire [François-Marie Arouet de], *Philosophical Dictionary*, trans. Theodore Besterman. Harmondsworth: Penguin, 1971.

Walvin, James, *Black Ivory: A History of British Slavery*. Washington: Howard UP, 1994.

Walzer, Michael, *Exodus and Revolution*. New York: Basic Books, 1985.

Watzlawick, Paul, P. Beavan, and D. D. Jackson, *The Pragmatics of Human Communication*. New York: Norton, 1967.

Weaver, J. Denny, 'Atonement for the Non-Constantinian Church'. *Modern Theology* 6, 1990: 307–23.

Webb, Eugene, 'The New Social Psychology of France: The Girardian School'. *Religion* 23, 1993: 255–63.

Weber, Max, *Ancient Judaism*, trans. H. H. Gerth and D. Martindale. Glencoe, IL: Free Press, 1952.

——, *Politics as a Vocation*. Philadelphia: Fortress, 1965.

White, Hayden, 'Ethnological "Lie" and Mythical "Truth"'. *Diacritics* 8, 1, 1978: 2–9.

Whitehead, Alfred North, *Science and the Modern World*. Cambridge: Cambridge UP, 1926.

Wilden, Anthony, *System and Structure: Essays in Communication and Exchange*. 2nd edn, London: Tavistock, 1980.

Williams, James G., 'On Job and Writing: Derrida, Girard, and the Remedy-Poison'. *Scandinavian Journal of the Old Testament* 7, 1, 1993: 32–50.

Wilson, Edward O., *Consilience: The Unity of Knowledge*. London: Abacus, 1998.

Wink, Walter, *Engaging the Powers: Discernment and Resistance in a World of Domination*. Minneapolis: Fortress, 1992.

Index

Lightning Source UK Ltd.
Milton Keynes UK
177262UK00001B/29/P